TRANQUEBAR PRESS

The Eye of the Serpent

Sundararaj Theodore Baskaran was born in Dharapuram, Tamil Nadu. After his Master's degree in History, he worked for a while at Tamil Nadu Archives and later joined the Indian Postal Service. A recipient of fellowships from the Tamil Nadu Council of Historical Research and Department of Culture, Government of India, he has written extensively on Tamil cinema, wildlife and conservation in academic journals and leading magazines and presented papers at several international conferences on media and popular culture. He was part of the jury for the National Film Awards, 2003.

Other titles by the author on Indian cinema

The Message Bearers: Nationalistic Politics and Entertainment Media In South India: 1881-1945 (1981)

Sivaji Ganesan: Profile of an Icon (2008)

History through the Lens: Perspectives on South Indian Cinema (2009)

The Eye of the Serpent:
An Introduction to Tamil Cinema

S Theodore Baskaran

TRANQUEBAR

TRANQUEBAR PRESS

An imprint of westland ltd

61 Silverline Building, 2nd Floor, Alapakkam Main Road, Maduravoyal, Chennai 6000 095
No. 38/10 (New No.5), Raghava Nagar, New Timber Yard Layout, Bangalore 560 026
93, 1st Floor, Sham Lal Road, New Delhi 110 002

First published in India by EastWest Books (Madras) Pvt. Ltd., 1996

Reprinted by TRANQUEBAR PRESS, an imprint of westland ltd 2013

Copyright © S Theodore Baskaran 1996, 2013

All rights reserved

10 9 8 7 6 5 4 3 2 1

ISBN: 978-93-83260-74-4

Typeset by Ram Das Lal

This book is sold subject to the condition that it shall not by way of trade or otherwise, be lent, resold, hired out, circulated, and no reproduction in any form, in whole or in part (except for brief quotations in critical articles or reviews) may be made without written permission of the publishers.

In loving memory of
Dhanalakshmi
My mother
From whose lap I watched my first film

The cinema tells its story to the illiterate as well as the literate; and it keeps its victim (if you like to call him so) not only awake but fascinated as if by a serpent's eye.

G B Shaw, ***Bernard Shaw on Cinema*** (1997)

Contents

	Acknowledgements	ix
	Introduction	xi
Chapter One	The Early Days—Silent Movies	1
Chapter Two	And Then Came the Voices	12
Chapter Three	Era of the Dialogue writer and the Cinema of Dissent	29
Chapter Four	Songs in Tamil Cinema	39
Chapter Five	Dialogue in Tamil Films	62
Chapter Six	Satyamurthi—the Link that Snapped	71
Chapter Seven	The Films	90
Chapter Eight	The Filmmakers	179
Chapter Nine	The Songwriters	221

Milestones of Tamil Cinema	235
Bibliography	241
Articles	245
Glossary	247
Index	249
Index to Film Titles	278

Acknowledgements

THE SEED FOR THIS PROJECT WAS SOWN WHEN ASHISH Rajadhyaksha persuaded me to write for *Encyclopaedia of Indian Cinema* published by the British Film Institute in collaboration with OUP, India. The many delightful conversations I had with my friend C S Lakshmi ("Ambai") gave me valuable insights into Tamil cinema. I cannot fail to acknowledge my debt to Satish Bahadur, formerly professor of Film Appreciation at the Film and Television Institute, Pune, who opened my eyes to the many splendours of cinema through a Film Appreciation course. P K Nair, former Director of National Film Archives, Pune, supplied me with video cassettes of films and books whenever required. Randor Guy willingly extended help and shared information whenever I called. Filmnews Anandan supplied the stills. The British Council gave me a grant to visit the India Office Library, London, thus facilitating access to records pertaining to Tamil cinema of the pre-Independence era. P Sankaralingam, Director, Roja Muthiah Research Library,

Acknowledgements

Chennai, helped in preparing the index for the first edition. I am thankful to V A K Ranga Rao who pointed out some errors in the book and helped me to correct them. Thilaka, my wife, viewed the films with me, shared her observations and provided an atmosphere of love and warmth in which I could pursue my interests.

S Theodore Baskaran

Introduction

THE IMMENSE POPULARITY OF FILM AS AN ENTERTAINMENT form and its emergence in Tamil Nadu as a major cultural preoccupation underscores the significance of the role of audio-visual communication in Tamil society. Over the years, films have become essential instruments for the conduct of any mass campaign that calls for manipulation of its target population. The quantum growth in television and video-viewing has further enhanced the influence of cinema as these media serve as virtual extensions of filmic exhibition. Obviously, such an important development in the cultural and communication environment—which has been under way for over twenty-five years now—merits examination and understanding.

Within three decades of its advent, Tamil cinema penetrated rural areas, piggybacking on the rural electrification programme, and began catering to predominantly illiterate masses. With its ability to reach vast audiences, its breadth of appeal widened. This appeal further increased, when

Introduction

the indigenous classical and folk traditions—sometimes called the "Great" and "Little" traditions respectively—were brought together and amalgamated in Tamil films. Today, Tamil films enjoy a very high exposure rate. There are 2,548 cinema houses, of which 213 are semi-permanent and 892 are "touring" cinemas. The last category operates in interior rural areas.* Bulk of the films screened in Tamil Nadu are made in the state capital, Chennai.

Over the ninety-six years of its existence, Tamil cinema has become one of the most domineering influences in the cultural and political life of Tamil Nadu. As filmmakers treated the subject of human beings in different situations, their films inevitably touched upon social and political issues. Various movements in Tamil Nadu, in turn, shaped the development of Tamil cinema. Even as it gave expression to the social comments and opinions of filmmakers, Tamil cinema also reflected the changing social concerns and moods of the period.

Popular films of any given period must try to satisfy the current desires and tastes of the masses to succeed; and the film industry, which is as vitally interested in profits as any commercial venture, adjusts itself as much as is possible and practicable, to the changes in the socio-political climate of society. Thus, cinema by its very nature mirrors the diverse strands of social thought and events during the various phases of a country's history. Many examples from the history of

---

* Figures from the Regional Officer, Film Censor Board, Madras, December 1994.

world cinema can be cited in support of this point of view; for instance the Great Depression and the Hollywood films of the 1930s. If Tamil cinema is studied as a socio-political force, then its dual role as a propagator of ideas and as a document of social mores will become evident.

Cinema is the only art form in Tamil Nadu, whose origin can be traced with some certainty. And this is the only secular art form, as distinct from traditional art forms which invariably have their basis in some modes of religious practice. Evolving in the context of a long and vigorous aural tradition, Tamil cinema developed some very interesting characteristics.

The diverse currents and crosscurrents of thought that went into various social and political movements in Tamil Nadu can be traced through a study of Tamil cinema.

Therefore, it was this connection between Tamil cinema and these movements that gave rise to the phenomenon of the star-politician and the use of films for explicit political propaganda.

Yet, there have been very few studies on Tamil cinema. In attempting to understand the performing arts of Tamil Nadu, such as Carnatic music or Bharatanatyam, including their social dimensions, there are numerous works one can turn to. In the field of Tamil literature too, there are many books which serve to provide an introduction. But when it comes to cinema, which has had a much greater impact on Tamil society, there is very little material. This apathy towards the study of cinema has been discernible right from the early years, and has been one of the factors that shaped the character of Tamil cinema. Film criticism and film studies did not develop

Introduction

and even after nine decades of its existence, this apathy still continues. The intelligentsia, which refused to take any notice of this new medium when it first appeared on the social scene, now fulminates against it for being escapist and shallow, long after its metamorphosis as a formidable force has come to pass.

While this indifference to the serious study of cinema is common to many other countries, in India it was further compounded by the rigidity of social stratification. In Tamil Nadu, where caste barriers are strictly defined, with exclusive entertainment forms for different classes, the appearance of an entertainment form that cut across all sections of society was, in the first instance, a development that the elite were not prepared to reconcile with. Early Tamil cinema, with its commercial orientation and sensational content, quickly endeared itself to the heterogenous mass audience and, by the same process, alienated the elite. How could an entertainment form, so avidly patronized by the plebeian masses attract the elite also to its fold? A position had to be taken by them vis-a-vis cinema and they took a rigidly negative one. This negative stance, in the course of its expression had many ramifications and continues to do so even now.

In recent years, however, one notices a shift away from this stance. Since I wrote *The Message Bearers* more than thirty years ago, scholastic interest in Tamil cinema has grown considerably. Elsewhere in the world, the relevance of cinema to historiography is being recognized. The conference on 'Film and Historian' organized by the University College in London in 1968 marked the recognition of cinema as an area of study. Film studies as a discipline, is in the process of acquiring an academic tradition as scholars are gradually awakening to this exciting possibility. Many academics, in India and abroad, choose cinema-related topics for their study of Tamil Nadu. Yet, we have very few works that can serve as an introduction to this interesting area of study. And, there is no baseline data available. If one intends to understand anything of Tamil cinema, it is not enough merely to watch films or write about their aesthetics. We need to study cinema. It is this need which justifies efforts such as this book.

In choosing the fifty films which are treated in this book, I have tried to make a representative selection. The films I have chosen are not all classics nor were they all successful films. They are instead illustrative of specific genres of films which are important for one reason or another. The availability of a film for viewing was also a determining factor. Obviously, this may have resulted in some significant omissions which the reader might readily notice. I would liked to have included *She Was Born to Live/Vazhapirandhaval* (1953); but I could not locate a print. The list of filmmakers was also subject to a similar constraint. It was difficult to obtain authentic information on the works of many filmmakers. The questionnaire I sent out to many contemporary filmmakers evoked very little response. And on some, like R Padmanabhan, I could gather only the barest details.

Chapter One
The Early Days—Silent Movies

1897. ARTHUR HAVELOCK WAS THE GOVERNOR OF THE Madras presidency. One evening at the Victoria Public Hall near Ripon building, a small group had gathered in great anticipation. In the centre of the hall, an Englishman named M Edwards was setting up a novel instrument and pushing strips of celluloid into its spools. This assembly of people had read about similar shows held the previous year at the Watson Hotel in Bombay (now Mumbai). Edwards' show had been advertised as kinemascope. The short films he screened were those which became familiar to film historians later: *Arrival of the Train* and *Leaving the Factory*. In less than two years after its birth on 28 December 1895 in Paris, cinema had appeared in Madras (now Chennai).

In many ways, it was a time of momentous change in Madras. Daily newspapers in Tamil, beginning with *Swadesamithran* in 1899, had been launched. In Madras city, a motor car could be occasionally sighted: a status

The Early Days—Silent Movies

symbol for the very rich. Just two years earlier, trams had been introduced in the city. Some affluent households and companies had telephones. People were getting used to the marvel of listening to recorded music from a rotating black disc on a spring-wound machine, the gramophone. The mechanical reproduction of works of art had begun. It was at this stage that the motion picture arrived on the scene.

That evening at the Victoria Public Hall, little did the audience realize that a new dimension to mass culture was being created or that they were witnessing the birth of a cultural colossus, which was to dominate all aspects of people's lives. Soon thereafter, similar shows of short films were held in various parts of Madras, bearing other names such as bioscope and kinema. Often the shows were held by the roadside or in a public park and the entrance fee was a quarter anna (the equivalent of 1.5 paise). There was no need for a licence or for electricity, since the film was projected with the aid of magnesium lamps. Gradually, these shows began to attract a regular clientele. One Warwick Major observed this growth and sensed its commercial possibilities. He had no doubt that it would be a worthwhile proposition to put up a permanent hall for such shows. He built the first cinema house in South India, Electric Theatre in 1900 on Mount Road in Madras. Regular shows of silent films were held here. A new mode of entertainment was born, signifying a landmark in the social history of Tamil Nadu.[1]

For the first eight years, these shows were confined to Madras city. It was Swamikannu Vincent, a draughtsman who worked for the Railways in Tiruchi, who introduced this newfangled entertainment medium to the interior of the Madras presidency. In 1905, quite by accident, he met Dupont, a Frenchman who was returning from Sri Lanka after holding film shows there. For a sum of Rs 2000, Dupont's equipment along with a copy of the forty-five-minute short film, *Life of Jesus Christ,* changed hands. Vincent screened the first show in St Joseph's School in Tiruchi. He called his unit Edison's Cinematograph and toured Madurai, Tirunelveli and Rameswaram holding shows of the film, using carbide jet-burners for projection. He came to Madras and screened the film for seventy-five days. Soon he tied up with Pathe of the United States, a well-known pioneering film producing company, and began screening short films all over the presidency. He also travelled to Bombay, Lucknow, Lahore and Peshawar, with his equipment. By 1909, he started using electric carbon for projection.[2]

Meanwhile in Madras, a photographer, R Venkiah, who owned a photographic studio on Mount Road, was attracted to this new venture. In 1909, he imported a chronomegaphone, which was a film projector attached to a gramophone machine. A gramophone record would be played as the film was screened. This gave the illusion of synchronized sound, and, in a way, anticipated the talkies. With this equipment, he screened the short films, *Pearl Fish* and *Raja's Casket,* in the Victoria Public Hall and in a tent set up in Esplanade. These films were each only 500 feet long, to match the duration of the gramophone. Venkiah later travelled with this unit to Myanmar and Sri Lanka and when he had gathered enough money, he put up a permanent cinema house in Madras—

The Early Days—Silent Movies

Gaiety in 1914, the first cinema house in Madras to be built by an Indian. He soon added two more cinema houses, Crown Theatre in Mint and Globe (later called Roxy) in Purasawalkam.

Most of the films screened then were short films made in the United States and Britain. In 1909, an Englishman called T H Huffton, founded Peninsular Film Services in Madras and produced some short films for local audiences. But soon, hour-long films which narrated a dramatic story, then known as "drama films", were imported, again mostly from the United States. From 1912 onwards, feature films made in Bombay were also screened in Madras. The era of short films ended. More cinema houses came up. The arrival of these "drama films" was a cornerstone in the history of cinema, because thereafter cinema was firmly and irrevocably established as a popular entertainment form.

Fascinated by this new entertainment form, an automobile dealer in the Thousand Lights area of Madras, R Nataraja Mudaliar, also decided to venture into film production. After a few days' training in Pune with cinematographer Stewart Smith, the official cinematographer of Lord Curzon's 1903 Durbar, he tied up with a business associate, S M Dharmalingam Mudaliar, and started India Film Company in 1916. A studio, the first in South India, was set up in Madras. Rangavadivelu, a stage actor from Suguna Vilasa Sabha, was hired to train the actors. Thirty-five days later the first feature film made in South India, *The Extermination of Keechakan/Keechakavatham* based on an episode from the Mahabharata was released in which the lead roles were played by Raja Mudaliar and Jeevarathnam. This was followed in 1917 by *Disrobing of Draupadi/Draupathi Vastrirabaranam*, also drawn from the same epic. At this point, Nataraja Mudaliar broke away from the company, went to Vellore and singlehandedly produced two films, *Mahiravanan* and *Markandeya,* both in 1919. All these films were each about 6,000 feet long.[3]

Although Nataraja Mudaliar was the first South Indian to have found a studio and produce films, it was Venkiah's son Raghupathy Prakasa, and A Narayanan, who put Tamil cinema on a firm footing. After a stint of training in England in filmmaking, Prakasa came to Madras and set up the Star of the East Film Company. The studio, which was located behind what is now Roxy Theatre, was modern by the prevailing standards. Beginning with *Bhishma's Vow/Bhishma Pratignai* (1921), Prakasa made a number of movies which were screened all over the country, with title cards in Tamil, Telugu, Hindi and Gujarati. Though the company lasted for no more than four years, it played a crucial role in the growth of cinema in this part of the country. Many pioneers of South Indian cinema such as Y V Rao (father of actor Lakshmi) and C Pullaiya were trained in this company.

In the first ten years of film production in Madras, Nataraja Mudaliar and Prakasa were the only two to make films. There was a lone exception—an Englishman named Whitaker who produced *The Wedding of Valli/Valli Thirumanam* in 1921 in Madurai. A reviewer in the English daily *The Mail* opined that this film was of a much higher quality than even Dadasaheb Phalke's works. This film, which had been made with the

The Early Days—Silent Movies

support of Madan Company of Bombay, was screened widely in South India.

The third Indian to step into film production in Madras was A Narayanan. After working for a few years in a film distribution company, A Narayanan founded his own outfit, the Exhibitor Film Services, in 1927, and supplied American films to Indian cinema houses. While on a trip to Hollywood, he developed an urge to make films and as a result, set up a production company in Madras, the General Pictures Corporation, popularly known as GPC. Beginning with *The Faithful Wife/Dharmapathini* (1929) GPC made about twenty-four feature films, the best remembered among them being the two-part film *The Star of Mangrelia* (1931) which was based on a story by G W Reynolds. Finally, GPC stabilized the film industry in South India and its alumni included names such as Sundararao Nadkarni and Jiten Banerji. Meanwhile, a colleague of Narayanan, R Padmanabhan, started his own film unit, Associate Films, and made a few films. The studio of this company was in the site now occupied by Paragon Talkies in Madras. It was here that K Subrahmanyam imbibed the basics of filmmaking.

It was learnt that at least seventy-three films were made in Madras during the silent era (Bangalore was the other film production centre in South India). *The Ways of Vishnu/ Vishnu Leela* made by R Prakasa in 1932, was the last silent film produced in Madras.

When one considers the many obstacles faced by filmmakers during this period, it is a wonder that the industry survived at all. Most of the films screened were from the

The Eye of the Serpent

United States, where they were produced in large numbers with several prints for each film. So, the rental for these films was, typically, much less than that for Indian films, of which only a few prints were in circulation. Moreover, the stunts and special effects in imported films were far superior to indigenous productions, and therefore were more popular and enjoyed better patronage. Often, it was difficult to lease a theatre to screen films made in Madras. In the face of this unequal competition, Indian filmmakers decided that one sure way to attract local audiences was to offer films depicting episodes from the Puranas.

Nor was the attitude of the British government in any way helpful. Not only did they discourage local film productions but tried to stifle them in order to promote "Empire films"— movies made in Great Britain—giving the latter special protection even as many filmmakers in India pleaded that indigenous productions should also be given privileges, as was being done in Germany. But the government's aim was to promote the commercial interests of British film companies. An interesting parallel can be drawn with another colony of Britain. It was during the same period that the fledgling film industry of Australia was killed by this policy and the local film industry could come into its own only in the early 1950s. In India, mythological films, and later, the advent of sound, saved the film industry from a similar fate.

There were also other impediments to the growth of cinema during this formative period. It was very difficult to get people to act in films. As film production during the initial decades was not stable and the income meagre and irregular, actors from commercial drama companies were not attracted by cinema. The theatre provided them more security as it ensured a regular income. In fact, there was no group of professional film actors in the early years. All employees of the companies, including on occasion the electrician, were called upon to act. Serukalathur Sama, who was an accountant in GPC and who also doubled as a make-up man, acted in many of its productions and his career as an actor lasted long into the talkie era. Similarly T S Mani, who was a painter in the same company, acted in GPC's films and later in many talkies. So, whoever the director could persuade among his friends and relatives, acted in his films. Once a doctor from the Adyar Theosophical Society, Dr Ernest Wood, acted in *Anadhaipenn/ Orphan Girl* (1931). In fact, the actors' names were not even mentioned in the advertisements. Only in the last two years of the silent era did the artistes' names appear in the publicity material. As the most popular genre was stunt films, gymnasts and stunt men were most sought after. Therefore, one had "Battling" Mani and "Stunt" Raju as leading actors.

It was even more difficult to get women to act in films. However, Nataraja Mudaliar solved this problem by persuading an Englishwoman—Violet Berry—and later, some Anglo-Indian women, to act. Another way out of the situation was to get men to play the role of women. This practice continued in the era of sound also. In the talkie *Menaka* (1935), actor T K Muthuswamy had to play the role of Perundhevi, a widow, since no woman was willing to accept the "inauspicious" role of a widow. In another talkie, *Baktha Ramdas* (1935) all female roles, including that of Sita, were played by men.[4]

The Eye of the Serpent

Some of the conventions that were set during the silent era continued to be followed long after the advent of sound and over the years, shaped the character of Tamil cinema. During the screening of silent films, extraneous programmes like group dances and even boxing matches were added to the show to make it more attractive. These group dancers travelled from place to place, performing wherever there was a cinema house. Sometimes, short plays were also staged. Even now filmmakers resort to the practice of adding extraneous features to pack more entertainment value into the film. Dances, fight sequences, plays and independent comic episodes in present day Tamil films, all belong to this category.[5] Since the literacy rate was very low at the time, some cinema houses engaged "explainers", men who stood by the side of the screen and read the title cards aloud. In addition to reading, they also provided a running commentary; and very often this became the chief attraction. Some of these explainers later blossomed into actors in the talkies.

Dependence on mythological subjects for film stories had a crippling effect on the development of indigenous cinematic vocabulary. Episodes from local mythologies were already familiar to the audience and saved a filmmaker the burden of narrating the story visually. Consequently, the scope for developing a cinematic language was severely curtailed. It has often been said that cinema was fortunate in having been silent in its formative years for the development of a film grammar of visuals. This opportunity was however lost to Tamil cinema because of its preoccupation with mythologicals. And when sound came, the Tamil filmmakers relied conveniently on

The Early Days—Silent Movies

verbal narration to tell the story. During the silent era, a few films were made on contemporary themes. A Narayanan made *Dharmapathini* (1929) and Raja Sandow, *Anadhaipenn* (1931). But we do not have access to any of these films; and hence a study of how these directors made use of visuals for the narrative is not possible.

Before the outbreak of the First World War, silent films from France, Holland and Germany were screened in Madras. Had this trend continued, the development of indigenous cinema would probably have been more wholesome. Local filmmakers might have been influenced by these films. Unfortunately, after the war, only American and British films were distributed here. This meant that the best of European cinema, like Fritz Lang's expressionistic classic *The Testament of Dr.Mabuse* (1933), was denied to the Madras audience and filmmakers. Russian films were subjected to severe censorship and a film that enriched the grammar of cinema, Eisenstein's *Battleship Potemkin* (1925) was banned. So, Tamil cinema had to perforce grow in cultural isolation.

In a society that was rigidly stratified, with each stratum patronizing its own entertainment forms, cinema appeared as mass entertainment, cutting across all strata. Anyone could buy a ticket and watch the show. Cinema's very accessibility to the lower classes alienated the elite from it. Added to this, the stigma that was attached to the popular stage and those working in it was extended to the world of cinema also. This apathy of the intelligentsia to cinema still persists, in many ramified forms. Attempts at introducing cinema studies at the university level in Tamil Nadu have failed continuously. Even today, there is no campus movement, and film society activity is restricted to a mere four or five centres.

Notes

1. Report of the Indian Cinematograph Committee 1927-28 (hereafter referred to as ICC) Vol. Ill (Calcutta, Government of India, Central Publications Division) pp. 359-354.
2. Souvenir of Vincent Light House (Coimbatore, 1946).
3. Nataraja Pillai, T B, *Cinemavin Thennatu Varalaru* (Tamil) (Thanjavur, published by the author, 1959).
4. *Anandavikatan* (Tamil), 15 September 1935.
   T H Huffton, deposing before the Indian Cinematograph Committee 1927-28, said on this practice of males playing females roles, 'We trust that this artistic atrocity will soon become extinct.' Report of ICC, Vol. Ill, p. 179.
5. T R Varadarajan, an associate of A Narayanan, interviewed by the author in Chennai, 19 April 1976.
   Some artistes, who acted in such plays later rose to become stars. Narasimhabharathi, hero of *Ponmudi* (1949) was one such.

Chapter Two
And Then Came the Voices

Although one does not have access to even a single film from the initial years of the sound era, some idea about the nature of these films can be gleaned from film reviews and magazine articles of that period. In the first six years of Tamil cinema, ninety-nine films were made, of which as many as eighty-eight were based on well-known episodes from various mythologies. That the thematic content of most of these films was mythological, contributed in no small way to the beginning of an uncritical tradition; after all, can Puranic presentations be subjected to criticism? Secondly, the choice of mythological subjects also resulted in the popularity of cinema as an entertainment form as it dealt with a subject which was familiar to the people and appealed powerfully to their sense of religious piety.

Most films of this early period were celluloid versions of stage plays which were already popular. The normal practice was to engage a drama troupe, have them enact the play and shoot the performance on film. Sarvotham Badami, who directed the second Tamil talkie, *Galava the Hermit/ Galavarishi* (1932), told me how a stage was erected, and the troupe enacted the play, scene by scene, in front of a static camera. It was thus a photographed version of drama.[1] Most of these films were shot in Bombay, Pune or Calcutta (now Kolkata) where studio floors were hired and were often made by directors and technicians who did not know Tamil. Therefore, at a very impressionable stage of its growth, Tamil cinema remained a total slave of the stage and there was little scope for cinematic conventions to develop. The long-term effects of that enslavement can still be observed. Referring to this tendency, a correspondent once wrote in *The Hindu* newspaper: '... that is inevitable until somebody courageously sets out to demolish the ranting, declaiming, rhetorical, superficially sentimental, wooden automatons—legacies of South Indian stage at its last and least creative epoch.'[2]

As these drama companies travelling to Bombay or Calcutta to make a film were operating in a new region and therefore had to bear the boarding and lodging expenses for the whole troupe, the tendency was to rush through and complete the project as quickly as possible. Sagar Movietone's *Harishchandra* (1932), the third Tamil talkie, was made in just twenty-one days in Bombay. As a result, not much importance was given to continuity or appropriateness. In *Kovalan* (1933), a film set somewhere between the third and fifth century AD, one of the characters appears in a few scenes wearing spectacles! In *The Exile of Sita/Sita Vanavasam* (1934), Rama opens an envelope with a postage stamp and postmarks on it.

Next to mythology, the most popular subject for films was the lives of saints. In this category, New Theatre's *Nandanar* (1933), the story of an untouchable farmhand who aspired to go to Chidambaram and worship Siva, was the first film and this was followed by *Siruthonda Nayanar* (1935). *Sankaracharya* was made in 1939. Parts of *Sankaracharya* made in 1939, were shot in Sringeri with the blessings of the Sankaracharya of that mutt. At the film's premiere in Madurai, the Sankaracharya of Jyothir Mutt presided over the function. On this genre of films, *The Hindu* wrote: 'The angle of cinematic treatment of their lives (saints) must change from the gross, objective to the imaginative and sensitively psychological.'[3]

Gramophone records were also gaining popularity at this time and many gramophone companies released recordings of songs from company dramas on a series of discs called "drama sets". Thus, when sound films arrived, a close commercial connection between the gramophone companies and cinema was promptly established. The complete soundtrack of the film *Alli Arjuna* (1935) was released as a set of seven discs (78 rpm), packaged neatly in a metal box. In fact, some companies—for instance, Orrs Gramophone and Talkies Limited of Madras—also produced films: *Vishnu Leela* (1938), directed by Raja Sandow, was one such film.

The first talkie with a contemporary setting—"socials", as they came to be called—was *Kausalya* produced by the South India Film Corporation, directed by P S V Aiyar and released in August 1935.[4] It was a thriller, with a pistol-wielding woman as the chief protagonist, and was made by a group of

The Eye of the Serpent

amateur actors. The second social, *The Playboy/Dumbachari*, adapted from a popular play of the same name, was released in September 1935. And the third, based on *Menaka*, also a popular play, was released in December the same year.[5]

Dumbachari told the story of a playboy who fritters away his wealth on women of ill-repute. Maharajapuram M R Krishnamurthy played the male lead and P S Rathnabai, the female lead. Samanna, who was known as the Charlie Chaplin of South India, was also in the cast. *Menaka* was adapted from a novel by Vaduvoor Duraisamy Ayyengar; the dialogue for the film was written by T K Muthuswamy, one of the TKS brothers, whose theatre group was engaged for filming this story. It was in this film that N S Krishnan and T A Mathuram—renowned actors of Tamil cinema—made their debut.

Following the success of these films, more and more were made on contemporary themes, though mythology continued to provide the subject for the bulk of the films. Of the thirty-seven films made in 1937, seven were on contemporary themes; in the next year, there were ten. The socio-political developments in the country was first reflected in films like *Child Saint/Balayogini* (1936) which criticized caste prejudices.[6] In the film, a Brahmin widow seeks refuge in a low caste servant's house; the Brahmins in retaliation set fire to the servant's house. The writer of the film, K Subrahmanyam, reinforced existing values, including religious beliefs, but attacked the irrationality of a hierarchical order decided by birth. Nearly all the members of the team, including the director, were Brahmins and this added a measure of authenticity to the anti-caste appeal of the film. Encouraged by the commercial success of *Balayogini*, Subrahmanyam followed up with *House of Service/Sevasadan* (1938), a story written originally in Hindi by Munshi Premchand, a Congress sympathizer. It was translated by Ambujammal and was published as a serial in the Tamil weekly *Anandavikatan*. Noting how well the story was received among the public, Subrahmanyam decided to film it. In this, in addition to reformist ideas, he introduced visuals of nationalistic symbols like the charka and portraits of national leaders.

But it is for *The Land of Sacrifice/Thyagabhoomi* (1939) that Subrahmanyam is best remembered. Here, he used all the elements he had so far successfully put to use—classical songs, child actresses, reformist and nationalist appeal and a story whose acceptability had already been tested when it appeared in a popular magazine. This story revolved around Sambu Sastri, a Brahmin priest with a Gandhi-like persona, his daughter and a Harijan farmhand, Nallan. Sastri's progressive ideas and his action in allowing the untouchables to take shelter in the temple after their huts are ravaged by a cyclone, infuriating other priests, leading Sastri to join the freedom movement. In this film, Subrahmanyam handled the theme of the freedom struggle directly. It must be remembered that at the time this film was being made, the Congress had come to power in the Madras presidency; and so there were no restrictions on nationalist propaganda in films.[7] The film opened with a song glorifying India and Gandhi and Sastri was hailed as the "Gandhi of Tamil Nadu". In fact, some of the sequences in the film, like the picketing by Congress volunteers and the marches, were semi-documentary in character.

In *Deliverance/Vimochanam* (1939) directed by T Marconi, all the roles were essayed by students of Madras Sangeetha Vidyalaya Girls School. The main thrust of the film was abstinence, one of Gandhi's programmes for national upliftment.[8] The film's release coincided with the intense temperance propaganda in Tamil Nadu in the wake of the Salem session of the Congress. The story revolved around Arumugam, who sells his wife's jewels to buy liquor; his family is pushed to the wall. Meanwhile, prohibition is imposed in Salem district; the whole town rejoices. Arumugam tries to brew illicit liquor and is imprisoned. Upon being released, he finds a tea stall in the place of his favourite toddy shop. When he sees his wife has become destitute, he reforms his ways and is united with his family.

As more and more contemporary stories were filmed, some of the issues that engaged the attention of individual filmmakers formed the themes of their work. Westernisation figured in quite a few of these films and it was always portrayed as evil where women were involved. C K Rajagopal's *Dharmapathini* (1935) revolved around a socialite and her Anglophile husband. *Fortune's play/Bagyaleela* (1938) was about a London-returned, westernised housewife who is adulterous.

Smoking cannabis was an accepted practice in the early Thirties, and this often featured in films as did betel chewing, without any judgmental comments. In the film *Tamil Mother or Maternal Duty/Thamizhthai alladhu Mathrudharmam* (1939) a group of men sing over a pot session:

And Then Came the Voices

Let us put this herb in a pipe and smoke
Let us drive our cares away

Three developments in the mid-Thirties gave a fresh impetus to the further development of Tamil cinema. The first was the setting up of the first sound studio in South India, Srinivasa Cinetone or the Sound City, by A Narayanan in Madras in 1934. This was quickly followed by Meenakshi Cinetone, Vel Pictures and a few other studios. Once the facilities for making a film became available in Madras, filmmakers did not have to travel all the way to Calcutta or Bombay to produce films. They could make them in Madras with editors, sound recordists and other technicians who were conversant with Tamil. This ensured a certain quality in the films they made.

The second factor was the new trend of making films on contemporary issues. Though many of these socials, like *Devotion to Husband/Pathi Bakthi* (1936), were film versions of successful plays, from the repertoire of company dramas, films were also made on stories that were written exclusively for them, for example *Balayogini*. The filmmaker had to structure his own mise en scene and a narrative technique that would suit the story; so, a format different from that of theatre was developed. The subjects chosen by these filmmakers were also very relevant to that period; some filmmakers turned their attention to social issues, studied and built their films around them. Thus, the concerns and conflicts of that period came to be featured in these films. The whole country was charged with the nationalist fervour, fuelled by the political activism of the Civil Disobedience movement and as a natural corollary, Tamil cinema benefited from this mood. The nationalists on their part used the press, the stage, the gramophone and the screen to communicate their ideas. As some filmmakers began to tackle these issues, first obliquely and later directly, Tamil cinema acquired a new relevance and respectability.

Thirdly, some filmmakers cast amateur actors in their films mainly because it was cheaper, and also because amateurs were easy to handle. This was yet another step that took Tamil cinema away from the ethos of theatre. Till then, all the actors, song writers and musicians were drawn from the world of commercial drama companies. When non-professionals made their entry, the style of acting obviously underwent a change. Highly stylized acting yielded place to attempts at realistic acting and the accent on songs was reduced. One such early attempt at casting amateurs was in the film *The Wedding of Sita/Sita Kalyanam* (Tamil, 1933), in which G K Seshagiri, acting as an agent of V Shantaram, the director of the film, started a trend which later caught on.[9] Many of these amateurs were persons who had other professions. For example, K Subrahmanyam's brother Viswanathan, who played the lead role in *Balayogini* under the name Vathsal, was a lawyer by profession.

The first two or three decades of this century also witnessed a revival of Tamil language and culture. The work of scholars like R Caldwell and G U Pope on Tamil language and literature in the latter half of the nineteenth century had created tremendous interest in the language. There were other developments which also contributed to this revival. Beginning with *Swadesamithran,* which was founded in 1880 as a magazine and later became a daily in 1899, around sixty periodicals in Tamil were launched in the next two decades. The rediscovery and publication of Tamil classics of the Sangam period—circa third to fifth century AD—by U V Swaminatha Aiyar in 1900, brought to light a glorious part of Tamil history. V Kanagasabai Pillai's *Tamils 1800 Years Ago,* published in 1904, was a part of this process. Somasundara Bharathi's *Tamil Classics and Thamizhagam* published in 1912 and M Srinivasa Ayyangar's *Tamil Studies* which came out in 1914 greatly added to this interest.[10] Poet Subramanya Bharathi's works brought poetry closer even to the semi-literate and gave a boost to the process of revivalism. To a society that had been humiliated by colonial rule and the attendant cultural hegemony, the nostalgic vision of a glorious past was almost like recompense and was zealously embraced. Gradually this ethos of revivalism began to manifest itself in films.

The writings and ideas of Ramalinga Swamigal alias Vallalar (1823-1874) was one of the motivating forces for Tamil revivalism as well as for the Self-respect movement. He later founded an organization —The Association of Equality, Purity and the Good Way/Samarasa Sutha Sanmarka Sangam— which had branches in many parts of Tamil Nadu. A film based on his life and ideas *Jothi or Srimath Ramalinga Swamigal/Jothi alladhu Srimath Ramalinga Swamigal* with dialogues by dramatist P Sambanda Mudaliar, was released in 1939. The film included ten songs from *Arutpa,* an anthology of devotional hymns by Ramalinga Swamigal.[11] *Baktha Kumanan,* also released in the same year—1939—told the story of a legendary king from the Sangam era who was renowned for his generosity.

The twin epics, *Silapathikaram* and *Manimekalai*, considered to be the earliest in the history of Tamil literature, were filmed during this period. These two epics are in sequence: *Silapathikaram* (The Story of the Anklet) revolves around Kannagi and her husband Kovalan. To avenge the injustice meted out to her husband, the enraged Kannagi burns down Madurai, the capital of the Pandyan kingdom. *Manimekalai* is about the eponymous daughter of Kovalan and Madhavi, a courtesan who eventually becomes a Buddhist nun. The film with dialogues by A A Somayajulu, was made in 1940 and *Kannagi*, based on the *Silapathikaram*, in 1942. While *Manimekalai* is Buddhist in character, *Silapathikaram* is Jain and the two faiths were popular during the Sangam era.

Thiruvalluvar, the author of *Thirukural*, an ethical work of 1,330 couplets, is also believed to have lived in the Sangam age. A film on his life, *Thiruvalluvar*, was made in 1941 with Serukalathur Sama as Valluvar and Tirunelveli Papa as his wife Vasuki. A year later, *The Bell of Justice/Araichimani* directed by Raja Sandow in 1942, was about a Chola king renowned for his sense of justice. When his son runs over a calf while driving his chariot, the king orders that the prince should also suffer a similar fate and be crushed under the wheels of a chariot.

Poet Bharathidasan, who under the influence of poet Subramanya Bharathi had given up his original name Kanagasubburathinam to call himself Bharathidasan, entered films as a dialogue writer and song writer for *Balamani* (1937). Bharathidasan, who was a sympathiser of the Self-respect movement— a precursor of the Dravidian parties— worked in other films too, such as *Sri Ramanujar* (1938), *Kalamegam* (1940) and *Ponmudi*. His dialogues and songs were imbued with rationalistic and reformist ideas.

Later, the arrival of dialogue writers like T V Chari and Ilangovan, who wrote flowery lines in chaste Tamil studded with literary allusions, further reinforced the process of Tamil revivalism in films. Ilangovan was identified with a group of writers associated with the Tamil magazine *Manikodi* who were committed to excellence in literature and other arts in Tamil Nadu and who recognized the possibilities of film as a medium. Ilangovan's dialogue for *Ambikapathi* (1937), a story about the eponymous son of poet Kambar, contributed in no small measure to the success of the film. He also wrote the dialogues for *Divine Poet/Sivakavi* (1943) which was the life story of Poyyamozhi Pulavar. Sivakavi, the protagonist, declares himself a poet who was fed by Thamizhthai (Mother Tamil), and as someone whose life was dedicated to the growth of the Tamil language. T V Chari wrote the dialogue for the film *Manonmani* (1942), based on *Manonmaniyam,* one of the earliest of Tamil plays, set in the classical age of the Cheran and Pandyan kingdoms. Written at the turn of the nineteenth century by Sundaram Pillai in verse form after the manner of Shakespearean drama, this play glorified the Tamil language and tradition. Another film *Tamil Savant Perumal/Thamizhariyum Perumal* (1942) set in the Chola times, told the story of a poetess played by M R Santhanalakshmi and Nakkiran, essayed by V A Chellappa, a legendary scholar in the court of the

Pandyan king who was known for his zeal in defending and protecting the purity of the Tamil language. Other legendary characters from ancient Tamil Nadu, Karikalcholan and Avvaiyar, were also also portrayed in this film.

By the end of Second World War, as India's Independence became imminent, and the freedom struggle reached its final stage, we observe that nationalist content gradually disappeared and was supplanted by Tamil consciousness in some films. In *Miser/Kanjan* (1947), a film dealing with a contemporary theme, the hero sings eulogies to the qualities of the Tamil people:

Of all the people who live on this earth
the Tamils are the best[13]

This film was directed by Kovai A Ayyamuthu, a staunch Congress leader and a lieutenant of C Rajagopalachari or Rajaji, who was influenced by the ideas of Ramalinga Swamigal. When I met Ayyamuthu in his village near Coimbatore, I asked him what prompted him to write this song. He thought for a moment and told me that such ideas were very much in the air at that time and that he thought that it would be quite in order to have a song on those lines.[14]

The apogee of this trend was seen in the film *Avvaiyar* (1953), a story woven around episodes from the life of the legendary eponymous poetess, whose works are considered to be one of the glories of Tamil literature. Every Tamil child is initiated into the language and culture through her poems. The film is dedicated to Mother Tamil and opens with a song praising Tamil Nadu. Avvaiyar herself symbolizes Mother Tamil and her deity, Murugan, is hailed as god of the Tamils. Other characters from the Sangam age, like king Paari and poet-saint Thiruvalluvar, are also depicted in the film. Gemini Studios was awarded a shield at the 6th Tamil Festival held in Delhi in recognition of its contribution towards the enrichment of Tamil life through this film. The main reason for the success of the film was the manner in which it combined religious appeal with Tamil revivalism. C P Ramasamy Aiyar, then vice-chancellor of Annamalai University, felicitating the makers of this film said, 'I regard the emergence of this picture as symptomatic of the recurrent, resurgent spirit of the Indian religion asserting itself.'[15]

The impact of the Second World War in 1939 was very perceptible on Tamil cinema. The popularly elected Congress government, which ruled the Madras presidency, resigned in protest against Britain's role in the war. As a result, censorship of "politically motivated" films which had been completely removed during the Congress rule, was made stringent, and nearly brought nationalist propaganda in films to an end. Wartime restrictions on the import of raw stock and machinery and rise in the cost of materials slowed down the pace of film production. Added to these, there was petrol rationing, frequent and erratic power cuts and cancellation of railway concessions. Studios closed down or were shifted. Due to the frequent blackouts, shows in cinema houses were cancelled. The war with Japan wiped out the market for Tamil films in Burma and some Far Eastern countries where a sizable Tamil population formed the audience. To regulate the

The Eye of the Serpent

supply of raw stock, the government laid down that the length of each film should not exceed 11,000 feet. As a result, song and dance sequences were drastically reduced. The number of films produced, which was thirty-seven in 1938 came down to fourteen in 1943 and then just ten in the next year.[16]

On the other hand, as was expected, the government encouraged filmmakers to lace their films with war propaganda. The Director of War Publicity, G T B Harvey, was nominated to the Film Censor Board to ensure that no anti-war sentiments were expressed in any film. It was easier to obtain supply of raw stock if the film supported the war. The government further ruled that at least one out of three films of a production concern should be a "war effort" film and extended cooperation in the making of such films. A few such wartime fictional films were released in 1945.

For instance, *Burma Rani* (1945), produced by Modern Theatres and directed by T R Sundaram, was about three British-Indian airmen, who, after making a forced landing in Burma, liberate the country from Japanese occupation and eventually escape with the help of some local Indians opposed to the occupation forces. The cast included Honnappa Bhagavathar, K L V Vasantha, N S Krishnan, T A Mathuram and T R Sundaram himself who played the role of a Japanese commandant. The film proved to be quite popular and had dialogues by the renowned Ilangovan, T V Chari and Ki Ra (Ki Ramachandran). *The Hindu* in one of its editions commented: 'Life in Japanese-occupied Burma is realistically depicted.'[17]

Yet another film, *Defence of Honour/Manasamrakshanam*

(1944) directed by K Subrahmanyam and featuring S D Subbulakshmi and Kali N Rathinam in the lead roles, was about Padmini, a woman from Burma who comes to Madras with a group of youngsters to trace the hide-out of some Japanese agents. She encounters Diraviyam, a call-girl and a Japanese spy. Padmini busts the spy ring and foils Japanese attempts to blow up some British ships in the Madras harbour. *Kannamma My Darling/Kannamma En Kathali* (1945), made by Gemini Studios and directed by Kothamangalam Subbu, was set against the backdrop of the war; the Japanese invasion of Burma was woven into the story with M K Radha and Sundaribai playing the lead roles.

The government hired some filmmakers to produce short feature films—usually three to eight reelers—to support the cause of the war. A number of such films were made between 1943 and 1946. P S Srinivasa Rao, a leading actor and a film director *(Shantha,* 1941) made a few in Tamil. Typcially, the propaganda was usually woven into the story and the films were shot in Bombay. W J Moylon, an American who was the manager at Gemini Studios, took over as the Chief of War Publicity in Madras and made a film titled *Madras Must Not Burn* explaining the work of the Air Raid Precaution Unit and civil defence procedures. Vittal made the film *Home Front* with Tamil commentary and *themmangu* (folk)songs, to propagate anti-panic measures in wartime. These were shown in villages through mobile vans fitted with projectors.[18] Evidently the Government had realized the power of cinema and endeavoured to use it for propaganda.

Unfortunately none of these films have survived.

Notes

1. Sarvotham Badami interviewed by the author in Bangalore, published *in The Hindu,* 20 July 1990.
2. *The Hindu,* 7 March 1939.
3. *The Hindu,* 7 March 1939.
4. *The Hindu,* 30 August 1935.
5. *Cinema Ulagam* (Tamil), 8 December 1935.
6. The lead role of Sarasa, in this film, was played by child actress R Balasaraswathi, who had made her debut in the film *Anasuya* (Telugu, 1935) and had acted in *Baktha Kuchela* (1936). Her role in *Balayogini* brought her fame She recorded songs for HMV Gramophone Company when she was just 9 years old. Later, she sang in many films as a playback singer. She was the music director for the film *Bilhana* (1948).
7. When the film was revived in 1941 after the resignation of the Congress government, it was banned by the British government. It was only in 1951 that the ban was lifted.
8. There were other westerners who had directed Tamil films. They were Michael Omalev and Ellis R Dungan.
9. "*Talkiyin Adhirshtam*", interview with G K Seshagiri, *Anandavikatan,* November 1936.
10. Christopher Baker, in the introduction to *The Message Bearers,* (Cre-A, Madras, 1981).
11. Irchick, Eugene F, *Tamil Revivalism in the 1930s* (Madras, Cre-A, 1986).
12. For more on this, see Richman, Paula, *Women, Branch Stories and Religious Rhetoric in Tamil Buddhist Text* (New York, Syracuse University, 1988).
13. This song proved very popular. It was broadcast over the radio from Tiruchi, Madras, and Colombo. The gramophone discs were sold in large numbers.

14. Kovai A Ayyamuthu interviewed by the author at Singarampalayam, Coimbatore, 21 October 1974.
15. *Filmfare,* 25 December 1953.
16. "Film Industry in 1941" in *The Hindu,* 6 February 1942.
17. *The Hindu,* 16 March 1945. *Burma Rani* was banned for a while due to objections from Buddhists on some scenes shot in a pagoda. It was banned for a second time after Independence as a pro-war film.
18. P S Srinivasa Rao interviewed by the author in Madras, 13 July 1975. In Hollywood also, the services of some stars and filmmakers were utilised for war efforts. Hedy Lamarr, Bob Hope, Bing Crosby and Ronald Colman supported the war effort. Frank Capra made a series of propaganda documentaries titled *Why We Fight?* (1942-44).

Chapter Three
Era of the Dialogue writer and the Cinema of Dissent

IN TAMIL NADU, IDEOLOGUES, WRITERS AND ARTISTES OF THE Dravidian movement used theatre for both propaganda and fund-raising. While production of films declined to an all time low during the war years, drama flourished, providing opportunities for many aspiring playwrights. A lieutenant of E V Ramasamy Naicker in the Self-respect movement, C N Annadurai, who later became the chief of Dravida Munnetra Kazhagam (DMK) and then the chief minister of Tamil Nadu in 1967, wrote the play *Moon Rise/Chandrodhayam* which was staged in 1943. This play, with both Annadurai and M Karunanidhi, who later succeeded Annadurai as chief minister of Tamil Nadu, in the cast, was used extensively for propaganda. The stage came handy as a tool for political propaganda when the Dravida Kazhagam (DK) was formed in 1944. A play was often the highlight of DK conferences;

many leaders in the movement routinely tried their hand at writing for theatre.

Some of these writers who aspired to work in films joined the story department at Modern Theatres in Salem which served as a kind of school for dialogue writers.[1] It was here that Bharathidasan, a Dravida Kazhagam sympathiser, made his mark as a dialogue writer for films. He wrote the dialogues for many films including *Subadhra* (1945) and set an example for other writers from the movement to emulate. These writers from the Dravidian movement worked in a number of films in the Fifties, films which can be described as the cinema of dissent: they were iconoclastic and radical towards certain traditional practices and beliefs. As one film historian put it, 'A cinema of dissent or disengagement makes comments no less revealing than one which whole-heartedly endorses the standards of its society.'[2] These films deserve a closer look for this reason.

Inspired by Frank Capra's *Mr.Deeds Goes to Town* (1936), Annadurai wrote the story and dialogue for *Nallathambi* (1949) and made a momentous entry into the film world. The original story by playwright Robert Riskin, set in the Depression years in America, suggested that the rich should share their wealth, with the poor.[3] This motif came in handy for some radical rhetoric in *Nallathambi*. Annadurai had already earned his reputation as a playwright through a successful play titled, *Servant Maid/Velaikari*. The basic idea for the play was taken from a newspaper report about a devotee in Sylhet, who, disappointed at his prayers remaining unanswered, had damaged a statue of the goddess Kali.[4] Jupiter Pictures of

Coimbatore, with a shrewd eye on the market, observed the full houses this play was drawing and decided to turn it into a film called *Velaikari* (1952). The hero Anandan, a devotee of Kali, returns from Sri Lanka to find his father hanging from a tree, victimised by his landlord's greed. He sets about planning revenge. This film's appeal lay in its rationalistic rhetoric and anti-priesthood slant.

Annadurai was an inveterate filmgoer and was much influenced by American films of that period. At the time, Hollywood films were going through a phase in which the spoken word was given importance, with pithy repartee and witticisms serving to entertain the audience. Robert Riskin's dialogue in *It Happened One Night* (English, 1934)[5] is a well-known example of this emphasis. Films for which Annadurai wrote dialogues stressed on the spoken word rather than dramatic action, reflecting the Hollywood trend of that time. Some sequences in *Velaikari* were modelled on those in *The Count of Monte Cristo* (English, 1934) and even had an identical sequence in which the hero Dantes, before escaping from prison and avenging himself on those who framed him, writes down his scheme of revenge chapter by chapter. Similarly the climactic court scene in which Anandan comes disguised as a lawyer was inspired by the film, *The Life of Emile Zola* (1937) starring the great actor, Paul Muni; even the hero's make-up was closely imitated.[6]

Rouben Mamoulian's film, *Queen Christina* (1935) in which a queen in seventeenth century Sweden, while trying to avoid a marriage she does not fancy, wanders around disguised as a male and falls in love with a man of her choice— inspired another film, *The Gateway to Heaven/Sorgavasal* (1954), written by Annadurai. This film, set against the backdrop of the spread of Buddhism in ancient Tamil Nadu, preaches rationalism and rails against ritualism and commercialisation of religious activities. *Gas Light* (English, 1944), another Hollywood film, whose hero inflicts mental cruelty on his wife in order to drive her insane, inspired Annadurai's novel *Rangoon Radha* which was later made into a film in 1956.[7]

Many other writers from the Dravida Munnetra Kazhagam entered the glittering world of cinema. A V P Asaithambi wrote the dialogues for *The Dictator/ Sarvadhikari* (1951). M Karunanidhi, who had earlier worked as a dialogue-writer in some films without being credited for it, wrote for *The Princess of Maruda Country/Marudanatttu Ilavarasi* (1950); but it was *The Goddess/Parasakthi* (1952), adapted from a popular play, that brought him acclaim as a dialogue-writer. He became much sought after and soon acquired a star status. The producers realized that the radical rhetoric and the elegant prose of these writers was a saleable commodity among Tamil audiences and were therefore hired as dialogue writers.

It is worth noting however that writers of the Dravidian movement were only employed as dialogue writers; control over a film remained with the director and the producer. When *Nallathambi* was under production, N S Krishnan, who played the lead, changed the story and Annadurai, the writer, though piqued, was in no position to resist.[8] The writer's job was to supply the lines; he exercised no control over the narrative sequences or visuals. He did not write the screenplay or shooting-script, but merely the dialogues.

While plays which met with popular success during conferences of the Dravidian movement were filmed, most of the radical content was jettisoned. The producers were theists; and they were wary of stretching the radical element too far and alienating the audience. Moreover, more money was at stake in a film than in a play. S K Mohideen and K Somasundaram, owners of Jupiter Pictures, were both believers and refused to allow any atheistic ideas in their film *Velaikari* as was its director, A S A Swamy, who was a devout Catholic. In fact, the anti-religious elements of the original play were greatly watered down when it was made into a film. K A Perumal, owner of National Pictures which produced *Parasakthi,* ensured that the first day's shooting began with a traditional puja. On another occasion, during the making of *Poongothai* (1953), when the Regional Film Censor Officer Stalin Srinivasan, pointed out that some scenes were likely to be perceived as anti-religious, Perumal readily agreed to remove them.

The visuals of this school of films were also organized in a way that ensured such a dilution. In *Velaikari*, the climactic scene where Anandan raves in the temple of Kali and goes to sit resignedly outside is immediately followed by another in which the solution to his problems offers itself, providentially as it were. Observing this, Kalki who was a conservative writer, approvingly titled his review of the film "The Grace of Kali".[10] The last sequence in this film is a wedding scene. The camera tilts up to a "welcome" signboard above the entrance to the wedding pandal which carries the legend 'There is only one God and only one community', as though intending to clarify the doubts of sceptics among the viewers. This reassuring message was the director's idea.[11]

In *Parasakthi,* when the priest tries to molest Kalyani inside the temple, she appeals to the goddess. The next shot shows the temple attendant, woken from his siesta by her cries, ringing the bell frantically; the priest releases Kalyani. The shots were edited in such a way as to make it seem that the bell was rung in answer to Kalyani's cries for help. This was clearly the idea of the directors, Krishnan and Panju.[12]

It has been argued by scholars that what was finally internalized and accepted by the audience, was not the radical ideas of these films but the cultural definition of what it meant to be a Tamil.[13] This view is supported by the success of many films with a heavy dose of religion that swept the box office, even as the films, of dialogue writers from the Dravidian movement were proving to be popular. *Avvaiyar* and *Gunasundari* (1955) are examples of successful films with an overt religious content.

Although the dialogue writers criticized social evils through the cast of characters, they did not suggest any agenda of political reform. They typically played the role of a gadfly attacking the establishment without offering an alternative political or economic ideology. It must be pointed out that this group of writers wrote the dialogue for scores of films and only a few are remembered for such rhetoric. Even these reformist ideas were not woven into the story but were merely spouted by the characters. Therefore, situational opportunities were contrived in a film where a character could be given scope for delivering long monologues, a courtroom scene, for instance. In many films written by this group, the courtroom scene was indeed the high point. This was so in *Parasakthi, Velaikari, Manohara* (1954) and *The Minister's Daughter/Mandhirikumari* (1950). Sometimes, a play-within-the-film was introduced to provide scope for some preachy monologues; the Socrates play in *King and Queen/Rajarani* (1956) written by M Karunanidhi, or Samrat Asokan drama in the film *Mother's Command/ Annaiyin Anai* (1958) written by Murasoli Maran, are examples. The ability to "deliver" these long monologues clearly and intensely was highly desirable in an artiste. Sivaji Ganesan's performance in these "dialogue heavy" sequences was acclaimed as one of his special talents.

Most of the other films written by this group had ordinary run-of-the-mill plots, in careful conformity with the existing beliefs and mores of the audience; as evident in *Treasure Trove/Pudhaiyal* (1957) written by M Karunanidhi. Kannadasan wrote the dialogue for films such as *The Soldier of Madurai/Madurai Veeran*, a folklore story and *Rama of Tenali/Tenaliraman*, the story of the legendary jester at the court of the Vijayanagar emperor, Krishnadevaraya, both made in 1956. However, in the dialogue, an occasional anti-establishment jibe was included, as in Annadurai's *A Honest Man will Prosper/Nallavan Vazhvan* (1961).

The films in which dialogue predominated were very stagy, with eye-level shots and horizontal exits and entries. Characters looked directly into the camera and delivered their lines.[14] The importance given to the spoken word tended to

Era of the Dialogue writer and the Cinema of Dissent

eliminate camera mobility and rendered the performance immobile. The capability of the camera to see from different angles and the consequent plasticity of cinema was not used in these films because of the importance given to spoken words. For the same reason, it was difficult for these filmmakers to get at the essence of the medium of cinema.[15] There was this preoccupation with just one aspect of cinema: speech. Cinema was largely perceived in literary terms. In fact, the dialogues of a few of these films were published in book form which sold well. Thus cinema, as handled in these films, was almost like an extension of literature, instead of belonging to its own realm.[16]

The popularity of rhetoric in films, which came into vogue in the early Fifties, lasted only a decade; its novelty then wore off. By then, these dialogue writers had earned enough fame and money to produce their own movies. A K Velan, A V P Asaithambi, Kannadasan, Rama Arangannal and Neelanarayanan all founded their own film companies and produced movies that were noticeably free from reformist propaganda. In the meantime, there was a significant development. The Dravida Munnetra Kazhagam, an offshoot of the earlier Dravida Kazhagam, decided to enter the electoral fray: and it was on guard against alienating any section of the voters by attacking their beliefs or values. As a result, the films they made at this point in time proffered entertainment with an eye on the box-office.

The early Fifties registered an unprecedented boom in production. The end of the war and the lifting of wartime restrictions facilitated an expansion of the industry. While in 1946, only sixteen films were made, the figure went up to thirty-six in 1953. During these years, in Tamil Nadu, the rural electrification programme widened the market for films and took cinema to the interior regions. The number of movie-goers increased manifold, creating a demand for more films. It was at this time that dialogue writers, and later actors, from the Dravida Munnetra Kazhagam consolidated their respective positions.

Notes

1. Kannadasan, *Vanavasam* (Tamil, autobiography, Madras, Kannadasan Noolagam, 1965) pp.105-111.
2. Housten, Penelope, *The Contemporary Cinema* (London, Penguin Books, 1963) p.125.
3. A S A Swamy interviewed by the author in Madras, 6 April 1975.
4. E V K Sampath interviewed by the author in Madras, 3 April 1975. The atheistic propaganda in the film created a lot of controversy. Two ministers of the Government of Madras viewed the film before it was cleared for exhibition. Kalki, *Kalaichelvam,* (Madras, Bharathi Pathippagam, 1959).
5. Corliss, Richard, *Talking Pictures: Screen Writers in the American Cinema 1937-1973* (New York, Harper & Row, 1974) pp. 241.
6. Alfred Dreyfus, a Jewish officer of the French Army, was accused of spying for the Germans and sentenced to long term imprisonment in an island. Many intellectuals, who believed that it was a case of anti-semitic prejudice, took up his cause which led to his acquittal in 1906. He died in 1935. Paul Muni played Emile Zola, the nineteenth century French

novelist, who supported Dreyfus. The film won 3 Academy Awards.
7. A S A Swamy, Interview.
8. Narayanan, V, *Kalaivanar Vazhvile* (Tamil, Madras, Parandhaman Pathippagam 1985).
9. K A Perumal interviewed by the author in Madras, 4 May 1975.
10. Kalki, *Kalaichelvam*.
11. A S A Swamy, Interview.
12. Stalin R Srinivasan, (the Regional Censor Officer who certified *Parasakthi)* interviewed by the author in Madras, 23 May 1975.
13. Barnett, Marguerite Ross, "Creating Political Identity: The Emergent South Indian Tamil", *Ethnicity*, Vol I (1971) pp. 237-265.
14. Kurosawa, Akira, *Something Like An Autobiography* (New York, Vintage Books, 1983) p. 195.
15. Das Gupta, Chidananda, *Talking About Films* (New Delhi, Orient Longman, 1981) p.118.
16. The tendency to look at cinema from literary point of view still persists. A cinema-related topic for Ph.D. or M.Phil degrees is quite popular in the Tamil language departments of the universities in Tamil Nadu, while the subject ought to come under the department of media studies, sociology or anthropology, if not of cinema studies.

Chapter Four
Songs in Tamil Cinema

ONE OF THE MOST STRIKING FEATURES OF CULTURAL CHANGE in Tamil Nadu over the past few decades is the growth and dominance of film music.[1] It is all-pervasive and enjoys a popularity that has few parallels in the history of music. 'Life is not what it used to be thirty years ago and one of the factors that has changed it is film music.'[2]

Film music, is in fact, another dimension of the hold cinema has on the social and political life of Tamil Nadu. The nexus between politics and films has attracted scholarly attention in recent years.[3] But film songs, which are a potent medium for propagating social and political ideas and a significant phenomenon on the cultural scene, have not been studied.

In India, film music's most predominant form is in songs.[4] Backed by a mammoth industry, film music is in the air constantly. Transistors and tape-recorders have contributed greatly to the spread and popularity of this music. On television, a programme featuring song sequences from films has been the most popular, practically since the inception of TV broadcasting in Tamil Nadu. During festivals, fairs and domestic functions such as marriages, loudspeakers blare out film songs. Even in remote villages, an amplifier and a box of discs are available for hire by the hour.

What are the historical, cultural and sociological factors which have brought about this situation? What are the divergent roots from which this film music has grown? How was the power of the ancient art of music harnessed to the new art of cinema? How do these songs affect the ideological content of a film?

While folk music forms, of which Tamil Nadu has a vigorous tradition, were people-oriented in character and appeal, the upper classes had their own exclusive forms of music.[5] Nurtured in palaces and temple courtyards, Carnatic music of South India is basically religious in content. It requires prolonged learning and discipline. Even to be able to respond to Carnatic music as a listener, exposure is necessary, which until a few decades ago only the privileged could afford. So, kings and landlords patronized Carnatic music while the others had their folk music, which to a great extent was secular in content.

By the beginning of this century the situation had changed with the arrival of the gramophone. When musical performances came to be mechanically multiplied through the medium of gramophone records, the sharp distinction between upper and lower class tastes began to blur and music was able to transcend the barriers of social stratification.

When classical music was recorded, the common man had the opportunity to savour it for the first time.[6]

A mass entertainment form had emerged by the end of the nineteenth century which contributed to the basic fabric of film music—the company drama. Though the tradition of theatre in Tamil Nadu goes back more than a thousand years, drama as we know it today, with divisions of acts, scenes and concealed orchestra appeared only in the middle of the nineteenth century. These were called company dramas as they were run on commercial lines, with professional actors.

The repertoire of these companies was limited to a few mythologicals which were written as musicals. The stories were narrated, in large part, through a series of songs. The playwright, called *vathiyar* (literally meaning teacher) in these companies, wrote the songs, composed the music and also directed the play. All the actors had to be singers, including the clown. The emphasis was on singing, not on drama. When a character died on stage after singing a lugubrious song, he would, in response to cries of "once more", unhesitatingly come back to life and start singing all over again.

Songs used by the drama companies were based on Carnatic music. In addition, they introduced a new strain of music into Tamil Nadu, natya sangeeth (drama music), a kind of Hindustani music appropriated from Marathi drama companies which toured Tamil Nadu at the beginning of the century. Through this strain, Hindustani ragas were assimilated; the resultant synthesis claimed a very large following. Another influence on drama and cinema music came from Parsi drama companies which toured the Madras presidency in the 1930s. They introduced a mixture of Hindustani music and Gujarati folk music called Parsi tunes which eventually found their way into cinema.[7] Folk songs were also featured in these dramas, usually performed by the comedian.[8]

Although silent cinema appeared in Madras in 1912,[9] it could attain the status of a mass entertainment form only by the middle of the 1920s. Even at that time, company dramas continued to draw large crowds with their music. Silent cinema produced in Madras, did not affect the company dramas; both were able to coexist without any conflict. In the absence of sound, silent cinema in South India specialized in stunt sequences; it needed men who could impress the viewers by jumping from tall buildings. So the singers and musicians stayed on with the drama companies where they were assured of a steadier income than in the spasmodic production of silent movies.

But the situation changed dramatically when sound films —"talkies"—came on the scene. The talkies produced in the first few years were all film versions of successful, song-laden plays staged by drama companies. Thus stage actors who were not classical musicians, but singers familiar with classical music, found themselves in the tinsel world of cinema. Here, the difference between classical musicians and stage singers familiar with classical music must be made clear. The former were basically classical musicians and sang in concerts. The latter only acted on the stage, though some of them, after gaining fame through dramas, gave solo concerts. S G Kittappa and Devudu Aiyar are examples of such singers.

Sound first came to Tamil cinema in the form of the four-reeler, which was just a series of sequences featuring semi-classical songs, folk songs and dances. It is significant that the very first Tamil talkie, *Kalidas* (1931), should have been a string of fifty songs; it was a continuation of the company drama tradition. It was understandable that an audience fed on music in all their entertainment forms expected the newfangled entertainment also to be fashioned on similar lines. In fact, it is this aspect of Indian cinema—the song-and-dance sequences—which lends it a distinct character.

For the first few years, all the talkies were only mythologicals and even later, only very few films of other genres were produced. In India, music has been used through the ages to commune with the supernatural, in worship and in mystic trances. The wandering minstrels narrated puranic stories to the villagers through songs in temple courtyards. So it was only logical that the early sound films—which were nearly all mythologicals—should have been mere vehicles for songs.

In a few years, regional films produced in Madras—Tamil, Malayalam, Kannada and Telugu—achieved commercial success. Talking pictures therefore carved out a safe market in their respective regional language areas, thus countering competition from films made in America and England. When sound arrived, Madras-made films were able to distinguish themselves from imported films through their language.[11]

The first sound studio in South India, Srinivasa Cinetone, was established in Madras in 1934. By 1937, there were nine such studios and the stampede for entry into the glittering world of cinema had begun in right earnest. Songwriters, musicians and instrumentalists, all drawn from the stage, vied for a position in studios which were springing up in Madras.[12] As baggage, they brought with them their learnings and skill honed in company drama music.

Movie business meant big money; its commercial prospects caught the attention of classical musicians, who had been dismissive of cinema as plebeian entertainment. There were other reasons also. Cinema had become somewhat socially respectable and primarily because of the money it made. It had grown and was now capable of providing facilities demanded by classical musicians who enjoyed independent status as vocalists. Afterall, when any art form is at an experimental stage, established artistes are naturally hesitant to make their entry into it. In the early days of the gramophone also, classical musicians had been similarly diffident about recording their performances.

Musicians like Papanasam Sivan, who wrote and composed more than 500 film songs, entered films and thereby seduced other classical musicians into following him. These musical luminaries of the late 1930s and Forties, like G N Balasubramaniam, M M Dandabani Desikar, Musiri Subramanya Aiyar and V V Sadagopan, did their stints in the film world. Some of their films became memorable solely due to the songs, like *Meera* (1945) in which M S Subbulakshmi played the lead role of the bhakti poetess.

However, classical music compositions had to be modified when they were adapted to films. One of the methods was to retain the essential features of a raga after which the duration of the songs were reduced and excluding the improvisations and innovative embellishments characteristic of the classical style of singing. This process of popularizing classical music and making it acceptable to a wider audience was set off mainly by the advent of cinema. Such modifications had been effected earlier when classical music was recorded on 78 rpm, 10-inch discs that played only for three or four minutes.[13]

The imperatives of sound technology also shaped the emerging trend of film music. Musicians responded to the challenges and utilized the new opportunities that were on offer. Stage singers, who were used to singing at the top of their voices in the absence of an amplifier, had to modify their singing technique to suit the microphone; a characteristic style of mellifluous crooning—in contrast to the full-throated expression on the stage—was born.

When recording was done through a single microphone, only one or two instrumentalists could accompany the singer. Interestingly, filming and recording had to be done simultaneously and a trolley carrying the instrumentalists would follow the camera in order to be within earshot of the microphone and the actor-singer. It was often difficult for the actor to sing while moving about and therefore, the camera remained static during song sequences. With better recording techniques, it was possible to use more than one microphone and therefore, more instrumentalists and a certain degree of complexity was now feasible.

When facilities for pre-recording music for films became available, it was no longer necessary to synchronize recording and picturisation. This had an interesting repercussion on cinema. As long as sound had to be recorded while the film was being shot, only those who could sing were hired to act. Once songs could be recorded independently and then synchronized with the lip-movement of the actors, there was no need for actors to possess singing ability. Artistes were chosen primarily for their good looks and acting talent and as a result, a distinct group of artistes known as playback singers who lent their voice to non-singing heroes and heroines emerged.

As film music became an industry in its own right, another strain found its way into this already mixed stream—western music. In the first few years, many Tamil talkies were made in the studios of Calcutta. The music directors of Calcutta were greatly influenced by western music; this paved the way for the use of western tunes in Tamil and Telugu films. Later in Madras, many sound studios acquired western musical instruments for use in film music. The use of these instruments, whose sounds were alien to the Indian musical tradition, was not conducive to the integration of music with cinema, particularly in period movies.[14] In the Thirties, the practice of using tunes of popular songs from Hindi films began; it persisted right up to the Eighties. In Asandas Classical's *Nandanar* (1935), K B Sundarambal sang three songs whose tunes were lifted from *Chandidas* (Hindi, 1934).[15]

Following the traditions of the commercial stage, characters in films also broke into a song, invariably in an intensely emotional context, as though spoken words would be inadequate for the occasion. Thus, songs were accepted as an essential ingredient of cinema right from the early

The Eye of the Serpent

years. Musicologist Ashok Ranade identifies a progression in which speech moved unobtrusively from pure prose to metrical patterns to simple tunes. The aim was not so much aesthetic as to clarify and help communication. He adds that songs from these early films were not really "film songs" in the sense we recognize them today, but mere extensions of speech. The film song, as a separate entity, was to evolve later. [16] In a manual on film making, published in 1937, dramatist P Sambanda Mudaliar wrote that, ideally, song sequences should take about one-fourth of the film's duration. [17]

The need to resort to a song in a given situation is perhaps a continuation of a literature-oriented aesthetic where versification or poetry is considered superior to the spoken or written form. The new medium of cinema probably appropriated the features of literature in order to gain initial validity as a medium. The song-dominated cinema was thus conforming to, and extending the framework of aesthetic value in Tamil society.

By 1944, the film song as we know it today, with a distinct set of characteristics, had emerged. So distinct were the characteristics of a Tamil film song, that ususally, listeners could identify a film song within the first few bars. It was a synthesis of various strains of music—Carnatic, Hindustani, folk and western pop. Soon film songs acquired an importance independent of cinema. *Haridas* (1944), which had a number of songs that were very popular, created a box office record with a continuous run of 133 weeks in Madras. This gave the music director star status.[18] It is now a ritual to begin work on a new film with the recording of a song. Songs can also endow a film with extra-regional appeal.[19] This was best evidenced by the successful run of the Telugu film *Sankarabaranam* (1981) in Tamil Nadu and the popularity of Hindi films with good musical scores in South India.

The gramophone industry has been closely allied with the development of film music in India. Since 1902, when the gramophone first came to South India, both classical and folk music were recorded and released as discs. The arrival of talkies coincided with the massive import of cheap (Rs.10-15) gramophone machines from Japan and film songs were released on graphite discs. To begin with, these songs were recorded separately, often by singers other than those who had acted and sung in the film. Later, songs from the soundtrack were reproduced on discs. Film songs could thus be listened to independently, without necessarily viewing the film.[20] Right from the beginning, film songs were composed with an eye on the gramophone record market. A song usually lasted some three or four minutes, the duration of a 78 rpm disc; this practice persists to this day.

The songbook of a film, a low-priced publication, was an important adjunct to film culture. From the earliest days of the talkies, these books, sold in cinema houses, contained the story line, the text of the lyrics and the credits. Today, these songbooks are a handy source of information for film historians, particularly when prints of the films themselves are not available.

The soaring popularity of film songs was given a massive thrust by a development in neighbouring Sri Lanka. In 1949, a commercial radio broadcasting outfit, Radio Ceylon, began beaming film song programmes across the sea for nearly six hours a day. The sale of radio sets soared film music was brought into the drawing room and in a large number of homes, film songs formed the background music for all household chores and leisure activities.

The state-owned All India Radio, which was the only radio broadcasting service in India then, also opened a commercial wing in 1967 for broadcasting film songs. On television also, song sequences from films are telecast in a programme called "Oliyum Oliyum" (Sound and Light), whose sustained popularity can be compared to that of the teleplays of the Fifties in America, like "Playhouse-90".

Recent developments in sound technology—audio cassettes, "walkman" and compact discs—have completed the picture. Now film music is a multi-million rupee industry. There are many recording companies in India, and most film songs are released as discs even before the film is released.

However songs for most part, have been socially and politically superficial in content. They are featured in stock situations in films—after the boy and the girl have met for the first time, when he is travelling alone or when she is worshipping, and so on. Most films have one or two song sequences of the hero and the heroine frolicking about and singing a duet and surprisingly, it is possible to compose such songs without any reference to the dramatic context. This is perhaps the reason why several film songs sound alike and their content is always trite and frivolous. The flow of the film is seldom affected if song sequences are excised, wholly or partly.

But film songs have also been used for propaganda

purposes by major political movements in Tamil Nadu. During the freedom struggle, when the British government had muzzled all mass media, film songs served the nationalist cause ably and songs like the one below were used to whip up patriotic feelings:

Let us vow to achieve freedom
This is the time to act.
Chanting the mantras taught by Gandhi,
We can realize our dream.
(Thamizhthai alladhu Mathrudharmam)

It may be recalled that the British government had either banned nationalist films or deleted certain sequences from them, but when nationalist songs were released on gramophone records, it was impossible to control their reach. In the post-Independence period, writers from the rationalist movements entered films. Their songs, with an anti-religious message, were released to the public.

There are lots of cheats in the country
Who exploit in the name of god.
Just for the sake of an empty stomach
They would mess about god's name in songs also
All those flaunting a beard, a stick, a jug
Or matted hairs are swamis.
All idlers, without the will to work,
But with a begging bowl, are swamis.
(Rajarajan, 1957)

Some song writers of leftist persuasion used film songs as vehicles for political comment, thereby lending them some measure of substance. In a film titled *Times Have Changed/ Kalam Mari Pochu* (1956), this song is addressed to the farmer:

Those who sell their farm and leave the village
Those who build bungalows in the cities
Those who hoard money in banks
They do not understand your strength.
Those who get frantic over positions of power
And those who forget you after the polls
They will all come to you, seeking your help, come
Times have changed, times have changed.

Film songs frequently reinforced existing value systems of the audience and can often yield insights into contemporary attitudes. Here is an example that typifies the attitude to women:

Man: A woman must be like this Even if she learns English.
Woman: Tell me and I will do as you say
You could change me the way you wish.
Man: Here chastity and modesty are the clothes of a woman
So woman should be like this
She must not show her body for public admiration—and
She must not dress exposing her midriff. She must not paint her lips red.
(*The farmer/Vivasayi*, 1967) [21]

The role and significance of film songs in popular culture was evident in 1984 when M G Ramachandran, chief minister of Tamil Nadu, was ailing in a hospital in the United States. In the film *The Bright Lamp/Olivilakku* (1970), when MGR, who plays the hero, is shown fighting for his life, a woman sings a plaintive song pleading with god to save his life:

Lord, there are many lamps in your temple
The light of my hope is at your feet.
I wash your feet with tears so that he may live.
If the heavens beckon unto this generous and noble man
What would happen to the earth?
I will come to you and lay down my life
So that he may live.

This song was played through amplifiers in public places and cinema houses all over Tamil Nadu as a prayer for MGR's recovery. [22] But most film songs are intended to be merely titillatory, often containing double entendres, like the following from a very popular film:

For desire there is no restriction
We have little else to do.
Here on the river bank when no one is looking
Let us discover that closeness.
(A knot in the Sari/Mundhanai Mudichu, 1983)

Like mentioned above, film songs often reflect certain social attitudes prevalent at the time the film is made, and can thus be a barometer for change over the years. In R R Pictures' *Gulebakavali* (1955), comedian Chandrababu cautions Allah in a song: *Be watchful or else, even you will be cheated.* He uses the metaphor of a *kulla* (cap) which rhymes with the word Allah. Such inoffensive and good-natured humour about certain sects and communities, quite common in the early decades, was progressively deleted from films due to increasing social distance and an implicit taboo on the slightest reference to caste or sect.

By the end of the first decade of talkies, some poets of repute, like Baskara Das, a nationalist, and Bharathidasan, who was radical and a rationalist, began writing songs for films. In the 1950s, Pattukottai Kalyanasundaram from the Communist movement and in the Sixties and Seventies, Kannadasan from the Dravidian movement dominated the scene. While the songs of the former were inspired by the folk tradition of Tamil Nadu, Kannadasan's songs were literary in flavour. For poets with ideological convictions, film songs also doubled as an instrument of propaganda. While they composed songs tailored to meet the requirements of films, they also managed to package their own ideas. The songwriter had to supply words to suit a tune which was composed earlier.

As songs became an essential ingredient of films, other professionals appeared on the film scene: the music director, and the playback singer. The songwriter from drama companies, who doubled up as the composer and music teacher, controlled all aspects of a film's music in the early sound films. Later, when music and recording grew complex, the music director was inducted as another professional resource person. The song-and-dance combination also gave rise to two more practitioners, the choreographer and the dancer. The roles of these five practitioners were for the most part an intrusion into cinema as songs and dances remain unintegrated with the filmic narration in most films. [23]

Along with the songs, dance inevitably made its entry into cinema but without any regard for the formal grammar of dance traditions. Invariably, each dance came with a song and was often an excuse for one. Each actress was free to create her own style, based on any type of dance she knew. Thus a new genre of dance, an arbitrary mixture of all schools of dance— often referred to as "oriental dance"— came into being. In the Fifties, oriental dance performances by well-known actresses were quite common.

Historically, film songs have supplanted folk music in the lives of the common people, exercising a much stronger hold on their emotions. Both have a simplicity that does not pre-suppose knowledge of music. Even when familiarity with the language of a film song is absent, an intense response is still feasible. The association of sound with images, of songs with certain film scenes and actors, is certainly another factor responsible for their popularity. Most of the songs revolve around the boy-meets-girl theme and every film has at least a duet or two, with much caressing and hugging. The lyrics are often unabashedly erotic. These love scenes endow the songs with direct sexual associations, thus increasing their appeal.

Film music is catholic in its approach, adapting continuously from other styles; and though such adaptation at times degenerates into plagiarism, its appeal is undiminished. This is one area of the Indian musical scene marked by constant experimentation and innovation.

Technological developments like microgroove, compact disc and the stereo revolution further accelerated the spread of film songs.[24] This omnipresent nature of film music has had an interesting effect on the cultural scene. While in many other parts of the world, changes in musical tastes affect the kind of music used in films, here the situation is exactly the reverse. It is film music which sets trends and moulds musical tastes. The cultural niche occupied by pop music in the West is occupied by film music in India.

The dominant hold of film music on society has hindered the development of any other kind of popular musical expression outside cinema. Even the little non-film music is patterned after film music. Songs in praise of gods or political leaders, which are normally played through the loudspeakers of a public address system, are churned out by the hundred, patterned after film songs. It is the same playback singers and musicians of the film industry, the culture-heroes of the masses, who are hired to sing these songs.

Symptomatic of the influence of film music in rural areas is a performance known as "record dance", a kind of poor man's cabaret, which is usually played at village fairs. An erotic film song, full of puns, is played on a turntable and a scantily clad girl gyrates to the music. Gate money is collected and often the dance degenerates into a striptease, much to the delight of the eager patrons.

Despite criticism, songs and dances have constituted an

important ingredient in Indian films right from the beginning of the talkies. Songs are often of greater importance than all the other cinematic elements in a film. One anthropologist has suggested that this feature relates directly to the semiotic function of music in the Indian cultural tradition.[25] It is this character, the predominance of songs in a film, which sets Indian cinematic tradition apart from others.

But, the effects of songs on a film, its cinematic character, and aesthetic implications, have not been examined thoroughly. The songwriters and music composers of the early years had all been trained for the stage. As a result, when they entered films, they did not learn the discipline required for film music. Film music is basically an applied art[26,] but in Tamil cinema, I reckon there was very little attempt at such application. The music was not adapted for cinema but was merely transferred as such, from the stage to the screen.

Most song sequences even today appear like commercials during a television show. They are unrelated to the main narrative. In the era of black-and-white films, these song sequences were in "real" time and no changes in costumes occurred during the course of the song. But by the end of the Sixties, black-and-white gradually gave way to colour, and this development affected the song sequences. They grew slightly more complicated as filmmakers tried to get maximum mileage out of colour. They began to shoot a single song sequence in different locales and in varied costumes. This meant a complete suspension of the logic of time and space for the duration of the song. In duets, which form the bulk of the songs, the man and the woman often sing one line standing on a hill! It is significant that the films that have won critical acclaim, both in India and in foreign film festivals, have been films without songs. To cite only two examples, *Some One Like You/Unnaipol Oruvan* (1964) and *House/Veedu* (1988) did not feature any songs. And in such films, there is a discernible attempt to integrate music with cinema.

There is also a sociological dimension to the predominant role of songs in films. By curbing the cinema-specific characteristics, songs keep films at the level of escapist entertainment, which has an ideology of its own. It ensures that the prospect of a truly political cinema's emergence remains bleak. Even films which espouse an ideology, however obliquely, have been diluted by the importance given to songs. The audience does not receive the message due to the distraction of songs and dances. The possibility of the movie-going public developing a sense of cinema is severely circumscribed by this practice.

The predominance of song as an element of Tamil cinema is exemplified by the long and illustrious career of music director Ilayaraja. He made his debut with the film *Annam the Parrot/Annakili* (1976), in which he used folk tunes; songs from that film have proved enduringly popular. He later went through a rigorous discipline and honed his sensibility to Carnatic and western classical music. Today, he is one of the most sought-after music directors in the country and has worked in more than 950 films in all the four South Indian languages. Many films have been commercially successful solely on the strength of his music. Even till recently, whenever new films are announced, prime importance is attached to his role as music director. He not only composes music, he also writes songs and is a singer to boot. Ilayaraja's music can be called a combination of Carnatic, western classical and western pop. His fidelity to a chosen form—folk or classical—and his musical imagination, combined with his brilliant orchestration are the factors behind his phenomenal success.[28]

Though the overwhelming popularity of the film song as a form of contemporary music and its widespread impact are so evident, there has been a continuing feud between film music on the one hand and classical music on the other. Classical musicians, who sneered at films first, came into it in a big way, lured by money and fame. But eventually they had to vacate their place in favour of more innovative and populist composers. Ever since then, film music has been subjected to hostile criticism by the classicists. In July 1952, B V Keskar, then Minister for Information and Broadcasting, Government of India, announced that broadcast of film songs by All India Radio would be progressively reduced. In seminars on music and culture, film music is not even mentioned; scholarly books and articles on Indian culture maintain a studied silence. But the fact remains that this music of the masses has always been—and will be—a significant phenomenon in the social and cultural history of Tamil Nadu.

Notes

1. This chapter is based on my article "Music for the Masses: Film Songs of Tamil Nadu" published in *Economic and Political Weekly*, Annual Number, Vol.XXVI, 1991.

2. Chandavarkar, Bhaskar, "Film Music and the Classical Indian Tradition", *Film Miscellany* (Pune, Film & Television Institute of India, 1976) pp. 108-112.
3. Hardgrave, Robert L, "Politics and Film in Tamil Nadu: The Stars and the DMK", *Asian Review*, Vol.XIII (1973).
4. Chandavarkar, *Film Miscellany*, p.109.
5. Somasundaram, M P, "Folk songs in Tamil Nadu", Souvenir of the II World Tamil Conference (Madras, Directorate of Tamil Development, Government of Tamil Nadu, 1968).
6. For a history of the gramophone industry in India, see Joshi, G N, "Phonograph Comes to India", *Journal of the National Centre for Performing Arts,* Vol.VI, No.3, 1972.
7. V A K Ranga Rao, musicologist, interviewed by the author in Madras, 28 September 1984.
8. Sambanda Mudaliar, P, "South Indian Talkies: Carnatic Music versus Hindustani Music", *The Hindu,* 18 July 1941.
9. Baskaran, Theodore S, *The Message Bearers: The Nationalistic Politics and the Entertainment Media in South India* (Madras, Cre-A, 1981) pp 67-94.
10. Ranga Rao, Interview.
11. Barnouw, Eric and S Krishnaswamy, *Indian Film* (Madras, Orient Longmans, 1963) p. 69.
12. Baskaran, Theodore S, *The Message Bearers,* p.99.
13. However, the classical musicians did not always sing classical songs in films. For example, M S Subbulakshmi in the film *Sakunthala* (1940).
14. In the film *Chenchulakshmi* (Telugu, 1944) Latin American music was incorporated as tribal music in a dance sequence. Ranga Rao, Interview.

   The donkey serenade music in the film *Chandraleka* (1948) was taken from R Z Leonard's film *The Fire Fly* (1937). This piece of music reappeared again in a recent movie, Peter Jackson's *Two Heavenly Creatures* (1994).

15. *Nandanar* film review by Kalki under the pen name Karnatakam in *Anandavikatan,* 21 July 1943. There were three film versions of *Nandanar,* one by the New Theatres in 1933, and another by Asandas Classical in 1935 and the third by Gemini Studios in 1942.

16. Ranade, Ashok, "The Extraordinary Importance of Indian Film Song", *Cinema Vision India,* Vol.I.No.4 (1981).

17. Sambanda Mudaliar, P, *Handbook of Tamil Talkie* (Madras, published by the author, 1937).

18. The earliest film credit I have seen for a music director is for the film *Ambikapathi* (1937).

19. Chandavarkar, Bhaskar, "The Great Film Song Controversy", *Cinema Vision India,* Vol.I, No.4 (1981).

20. For details of recording industry see Mathur, Asha Rani, "Marketing Music", *Swagat* (Inflight magazine of Indian Airlines) March-April, 1982.

21. I am thankful to C Manee of Salem for the translations.

22. Pandian M S S, *The Image Trap* (New Delhi, Sage Publishers, 1992) pp.120-121.

23. Mahmood, Hameeduddin, *The Kaleidoscope of Indian Cinema,* (New Delhi, Affiliated East-West Press Pvt. Ltd., 1974) pp.190-191.

24. Technology has adversely affected folk music also. The oral and the aural richness of folk songs and the scope for improvisation have been neutralized by mechanical multiplication of music.

25. Beeman, William, O, "The Use of Music in Popular Film: East and West", *India International Quarterly,* Vol 8, No1 (1981).

26. Huntley, John, and Roger Manwell, *The Technique of Film Music,* (London, Focal Press, 1957) p.197.
27. Venkatesh Chakravarthy interviewed by the author at Madurai, 5 May 1990.
28. "Troubled Genius", *Aside,* (cover story) 16-28 February, (1988).

Chapter Five
Dialogue in Tamil Films

SINCE THERE IS LITTLE OR NO ACCESS TO FEW FILMS FROM the silent era, it is extremely difficult to assess whether filmmakers of that era depended on words—in the form of title cards—for narrative flow. But as mentioned in an earlier chapter, there were narrators or "explainers" in cinema houses who explained the story to the viewers as it unfolded on the screen. Even after the advent of sound films in the Thirties and Forties, title cards were still in use. The very first talkie, *Kalidas,* opened with a lengthy "preface" (*munnurai*) written on title cards. In *Gulebakavali* (1935), a sequence in the narrative has the hero Tejanmulk meandering through the clouds on his magic steed. As this effect could not be achieved cinematographically, a title card announced to the viewers that the hero was flying across the sky on his magic horse.[1] The practice of using title cards persisted even up to *Marudanattu Ilavarasi,* where at the beginning, a lengthy title card was scrolled on the screen to narrate the prologue.

The Eye of the Serpent

Here too, the narration was through words, though not of the spoken variety.

From the very beginning of the sound era, Tamil cinema was aurally oriented and could be viewed as part of the continuum of the aural tradition in Tamil Nadu. The traditional mass media, like ballads, performances of wandering minstrels and folklore, all testify to the predominance of the oral tradition in South India. In the early years of talkies, it was song which reigned supreme and typically a film from the 1930s had about forty to fifty songs. It may be recalled that the stories were mostly episodes from the Puranas and epics which were already popular with the audience because of religious discourses and later, through company dramas. Therefore films were used as mere vehicles for songs. There was of course some dialogue which was often written by the songwriter himself. What made *Kalidas,* which is referred to as the first Tamil talkie, a Tamil film, was that its songs were in Tamil, while the characters spoke in Telugu and Urdu. In *Baktha Ramdas* (1935) also, while the characters spoke in Tamil, Telugu and Hindi, it was ensured that all the songs were in Tamil. Song was the most important factor which determined the character of a film. Commenting on the state of Tamil films, a correspondent wrote in *The Hindu* in 1935, 'the predominant element is music but it is mostly music of such a sort that one is apt to be quickly cloyed with it. What little speech there is, is turgid or stilted, bereft of all harmonious emotions and content.'[2]

Spoken words were totally neglected in the early years of sound cinema. It was only when Ilangovan (aka

T K Thanikachalam), a dialogue writer, arrived on the scene that the spoken word became important as an ingredient of cinema. Ilangovan wrote in a flowery style, replete with witticisms: for the first time, the dialogue-writer began to be noticed. He wrote for many successful films which included *Ambikapathi* (1937) and *Ashokumar* (1941). In *Thiruneelakantar* (1939), an argument ensues in the scene when the courtesan, Kalavalli, tries to seduce the devout Neelakantar. The lengthy rhetoric written by Ilangovan for this scene endowed the spoken word with a significance hitherto unknown on Tamil screen. But it was the film *Kannagi*, also scripted by Ilangovan, which marked the arrival of the dialogue-writer, in which Kannamba as Kannagi reeled off paragraph after paragraph in high flown Tamil. Ilangovan's dialogue was identified as the chief reason for the success of the films he wrote.

There were also other writers who adopted this style of dialogue writing on their way to fame and success. T V Chari *(Manonmani)* and A S A Swamy *(Valmiki,* 1946), along with Ilangovan, ushered in the era of the dialogue-writer. S D Sundaram *(The Virgin's Love/Kanniyin Kathali,* 1949), Jalakantapuram Pa Kannan *(The Dream of Athithan/ Athithan Kanavu,* 1948) and Bharathidasan *(Ponmudi)* continued the trend. In addition to florid and long-winded sentences, they employed alliteration to make the dialogue more witty and entertaining. Thus, along with songs, dialogue emerged as another ingredient of filmic entertainment.

However when writers began using dialogue to reflect the ideology of the Dravidian movement, the spoken word gained more importance as films were now replete with political content. The importance of dialogue reached its apogee when some leaders of the Dravidian movement entered the film industry as dialogue writers and used films as propaganda vehicles, as C N Annadurai did with *Velaikari*. M Karunanidhi made his debut as a dialogue writer with the film *Marudanattu Ilavarasi*. He set the pattern for long, alliterative monologues which made *Parasakthi* a landmark in Tamil cinema as far as dialogue was concerned. The evolution of rhetorical dialogue in Tamil cinema added a distinct dimension to films of this period.

The language spoken by the characters in Tamil films at the time can be described as "written Tamil" which is different from "spoken Tamil". In linguistic terminology, Tamil is characterized as a diglossic language. In such a language, there are two forms—the high and the low. The high is used on certain occasions and is grammatically more complex. It is this form which is codified and legitimised. This is also the written version which can be used in a few spoken contexts also, such as oration. On the other hand, the spoken variety is the low form which takes a lot of liberties with grammar and form. In a diglossic language like Tamil, the distance between the written and the spoken form is great and the two categories are sharply defined: it is a case of the formal as opposed to the informal. In a spoken context which is formal, the high variety would be used. On the other hand, a personal letter can be of the low variety while an academic paper can be of high variety. What defines the form here is the relationship between the speaker and the audience.[3]

Dialogue in Tamil Films

It is interesting to note that the language in Tamil films belonged to this formal domain. Most of the principal characters spoke the formal or the written form and one of the reasons for this was that dialogue in Tamil films was intended to be a one-way communication, as in more of a monologue like a speech from a podium. Such one-way communication opted for the high variety as more befitting to the speaker's status. In mythological films, the kings always used the high variety which was in keeping with their royal position. The comic characters and menials used the low, informal variety, like the two fishermen in *Sakunthala* (1940), played by N S Krishnan and T S Durairaj. The kind of language spoken—high or low—depended upon the status of the character, very much like the implicit social regulations regarding the dress and bearing of various social strata.

The dialect used by Brahmins was considered superior because it was spoken by the high caste group. In the early films, even royal characters often used this form. In the film *Gulebakavali* (1935), a story about a Muslim prince, which was apparently set in the Middle East, all the lead characters spoke Brahmin Tamil. In fact, this practice lasted even up to *Chandraleka*.

With the appearance of films scripted by leaders of the Dravidian movement, this characteristic of one-way communication and the use of high variety of Tamil was accentuated. In their films, each piece of dialogue was long and very much like an oration. *Manohara*, which had dialogues by M Karunanidhi, has a durbar scene in which Sivaji Ganesan, playing the role of Manoharan, delivers a long, alliterative monologue; the soundtrack of this scene was released on a gramophone record and later, on audio-tape. These monologues were remarkably like formal speeches. Even the camera angles were such that the characters appeared to be directly addressing the vast multitudes in cinema houses when compared to other characters in the scene. These long monologues were always delivered standing, and with gesticulations typical of stage oratory. The actors did not even modulate their voices to suit the soundtrack of cinema. A speech that was meant for crowds at a political rally was delivered to the film audience.

Gradually, writers belonging to the Dravidian movement developed public speaking into a finely honed art and used it effectively for political mobilization. In fact, it was common practice to charge an entrance fee for their speeches. When they sat down to write scripts for films, they used exactly the same structure and style. Here however the larger question is: which communication should be given importance—that between the characters in the film, or the one between a character in the film and the audience? If a film has a message, it should be woven into the filmic narrative for the audience to receive it through a cinematic experience, by their becoming active participants in the film at the level of imaginative experience and not as passive listeners. But this is precisely what does not happen when long monologues become a major part of the film—as in *Parasakthi*. To these dialogue writers, a film was just a public address system. The characters addressed the camera—in other words, the audience and not their fellow characters in the scene.

Dialogue in Tamil Films

In Tamil Nadu, although each caste group and region has its own variant of the spoken language, written Tamil does not have these differentiations. In most instances, the high language used by dialogue writers is caste-neutral and region-neutral and therefore, characters in films are not authentic and lifelike. In some novels, regional dialects *(vattara vazhaku)* have been used. In recent years, there have been similar attempts in films also. One of the earliest films to adopt a region-specific variant of spoken Tamil was *The Blessed Mother/Makkalai Petra Makarasi* (1957) in which some of the characters spoke Kongu Thamizh, the variety of Tamil spoken in the Coimbatore region where the story is set. Even in films when an effort was made to give a regional flavour to the spoken language, this was achieved only partially and the formal variety invariably predominated. During the Eighties, in some films with a rural setting, there were similar attempts made, but not one film was consistent in this respect. Moreover, however colloquial or regional the Tamil spoken by the characters in the film might have been, when they started singing, they became very literary. However, mention must be made of *Unnaipol Oruvan* and *Hunger/Pasi* (1979) in which the Madras working class dialect was consistently used in an authentic manner.

The patois notwithstanding, spoken word in films must have a realistic quality. Satyajit Ray once wrote, 'Film dialogues must have the feel of life-like speech. Only then can it have the true plastic quality which can enhance a film instead of stultifying it.' When this quality is absent and formality of language takes its place, as it does in most Tamil films, cinema, instead of being strengthened by the spoken word, is thwarted. The cinematic quality of a film is enhanced by the manner in which words are combined with significant action and behaviour. This quality is often absent in Tamil films where dialogue is delivered as though it were a piece of oratory. In real life, it is the educated urbanites who tend to use words to express themselves while the illiterate and rural people are more likely to act out their reactions and feelings. But in Tamil films, even the rustic folk use the ornate, high variety of Tamil, as does the ghetto dweller, played once by Sivaji Ganesan, in *Forgiveness of Sins/Pavamannippu* (1961).

As long as there was dependence on the spoken word for the flow of filmic narration, there was no effort to stretch the visual range of cinema. During the Fifties, the heyday of the spoken word in Tamil cinema, the works of K Ramnoth were an exception. In *The Plight of the Poor/Ezhai Padum Padu* (1950) there is a sequence in which Kandhan escapes through a storm drain, carrying the wounded Umakanth. The short-statured police inspector, Javert, is not able to follow Kandhan as the water is too deep for him, while the tall Kandhan, played by Nagaiya, wades through with ease. This portion is told only through images as Ramnoth had the cinematic sense to contain the dialogue-writer.

However, domination of the spoken word in Tamil films still continues, militating against any development of a visual sense. A common feature is to resort to short soliloquies when the filmmaker is unable to visually depict a certain turn of events in the film. When the filmmaker wants to reveal the intentions of a character to the viewers, he/she sometimes resorts to "direct address" in which the character looks into the camera and addresses the audience. In the film *Pudhaiyal,* Tukkaram, speaks aloud the reason for his being there, even as he waits alone on the beach for the heroine to arrive. This practice is reminiscent of the folk theatre convention where the performer addresses the audience directly.

Notes

1. *Anandavikatan,* 7 July 1935.
2. *The Hindu,* 5 July 1935.
3. Dr E Annamalai, Director, Central Institute for Indian Languages, Mysore, interviewed on 10 June 1990.

Chapter Six
Satyamurthi—the Link that Snapped

THE INTERACTION BETWEEN POPULAR ENTERTAINMENT AND politics in Tamil Nadu has intrigued observers for long. By a historical process unparalleled elsewhere, all five chief ministers who have ruled Tamil Nadu since 1967 have been associated with the film world. They also have a second commonality: they belonged, in one way or another, to the Dravidian movement. But the association is not just a post-Independence phenomenon, but has a long history, which goes back to the early days of the freedom movement. This association was in fact established by S Satyamurthi, the nationalist leader, who belonged to the Congress party. This crucial beginning and Satyamurthi's role in it has not been studied so far. Had this association between the leaders of the Indian National Congress and the entertainers of Tamil Nadu continued beyond Satyamurthi's time, the history of the Dravidian movement, and of Tamil Nadu, could well have been different.

Satyamurthi—the Link that Snapped

Born in 1887 at Tirumayam, near Pudukottai, in a lawyer's family, Satyamurthi pursued his higher education in Madras and graduated from the Madras Christian College. After earning a degree in law, he joined the bar in Madras but was soon drawn to active politics. He made his political debut in 1919 at a Congress conference in Kanchipuram where his spirited attack on the ideas of Annie Besant attracted the attention of Sarojini Naidu and other leaders of the Congress, who identified him as a potential publicist for the party. Soon he came to lead the nationalist faction of the Congress, which was then based in Madras.[1]

His fluency in both English and Tamil, coupled with oratorical abilities, helped him play his assigned role with confidence and aplomb and his speeches during his 1925 tour of England projected the Congress' point of view clearly and forcefully. Satyamurthi's role in the nationalist movement grew steadily: from 1923 to 1930, he was a member of the Madras Legislative Council and was also very active in the Civil Disobedience movement in the late 1920s. During this period, he developed close relationships with artistes of the entertainment world, and subsequently brought many of them into political activism.

In 1935, Satyamurthi was elected to the Indian Legislative Assembly in Delhi where he made a considerable impact as a debater and as the deputy leader of the Congress party. When the Congress contested the elections in 1937, he led the party's election campaign in the Madras presidency and in an astute move, harnessed the talents of stage and screen artistes in support of the campaign. Later as the Mayor of Madras, and right up to his premature death at the age of fifty-six in 1943, he maintained an active association with artists .[2]

Satyamurthi was first drawn to the world of entertainment when he started his legal practice in Madras. The amateur drama club, Suguna Vilas Sabha of Madras, founded by Judge P Sambanda Mudaliar in 1891 offered a forum for those interested in theatre activities. Suguna Vilas Sabha was an elitist outfit in which bureaucrats, lawyers and other professionals took part, as distinct from commercial drama companies popular with the masses at that time. Satyamurthi joined this troupe and acted in many productions; his performance as the jester in the Sanskrit play *Clay Cart / Mrichakatika* and as Manoharan in *Manohara,* both within a week of taking over as the president of the Tamil Nadu Provincial Congress Committee, received highly favourable notice.[3] After watching a performance of *As You Like It* at the Memorial theatre at Stratford-on-Avon in England, he had said, 'I visited the place as a pilgrim from Suguna Vilas Sabha.'[4] He was soon elected as the vice-president of the Sabha and later held the office of Tamil conductor, a designation assigned to individuals entrusted with the responsibility of directing Tamil dramas.[5]

As he grew more active in politics, Satyamurthi realized that for building up a popular political base for the Congress, he needed a different set of connections with the people: the world of commercial drama could serve his purpose. In fact, as early as 1922, Motilal Nehru had written to Satyamurthi emphasizing the need to gather support for the nationalist faction in the Congress, 'Yours is truly a benighted province

Satyamurthi—the Link that Snapped

in this matter... I doubt very much that we shall have any appreciable number to support us unless an intensive propaganda is at once started.'[6]

The performances of commercial drama companies were the most prevalent form of popular entertainment during this period. These troupes had first appeared during the last decade of the nineteenth century; and in just two decades had popularized drama as a major entertainment form. Soon, many newly established companies were touring the presidency. Typical of a form that was trying to make its advent in a culture marked by orthodoxy, commercial drama companies had certain peculiarities initially: there were companies which employed only boys, and others, only women. Their repertoire was quite limited, mostly episodes from Indian mythology and their plays mere vehicles for songs, resembling European operas, and so the actors were required to be singers also. There grew a corpus of songs which enjoyed popularity on stage; and stage actors often gave independent concerts featuring these songs. The nascent gramophone record industry, together with the import of inexpensive gramophones from Japan, spread the appeal of these songs. In spite of such popularity, company dramas were looked down upon by the upper classes; artistes from these drama companies were treated like social outcasts by them.

The surge of anger that erupted all over the country over the Jallianwala Bagh massacre of 1919 drew these entertainers into a vortex of political activity. With the print media coming under severely restrictive censorship, the stage became a convenient and relatively independent forum for mounting attacks on the policies of the British government. Songs from these plays spread the message of nationalism. Offstage, stage actors participated in demonstrations and pickets. Satyamurthi, recognizing the tremendous potential of the stage as a medium for nationalist propaganda, began to associate himself with this group. They, in turn, responded positively. One of Satyamurthi's favourite statements from political platforms was: 'We shall sing our way to freedom.'[7] Stage artistes found themselves leading an active political life, acquiring in the process a new respectability which they had hitherto lacked. They found that they often appeared on political platforms along with nationalist leaders, a possibility they could scarcely have dreamt of earlier. This was an added incentive for their political activism. It must be noted here that political leaders had till then been dismissive and contemptuous of these artistes as people of no consequence. It was Satyamurthi who first established what had then seemed like an improbable nexus between political leadership and the world of popular entertainment.

One of the earliest links Satyamurthi forged among entertainers was with M M Chidambaranathan, an actor in company dramas who had been trained and inspired by the nationalist poet, Udumalai Sarabam Muthusamy Kavirayar. In 1921, when Satyamurthi led pickets in Madras as part of the Non-cooperation movement, Chidambaranathan organized many performances of patriotic plays. In addition to these propaganda efforts, he donated the gate collections for financing the demonstrations.[8] Other troupes also began staging nationalist plays. When the British government imposed a ban on some of these troupes, Satyamurthi, who had by this time been elected to the Madras Legislative Council, raised the matter on the floor of the House. When neither the press nor the political leadership was prepared even to acknowledge the existence of these artistes, Satyamurthi, who advocated their cause, won their loyalty and they looked upon him as their spokesman and leader. From then on, he involved these artistes in all his political programmes. In 1928, when Satyamurthi was appointed the president of the Simon Boycott Propaganda Committee of the Tamil Nadu Provincial Congress to carry out an intensive campaign, his contact with the entertainers proved very valuable.[9]

Gradually, Tamil talkies emerged as a popular entertainment form in the early 1930s, and artistes from the stage—playwrights, actors, song writers and musicians—moved en masse into the glittering world of cinema where the advent of sound had created a demand for their talents. Many well-known names from the stage quickly gained screen fame. When they entered cinema, they brought with them their repertoire of nationalist dramas and songs. The very first Tamil talkie *Kalidas* had a song totally unrelated to the story of poet Kalidas, a song which extolled the charkha or the spinning wheel, a Gandhian symbol of nationalism. Soon, several films also began to be infused with nationalist propaganda.

Satyamurthi recognized the potential of cinema as an instrument of change and showed keen interest in its development. He used his powerful writing talent to promote the growth of cinema as a social force and predicted that cinema would play a major role in the next thirty years and that in a country with such high rates of illiteracy its influence was bound to be strong. In an article in a daily, he wrote, 'I hope there will be a synthesis established between the film producers in India, the directors, and the leaders of the nation. The film should be made to comprise a purposeful part in Indian Renaissance.'[10] When the film *Nandanar* (1935) was released, he wrote about its implications for the Non-Brahmin movement, with whose protagonists he was engaged in a bitter political battle.[11]

Among the political leaders of India at that period, Satyamurthi had established a reputation for being fiercely independent. His association with film artistes was only one such factor which gave rise to this image. He openly opposed Gandhi in the All India Congress Committee meeting at Ahmedabad on 1 March 1930 and did not think that Prohibition was an important cause or that it should be given priority over other issues. He confessed in public his disillusionment with non-violence as a political weapon.[12] Speaking at the meeting of the European Association in Madras on 20 May 1936, he was highly critical of socialism.[13] When the Congress decided to resign from power in 1939 in protest against the war, Satyamurthi openly opposed the idea.

At a time when the educated elite despised cinema as a plebeian preoccupation and refused to consider it seriously, Satyamurthi, with great foresight, took pains to elucidate its importance. In 1939, in the Senate of Madras University, he pleaded for the introduction of cinema as a subject for study, but his idea was rejected, much to his anger and disappointment.[14] He had hoped that the Indian film industry would be able to usher in an era of cultural swaraj (self-rule) and argued that educated women should join films and improve its quality. He was often invited to preside over the premiere of a film or to inaugurate a film's shooting. When the film *Iru Sakodarargal* (1936) was released in the Elphinstone cinema house in Madras, Satyamurthi was able to persuade a leader of Rajaji's stature to attend the premiere show. The proceeds of this show went to the Patel Purse Fund. He also took note of the charisma these film actors were beginning to acquire; and he used it effectively.

Satyamurthi exercised considerable influence over film stars. Though cinema was looked down upon as low class entertainment, he could persuade classical musician Maharajapuram Viswanatha Aiyar to act in Asandas' classical film *Nandanar*.[16] While honouring the artistes of the film *Thiruneelakantar,* Satyamurthi requested M K Thyagaraja Bhagavathar, the leading male star of the 1940s, to give up silk and wear only khadi; Bhagavathar readily deferred to this request.[17] When a felicitation function was organized for the eminent actor-director Raja Sandow, it was Satyamurthi who was called upon to preside. He won over film actor V Nagaiya to the nationalist cause and sent him as a delegate to the Congress session at Guwahati. All these artistes, in turn, lent their charisma in support of the party.[18] However, Satyamurthi's fascination with film stars at times went beyond their utility for propaganda efforts. He requested Gohar of Mumbai, a star of the silent era, to send him an autographed photo; she did, along with a note which said, 'I will be greatly delighted to meet you whenever you come to Mumbai.'[19] They did eventually meet in 1939, when Satyamurthi was in Bombay to participate in the silver jubilee celebrations of Indian cinema.

During the Civil Disobedience movement, with all the other leaders in jail, Satyamurthi found himself the president of the Council of Action.[20] Many celebrities from the screen and stage now took part in direct political action. Dramatist Akkur Ananthachari was in charge of the movement in North Arcot district. Famous film artistes of the period like K S Ananthanarayanan, who had acted in films like *Alii Arjuna,* K S Devudu Aiyar *(Radha Kalyanam* 1935), M V Mani *(Sathi Leelavathi,* 1936) and M G Nataraja Pillai[21] (*The Fire Sacrifice of Daksha/ Dakshayagnam,* 1938) all participated in anti-government pickets and courted arrest. Filmmaker and founder of the first sound studio in South India, A Narayanan, a friend of Satyamurthi, lent his support to the movement and organized a bonfire of foreign textiles.[22] K S Gopalakrishnan, actor-director (*Jalaja,* 1938) organized the All India Swadeshi Exhibition in Madras to subsidise the Salt Satyagraha campaign in Madras; he also conducted a music festival in which the great exponent of Carnatic music, Semmangudi Srinivasa Aiyar sang and renowned Bharatanatyam danseuse, T Balasaraswathi performed.[23] By identifying themselves with such popular causes, these artistes increased their own popularity among the people.

Satyamurthi's sustained interest and involvement in the world of cinema culminated in his election as the first president of the South Indian Film Chamber of Commerce in 1939 for a term of three years. It was he who drafted the Memorandum of Association and gave the organization its initial momentum.[24] In the same year, he led a contingent from the Chamber to the silver jubilee celebrations of Indian cinema and the Motion Picture Congress at Bombay; he presided over the latter. In his address he declared, 'The propaganda value, the technique and the appeal of the films will thus be the very best possible. It can in fact be made into a nation-building force in the true sense of those words. With popular governments and Congress governments functioning in the various provinces, there is unlimited scope.'[25] He believed that cinema could be used to drum up mass support for the Congress and for tackling social problems like illiteracy.

Satyamurthi had a flair for election campaigns and from 1921 onwards, he insisted that the Congress should enter the legislatures. This was the plank of the Swarajists, a faction of nationalists with which Satyamurthi identified himself. He received financial assistance from C R Das and Motilal Nehru, which enabled him to start a newspaper and to build a cadre of publicists.[26]

One of Satyamurthi's principal aims in contesting the elections was to displace the Justice Party, the genesis of Dravidian parties, from the legislature. When the 1935 Constitution brought in provincial autonomy and liberally expanded franchise, the need for using mass media in electoral campaigns was self-evident. He realized that in this changed scenario, film and stage artistes, with their unprecedented popularity, could be used effectively. Many well-known figures from the world of entertainment extended their support to the Congress in its campaign when the party decided to contest the elections in 1937. T K Shanmugam, the lead actor from one of the most successful troupes of the period, TKS Brothers Drama Company, and a film actor *(Menaka)*, campaigned for the Congress in the villages around Coimbatore. Their method of campaigning was to sing or make a political speech; their popularity as actors ensured that their very presence drew large crowds.[27]

The film artiste who played the most high profile political role was K B Sundarambal, the star of the film *Nandanar* (1935). Influenced by her uncle, Marikozhundu Gounder, a Congress worker, Sundarambal joined the nationalist movement and became a close associate of Satyamurthi. Earlier, when she was reluctant to enter the world of cinema and was still mourning the death of her husband, stage-star S G Kittappa, it was Satyamurthi who persuaded her to sign the contract for the film *Nandanar* (1935).[28] Similarly, to persuade her to campaign for the Congress, Satyamurthi accompanied Gandhi during one of his visits to Madras to Sundarambal's house.[29] She campaigned hard for the Congress in the 1937 elections. The pattern followed was for her to sing patriotic songs first; which was followed by a speech by Satyamurthi. A gramophone record was also released with a song by Sundarambal on one side, which appealed to the voters to support the Congress, and a speech by Satyamurthi on the reverse side. Throughout her life, she wore only khadi and remained a loyal supporter of the

Satyamurthi—the Link that Snapped

Congress. In 1958 she was nominated as member of the Legislative Council in Madras.

Pioneer filmmaker A Narayanan made a short film supporting the candidature of Satyamurthi in Madras. The film, lasting a few minutes, featured Bhulabhai Desai and Satyamurthi appealing to voters.[30] Thus Satyamurthi harnessed all the three popular entertainment forms—cinema, drama and gramophone—in widening and deepening political activism for the nationalist cause in Tamil society. In this process, the entertainers were brought under one flag and given a cause to work for. At a more practical level, Satyamurthi also pressed into service the most widely used contemporary media artefacts— songs, discs and film. Finally, these unorthodox instruments of electioneering proved quite successful. The Congress emerged victorious with a phenomenal majority in the Madras presidency; its margin of victory was not so decisive in the other provinces where it had won. Out of the 215 seats in the Madras presidency, Congress won 159.

In the Congress party, Satyamurthi acted as a bridge between the field worker and the top leadership. He observed the cultural experience of a vast majority of the people and thereby realized, with remarkable foresight, that popular culture was rapidly emerging as a force that could transform the political scene. The Congress leadership, on the other hand, refused to take cognisance of this development and treated the artistes with contempt as purveyors of cheap entertainment. This was one among the many ramifications of early elitist apathy to popular culture.

In spite of the support extended to the Congress by drama

and cine artistes, the other leaders failed to appreciate the role played by these artistes in building up a strong, populist base for their party. Nor were they able to foresee the political dimensions cinema was to assume later. Gandhi, whose arrival on the scene marked the politicisation of the masses, failed to take note of the work of these artistes. His attitude to the entertainment media was typical of many Congress leaders. For its issue commemorating the 25th anniversary of cinema in 1938, a Mumbai film journal requested Gandhi for a message and received the following reply from his secretary, 'As a rule, Gandhi gives messages only on rare occasions and these only for causes whose virtue is undoubted. As for the cinema, he has the least interest in it and one may not expect a word of appreciation from him.'[31] Satyamurthi's political rival in the Congress, Rajaji, who was seen to undermine Satyamurthi's power base in Tamil Nadu, did not take kindly to the entertainment world which was so supportive of Satyamurthi.[32] While the British government at the Centre and the Justice Party at the provincial level were targets of Satyamurthi's attack, Rajaji was his chief rival within the Congress. Even in the early 1920s, when Satyamurthi had led a faction known as the Nationalists while Rajaji had headed the other faction, Satyamurthi had hoped to be chosen the prime minister of Madras province and was disappointed when he lost it to Rajaji. In their approach to the world of entertainment also, their opinions were diametrically opposed. Rajaji's views on cinema were puritanical—as were his views on most other aspects of life—and he had asked people to refrain from watching films. In 1953 as chief

Satyamurthi—the Link that Snapped

minister presiding over a meeting of film celebrities, he described cinema as "poison" and said that if cinema could terminate itself, it would be an extraordinary service.[33] Even K Kamaraj, a protege of Satyamurthi who succeeded Rajaji as the chief minister of Tamil Nadu, was quite disdainful of this group and contemptuously referred to them as *koothadigal* (Mountbanks).[34] When Satyamurthi died in 1943, the leadership of the Congress in the Madras presidency passed on to Rajaji, his bitter political rival from the early years of his career.

While fighting the British government at the national level and at the provincial level, Satyamurthi was also constantly trying to out-manoeuvre the Justice Party, the ideological forerunner of the Dravidian parties, and he managed to keep it at bay. As long as he was active, they could not make much headway in the face of his campaigning skills. As mentioned earlier, his principal objective in persuading the Congress to enter the legislature was to evict the Justicites. He fought the Justice Party in the 1926 elections for the provincial council and defeated it, bringing to an end the first six years of its rule in Madras. The Justice Party's opposition to the Congress, was because it feared that if the British handed over power to that party, it would only perpetuate the dominance of Brahmins in the province.[35]

Satyamurthi had consistently opposed all that the Justice Party and the later the Self-respect movement had stood for. He, who had studied Tamil only up to fourth standard in school, believed that Sanskrit should be accorded a prime place in education and declared that he looked forward to the day when Hindi would be the national language. He was orthodox in religious matters and believed in astrology and horoscopes. He advocated early marriage for women recommending that about fifteen years was the ideal age, and opposed inter-caste marriage.[36] He therefore clearly took a position against the efforts that were on in the province to establish a Dravidian identity.[37] After his death, artistes from the world of entertainment, now leaderless and directionless, gravitated towards the Dravidian movement, whose leaders offered them recognition and patronage. In fact, many of the leading lights of the movement, including C N Annadurai and M Karunanidhi, were themselves playwrights and often acted in plays. It was they, the Dravidian leaders, and bitter political enemies of Satyamurthi, who eventually inherited the force that he had assiduously nurtured, and used it in their journey to power, creating the phenomenon of star-politicians.

The Dravidian movement, which was then expanding its mass base, first began using the stage for propaganda, with many artistes joining the movement. Later, when Dravida Munnetra Kazhagam was formed in 1949, stage and film artistes also came in handy as tools for propaganda; the party's first organizing committee included K R Ramasamy, a film star, and T V Narayanasamy, a drama actor. N S Krishnan, yet another actor was also one of the main supporters of the party.[38]

In fact, the career of N S Krishnan, who dominated the Tamil film scene for more than two decades as a comedian and acted in more than a 100 films, epitomizes the fortunes

Satyamurthi—the Link that Snapped

of stage and screen artistes in the political arena during that crucial period in history. Since the time of the Civil Disobedience movement, Krishnan had been actively carrying on political propaganda for the Congress. He wrote the story of Gandhi's salt satyagraha as a *villupaatu*, a traditional form of musical narration, and performed it as a part of Swaminatha Sarma's famous play *Desabakthi*, and later, as a separate show. After Independence, for the first general election in 1952, Durgabai Deshmukh persuaded him to contest as a Congress candidate from Madras. When Krishnan was in Delhi to finalise his candidature, some Congress leaders from Madras ridiculed the idea, saying that a *komali* (clown) should not enter the legislature. Piqued, Krishnan refused to contest.[39] In the 1952 general elections, N S Krishnan, along with actor M R Radha and K R Ramasamy, campaigned against the Congress candidates.[40] Later, he lent his support to the Dravidian movement and was of invaluable assistance in building up the Dravida Munnetra Kazhagam, though he was never a member of that party. S S Rajendran, a lead player of the nationalist TKS Brothers Drama Company, joined the DMK and became the first film star to be elected to a legislature when he won the election to the Tamil Nadu Assembly in 1962 from the Theni constituency. Later, he also became a Member of Parliament.

M G Ramachandran, the best known star-politician of the Dravidian movement, had acted in the nationalistic play *The Triumph of Khadi/Kadarin Vetri* as a company drama artiste and was a khadi-wearing Congress sympathizer before he joined the DMK.

Notes

This chapter is based on an article of the same tide, published in *The Economic and Political Weekly*, Vol.XXIX, No. 38 (1994).

1. The building housing the headquarters of the Tamil Nadu Congress Committee in Madras is called Satyamurthi Bhavan, largely due to the efforts of K Kamaraj.
2. Parthasarathy, R, *S. Satyamurthi* (Builders of Modern India series) (New Delhi, Publication Division, 1979) pp 193-201.
3. See Satyamurthi, S, "Mrichakatika—A Sanskrit Drama", in *Indhunesan,* Annual (1923).
4. Parthasarathy, S, *Satyamurthi,* p.62
5. Satyamurthi Papers, Jawaharlal Nehru Memorial Library, New Delhi.
6. Copley, Anthony, *C.Rajagopalachari: Gandhi's Southern Commander* (Madras, Indo-British Historical Society, 1986) p.74.
7. Parthasarathy, S, *Satyamurthi,* p.196.
8. Chidambaranathan, M.M., "*Sudhanthira Poratathil Kalaignargal*" in *Nadigan Kural* (Tamil) August 1957.
9. Visswanathan, E Sa, *The Political Career of E.V.Ramasami Naicker: A Study in the Politics of Tamil Nadu. 1920-1949* (Rau & Vasanth Publishers, Madras, 1983) p. 113.
10. *The Mail* (Daily), 26 December 1936.
11. *Cinema Ulagam* (Tamil), 11 August 1935.
12. Copley, *C.Rajagopalachari,* p.99 and p.143.
13. Parthasarathy, S, *Satyamurthi*, p.181-182.
14. *Film Gazettee,* Vol.1, No.2, December 1939.
15. *The Hindu,* 8 January 1937.
16. *Cinema Ulagam,* 21 April 1935.
17. *Dinamani Kadir* (Tamil), 27 May 1990.
18. *Dinamani Kadir,* 9 February 1973.

Satyamurthi—the Link that Snapped

19. *Satyamurthi Papers,* Letter dated 26 December 1928 from Gohar to Satyamurthi.
20. Parthasarathy, S, *Satyamurti,* p.94
21. Known as "Salt Satyagrahi Nataraja Pillai", a street has been named after him in his home town Mannargudi. *Adal Padal* (Tamil), 3 June 1939.
22. Dr N Kalavathy (daughter of A Narayanan), interviewed by the author in Madras, 25 April 1976.
23. This incident paved the way for the founding of Music Academy. K S Gopalakrishnan interviewed by the author in Madras , 19 January 1976.
24. Lakshmi Krishnamurthy (daughter of Satyamurthi), interviewed by the author in Delhi, 27 March 1986.
25. Indian Motion Picture Congress, Presidential address, (Pamphlet) Mumbai, 7 May 1939.
26. Baker, Christopher, *The Politics of South India 1920-1937,* (London, Cambridge University Press, 1978) p. 158.
27. Shanmugam, TKS *Enadhu Nataka Vazhkai,* (Madras, Vanadhi Pathipagam, 1972) p. 135.
28. K B Sundarambal interviewed by the author in Madras, 9 April 1975.
29. Kumari Anandan in *Kumudam* (Tamil), 9 May 1991.
30. P G Sundararajan alias Chitti (Tamil writer and associate of Satyamurthi) interviewed by the author in Madras, 28 April 1975.
31. Dogra, Bharat B, "When the Censors Tried to Block Out the Congress", *Filmfare,* 27 July 1975.
32. Copley, *C. Rajagopalachari,* p.147. For a detailed account of the Rajaji-Satyamurthi rivalry, see Copley's book.
33. Bamouw, Eric, and S Krishnaswamy, *Indian Cinema* (New York, Oxford University Press, 1963) p. 176.

34. Pandian, M S S, *The Image Trap*, (New Delhi, Sage Publications, 1992) p.38.
35. Sattanathan, A N, *The Dravidian Movement in Tamil Nadu and its Legacy*, (Madras, University of Madras, 1982) p.14.
36. *Satyamurthi Pesugirar* (Tamil, collection of speeches), (Madras, Thamizh Pannai, 1945) see chapters "*Namadhu Latchiyam*" (Our Goal) and "*Indhu Vivaham*" (Hindu Marriage).
37. Irschick, Eugene F, *Politics and Social Conflict in South India: The Non-Brahmin Movement and Tamil Separatism, 1916-1929*, (Berkley, University of California Press, 1969) p.249.
38. In his last public function as chief minister, in 1969, C N Annadurai unveiled a statue of N S Krishnan, in an important road junction in Thyagaraya Nagar in Madras.
39. Subrahmanyam, K, "*Viruppum Veruppum Atra Kalaivanar*" in *Kalaivanar Malar*, Souvenir marking the 13th death anniversary N S Krishnan (Madras, 1968).
40. Sivagnanam, Ma Po, *Enadhu Porattam*, (Madras, Inba Nilayam, 1974) p.559.

Chapter Seven
The Films

Kalidas

B&W	1931	Not Available
Producer:	Imperial Movietone Company, Bombay	
Director:	H M Reddy	
Cast:	T P Rajalakshmi, Thevaram Rajambal, J Sushila, T Susheela Devi, P G Venkatesan	

THE FIRST TAMIL TALKIE *KALIDAS* WAS RELEASED ON 31 October 1931 at Kinema Central, now Sri Murugan Talkies, in Madras. Like all the Tamil films released in the first four years (1931-34), this was also shot in Bombay. This film was about Kalidas, the legendary Sanskrit poet who wrote classics like the *Abijnanashakuntalam*. The story revolved around Vidhyadhari, the daughter of Vijayavarman, king of Thejavathi whose minister suggested to the princess that she marry his son. But Vidhyadhari declined. Piqued, the minister set out in search of a suitable groom for her.

In the forest, he found a cowherd on a tree, trying to cut down the very branch on which he was sitting. The minister persuaded him to come to the palace and got him married to the princess. When Vidhyadhari realized that she had been cheated and married to a cowherd, she prayed to goddess Kali for redressal. The deity appeared before her, named her husband Kalidas and endowed him with literary talents.

While most of the characters in the film spoke Tamil, some spoke in Telugu also. All the fifty songs in the film were in Tamil and set to classical Carnatic ragas. It was because of the songs that the film is recognized as "the first Tamil talkie". The heroine, T P Rajalakshmi, who was then a star in the commercial drama companies, sang some of the songs in the film which had made her popular on the stage. She also sang two nationalistic songs, quite unconnected with the story; one on the need for unity among Indians and the other praising the charkha which had become a symbol of nationalism. Both songs were written by the nationalist poet, Baskara Das. T P Rajalakshmi, later authored two novels in Tamil, *Kamalavalli* and *Vimala*. The former was made into a film titled *Miss Kamala* and was directed by Rajalakshmi herself.

1931 was incidentally also the year in which the Indian freedom struggle had gained fresh momentum with the launching of the Civil Disobedience movement.

There had been an earlier attempt at producing a Tamil sound film, a short four-reeler, titled *Korathi Dance and Songs,* in which a little-known actor called Jhansi Bai had featured. The film was screened along with *Kalidas* as a side attraction.[1]

The Films

Two Brothers/ Iru Sakodarargal

B&W 1936 Not Available
Producer: Parameshwar Sound Pictures, Coimbatore
Director: Ellis R Dungan
Cast : S N Vijayalakshmi, K P Kesavan, K K Perumal, T S Balaiya, M K Radha

One of the earliest films on a contemporary theme, as distinct from mythologicals, this film was scripted by S D S Yogi. In addition to other social issues, the film depicted the conditions prevailing in a commercial drama company: one of the two lead characters was a drama buff. (Commercial drama was the most popular form of entertainment in the Thirties.)

The story was about the conflicts and values of the joint family system and revolved around two brothers, Sabapathy and Pasupathy. The problems in the household are aggravated by the wife of the elder brother and a fight for the family property ensues. After a series of tribulations, the brothers are reconciled and once again come together as a family. A supernatural element is introduced in the form of a family angel (in the garb of a maid servant) who is a trouble-shooter.

The film was shot in Sagar Movietone in Bombay and was directed by an American, who had been trained in Hollywood, Ellis R Dungan. He drastically reduced the number of songs, from the usual thirty to thirty-five to a mere thirteen, and laid emphasis on acting. For some sequences, his rehearsals lasted as long as three hours. He encouraged the actors to speak their lines extempore, after briefing them about the scene to be shot and shot more footage than was the practice and edited the film himself. He also integrated the humorous sequences into the film rather than keep them separate as a parallel plot.

The film's producer Ramasamy, a businessman from Coimbatore, was a Congress party sympathizer and therefore had nationalistic songs inserted in the film. S Satyamurthi, was so impressed with it that he wrote a letter of praise to *The Hindu*. He also persuaded Rajaji, then the prime minister of Madras presidency, to see the film in a special show at Elphinstone Talkies on Mount Road.

Ambikapathi

B&W	1937
Producer:	Shankar Films
Director :	Ellis R Dungan
Photography:	Krishna Gopal
Music:	Papanasam Sivan and K C Dey
Cast :	M R Santhanalaksmi, T A Mathuram, M K Thyagaraja Bhagavathar, Seruka athur Sama, P B Rangachari, N S Krishnan,

One of the earliest films dealing with historical fiction (there had been just two earlier, *Raja Desingu* and *Baktha Kabirdas*, both in 1936) this film is set in the days of the Chola kingdom. Poet Kambar, who translated the Ramayana in Tamil, is in the court of King Kulothunga Cholan. His son Ambikapathi falls in love with princess Amaravathi. But the couple is not able to unite because Ambikapathi fails in a test of will power laid down by the king as a precondition for their marriage. The director Dungan was quick to see the parallel between this and Shakespeare's *Romeo and Juliet* and therefore organized some of the sequences on the pattern of that famous play. The balcony scenes showing the hero climbing up to meet his beloved were particularly similar. Although love sequences between lovers were considered bold by those standards, not much care was taken about the historical accuracy of costumes and customs.

The film was made in the New Theatres studio in Calcutta and the background music was composed by the blind singer-composer K C Dey. Another high point of the film was its music, written and composed by Papanasam Sivan. The voice of M K Thyagaraja Bhagavathar, who, as Ambikapathi, sang a number of songs including the famous *Bajanai seivai maname,* was a major attraction. This film proved a landmark in his career.

The film opens with the scene of Kulothunga Cholan returning victoriously from battle. His entry into the city of Woriur was filmed quite spectacularly. In fact, such scenes depicting groups of people moving in the open was a favourite with Dungan. Sage Kanwar returning from his pilgrimage in *Sakunthala* and the marriage party returning home in the film *Mandhirikumari* are other examples from his work.

The importance given to dialogues set this film apart from the others made in the Thirties in which songs dominated. Ilangovan, the scriptwriter, started this trend—and was evident both in the balcony scene and in the one where the friend of the princess brings a message from Ambikapathi-- in which he had borrowed liberally from Shakespeare. Mumbai-based filmmaker Karan Bali has produced a documentary on the life and works of Dungan titled "An American in Madras".

Streak of Lightning/ Minnalkodi

B&W 1937 Not Available
Director: K Amarnath
Cast: K T Rukrnani, P S Srinivasa Rao, S S Kokko

Influenced by English serial films like *Flash Gordon* and *Captain Marvel,* which were screened widely in South India, a number of stunt films were released in the late Thirties. *Minnalkodi* is typical of this genre. (There were others like *Danger Signal* and *Pucca Rowdy,* both in 1937.) In these films, the heroine often dominated by indulging in daring acts on the screen.

Minnalkodi was a story about a young girl Mohini, whose father dies, leaving her and a man-servant homeless. A wily uncle misappropriates her property. In their wanderings, Mohini and the servant come across the dacoit Minnalkodi and protect him from the police. The injured Minnalkodi declares Mohini as the leader of his gang and dies. Mohini goes about in the guise of a man as Minnalkodi and kills her uncle and others who had harmed her earlier.

But, she plays a "good" thief who robs the rich only to help the poor. Meanwhile, Police Inspector Jayakumar tries to capture her but is unable to make much progress. Once while pursuing her in the jungle, he comes across Mohini, without her disguise, and falls in love with her. When he learns that she is, in fact, the dacoit, he persuades her to change her ways and they finally get married.

Stunt films were mostly produced by Mumbai-based producers like Ramaniklal and Mohanlal; most of the artistes were also from Mumbai and therefore the Tamil they spoke in these films was very crude. Moreover, the plausibility of events was also totally discounted. For instance, as soon as she becomes a dacoit, Mohini, a country girl, rides a horse and a motorbike and handles weapons with ease. However, the accent in this film was only on action sequences, like fights and daredevil acts and the film had only three songs. K T Rukmani, who played Mohini, modelled her screen mannerisms on Gohar of Hindi cinema. In fact, she even draped her sari in the Gujarati style.

Another draw of the film was S S Kokko (aka Pasubuleti Ramulu Naidu), a very popular stunt-comedian who entered films from the world of circus. He played the role of the servant in *Minnalkodi*.

Rajamohan

B&W	1938	Not Available
Producer:	National Movietone	
Director:	Fram Sethna	
Photography:	Bomman Irani	
Music:	Yanai Vaidhyanatha Aiyar and H H Sarma	
Cast:	M M Radha Bai, K P Kesavan, P U Chinnappa, Kali N Rathinam	

Vai Mu Kothainayaki Ammal was a popular novelist of the

Thirties. Some of her novels were adapted for films and this was one of them. Although the adaptation marked a break from the practice of filming only popular stage plays, most of the artistes in this film were from the stage.

The story focused on Mohan's mother who eked out a precarious living as a vendor of vegetables. When she grows too frail to work, Mohan drops out of school and gets a job as a proofreader in a magazine. Dharmalingam, who runs the magazine, has a daughter called, Rajam who falls in love with Mohan. He soon rises to be the editor of the magazine much to the annoyance of Krishnan, Rajam's brother, who is a wastrel. Due to Krishnan's machinations, Mohan loses his job. When Dharmalingam is found murdered, Mohan stands accused. Eventually, Mohan is acquitted and is united with Rajam.

K P Kesavan, the popular hero of the Thirties played the role of Mohan and P U Chinnappa, who later became a singing star specializing in mythological roles, played Krishnan in one of his rare roles as a villain that too in a film set in contemporary times.

The music for the film was composed by Carnatic music pundits and out of nine, eight songs were set to classical tunes. However, the songs were in an abridged form lasting only four or five minutes and one tune was copied from a popular Hindi film song. There were separate comic sequences played by Kali N Rathinam, a characteristic of commercial dramas in which the comedian had his own plot, often quite unrelated to the main story. And like commercial dramas, the film opened with a song in praise of the producers of the film, National

Movietone, and invoking the blessings of Lord Ganesa for the success of the film.

The director of this film, Fram Sethna, was Calcutta-based and had earlier directed two Tamil films, *Good Sister/ Nallathangal* and *Dhuruva,* both in 1935, for Pioneer Films.

Motherland/ Mathrubhoomi

B & W	1939	Not Available
Producer:	Al Rm Company, Madras	
Director:	H M Reddy	
Photography:	E R Cooper	
Music :	K Subba Rao	
Cast:	T V Kumudini, P Saradambal, T S Santhanam, P U Chinnappa, C S D Singh, K K Perumal	

The late 1930s was the era of patriotic cinema in India and filmmakers used allegorical format to attack the British rule. This film, set during the period of Alexander's invasion of India and the resistance offered by Indian kings, is typical of the time.

After Alexander, his commandant Minander gains control over the Indus area. The King of Udayagiri, Ugrasenan, with the help of some smaller kings, opposes Minander. Admiring his valour, Minander's daughter, Helen, falls in love with him and joins him. After much palace intrigue and fighting, Minander returns to Greece, leaving the Indian kingdoms to themselves. Helen marries Ugrasenan.

T V Kumudini, who made her debut in this film as a heroine, played the character of the same name. When she learns that her husband was a spy for the Greeks, she throws her *thali* (wedding chain) at him and turns against him. She also had battle scenes in the film. T S Santhanam played the dual roles of Ugrasenan and Jayabalan, the spy, one of the earliest examples of double acting.[7] P U Chinnappa played the role of Prathapan, brother of Kumudini.

Though the costumes were not historically authentic, the battle scenes were shot in actual forts, in Gingee and Krishnagiri. Papanasam Sivan wrote all the songs in the film and all of them proved very popular, including *Bharatha desam* (The country of Bharat) and *Namadhu jenma bhoomi* (The land of our birth). The latter was used as a marching song in schools for many years.

S Satyamurthi, the nationalist leader presided over the premiere of the film and praised its nationalistic appeal. As was expected, the British government banned the film; Satyamurthi had to intervene and get the order rescinded. D L Roy, a Bengali playwright, had used the same theme for a patriotic play titled, *Chandragupta*.[8]

The Land of Sacrifice/ Thyagabhoomi

B&W 1939
Producer: Madras United Artistes Corporation
Director : K Subrahmanyam
Photography: Sailen Bose
Music: Papanasam Sivan
Cast: S D Subbulakshmi, Baby Saroja, Papanasam Sivan, K J Mahadevan

The Films

This film is a good example of patriotic cinema. The story is woven around Sambu Sastri, a poor Brahmin priest and his daughter Savithri. Sastri is ostracized for sheltering cyclone-hit dalits inside the temple. So he moves to Madras, where he teams up with Nallan, a dalit, and starts Gandhian social uplift programmes in a ghetto. His daughter, recovering from a broken marriage, is also inspired and joins the movement.

The film opens with shots of the cyclone and of the stranded dalits waiting in front of the closed doors of the temple. Gandhi's programme of temple entry, anti-untouchability and temperance—all form part of the film. Political awakening in Tamil Nadu was dramatized through a series of low angle shots of nationalists marching, which inspires Sastri to join the movement. The marchers, led by Sastri, pull down liquor shops. There is a scene of a mass spinning session, a symbolic act that was given the status of a ritual by Gandhi. The last sequence, a long tracking shot of a march, ends with police intervention. The film closes with Savithri being imprisoned and a flag-hoisting ceremony in the ghetto.

The filmmaker, K Subrahmanyam established his credibility by conforming to the basic religious belief-system of Indians; and then, by questioning social evils, created an impact through the film. In the film, Sastri believes that it is because of the will of goddess Ambikai that he joins the national movement. Thus the message of nationalism and social reform was infused with a religious flavour. The anti-caste appeal of the film gained greater authenticity due to the fact that most of the people who worked in the film were Brahmins.

The Eye of the Serpent

Papanasam Sivan, well-known musician and songwriter of the times, was appropriately cast as Sambu Sastri who symbolizes Gandhi. In fact, he is referred to as the Gandhi of Tamil Nadu in the film and, in one scene Sastri sits on a dais, spinning on a charkha, in a posture strongly reminiscent of Gandhi. As the camera dollies up to him, the scene is interspersed with documentary footage showing Gandhi.

The story had been written by Kalki (R Krishnamurthy) and had been serialized in the weekly magazine, *Anandavikatan*. The performance of child actress Saroja, who played the granddaughter of Sastri, endeared her to filmgoers. Later, Saroja became such a legend that songs were composed on her.

When the film was revived in Madras in 1944, it was banned as a part of tightening of censorship during the War years, It was revoked after Independence in 1951 and was screened in Chithra talkies in October that year. (When it was released in 1939, Congress party was in power in the Madras presidency.)

Ashokumar

B&W	1941
P:	Murugan Talkies
Director:	Raja Chandrasekhar
Photography:	M R Purushothaman
Music:	Alathur V Sivasubramanyan
Cast:	P Kannamba, M K Thyagaraja Bhagavathar, V Nagaiya, N S Krishnan, T A Mathuram, M G Ramachandran

The Films

This story, set in the era of the Mauryan dynasty (3rd century BC) revolves around Emperor Ashoka's son, Gunalan. The emperor's second wife is enamoured of the prince and when he spurns her advances, she manages to have him exiled and later, blinded. The prince wanders around before he is reunited with his wife. The father repents and the family assembles at a Buddhist vihara where the Buddha appears in the flesh and restores sight to the prince. The grateful prince vows to spread the message of the Buddha.

This unusual theme of a woman falling in love with her stepson and the Buddhist backdrop set the film apart. Buddha and his disciple Upagupta were featured in the film; ideas of non-violence and vegetarianism were expressed through them. However, the costumes and sets had no relation to the period or to the historical background of the story.

M K Thayagaraja Bhagavathar was at the height of his glory at the time. This was his seventh film. His songs in the film, all written by Sivan, have become part of the social history of Tamil Nadu, particularly *Bhoomiyil manida jenmam* (Life on this earth as humans). In a quaint way, this song featured in a Hollywood movie also, *Elephant Walk* (English, 1954), in which tea plantation workers in Sri Lanka sing it. *Ashokumar* was one of the earliest films in which the songs were pre-recorded. The practice of using popular tunes from Hindi films was just beginning. The tune of the song *Pia milan ko jana*, sung by Pankaj Mullick in *Kapal Kundala* (1939) was therefore used in this film.

A textile engineer-turned-filmmaker, Raja Chandrasekhar, as director of the film, gave it a vibrant quality by his camera movements and angles and made good use of close-ups, dolly and crane shots. In a court dance sequence, the influence of Busby Berkley is evident. But the dominance of the spoken word continued (dialogue was by Ilangovan). There was also a comic sub-plot featuring N S Krishnan and T A Mathuram, the pair that strode the Tamil film scene for twenty-five years in comedy roles.

We Two/ Nam Iruvar

B&W	1947
Producer:	AVM Productions
Director:	A V Meyyappa Chettiar
Photography:	T Muthusamy
Music:	R Sudarsanam
Cast:	T A Jayalakshmi, K R Chellam, Kumari Kamala, T R Mahalingam, B R Panthulu, T R Ramachandran,

This film, the last of the genre of patriotic films, was made on the eve of India's Independence. By 1945, after the formation of a popular government in Madras, political censorship had been lifted and nationalist symbols became saleable commodities in films. In this film, characters used "Jai Hind" to greet each other and portraits of nationalist leaders were shown, one after the other. It opened with poet Bharathi's death anniversary and ended with the 77th birthday celebrations of Gandhi.

The film was a modified version of the earlier, *Iru Sakodarargal*. Vijayakumar and Sukumar, sons of a rapacious black marketeer, protest when their father plans to marry a young girl. Sukumar is in love with Kannamma, daughter of a business associate of his father. He falls in evil ways, gets the family property divided and squanders his share of the money in making a film. He comes back in the style of the prodigal son and is accepted by his brother. Devaluation of currency hits the black marketeer who kills his partner and is imprisoned. Sukumar marries Kannamma.

For many years a successful play of the NSK Drama Company, much of its original stage flavour was retained when it was made into a film. It was shot in a make-shift studio in Karaikudi where this film company had moved in the wake of the war. Painted backdrops and cut-out trees added to the "staginess". Characters spoke chaste (the written form) Tamil and the dialogues were pedagogic. There were no outdoor shots at all except the one showing lovers riding bicycles outside the sets, but within the studio compound.

The main draw of the film was poet Bharathi's nationalist songs; the producers had bought the copyright of these songs for 10,000 rupees from Messrs Surajmal & Company, a recording concern. The heroine is called Kannamma, after the subject of many of Bharathi's love poems. Kamala, who plays the character of the same name, as the younger sister, dances on drums for Bharathi's famous song *Kottu murase* (Let the drum sound). This dance, incidentally, was the precursor to the famous drum dance in *Chandraleka*. During this dance, in what was supposed to be a stage performance, two images of Kamala were shown.

After a series of mythologicals, this film with a contemporary theme dealing with issues like black marketeering and price-rise was received very well. This was also the first Tamil film which showed actual sequences of film shooting as part of the narrative.

Miser/ Kanjan

B&W 1947 (Not Available)
Producer: Jupiter Pictures
Director: Kovai A Ayyamuthu and T R Gopu
Photography: P Ramaswamy
Music: S M Subbaiya Naidu
Cast: M S S Packiam, K Angamuthu, S V Subbaiya, M N Nambiar, P V Narasimhabharathi

Kandasamy, a miserly zamindar, is a womaniser. His son Kumarasamy and daughter Amaravathi do not approve of his ways. Kandasamy stores his jewels and money in a vessel and buries it in the house. Velappan, an orphan who had lost his parents in a boat accident, reaches the village. Through a common friend he comes to stay in Kandasamy's house and falls in love with Amaravathi. Kumarasamy is fond of Maragatham, a drama artiste. His father Kandasamy also fancies Maragatham. He also plans to get his daughter Amaravathi married to an old man in return for 50,000 rupees. All problems get sorted out in the end and the lovers unite.

Kovai Ayyamuthu, a nationalist leader and a great campaigner for khadi, wrote the story, script and seven songs, in addition to directing the film. He was originally a playwright and his famous play, *Inbasagaran* was staged by the Nawab Rajamanikkam Drama Company. He presented khadi to all the workers after the shooting was completed. Gandhi's visit to Palani and the Independence Day celebrations at Coimbatore were shown in two reels along with the main film, which was released in November 1947.

Protest against old men marrying young women was a frequent theme in films of the Forties. This film also attacked black marketeering, a major issue in the post-war years. Though the film had nationalistic overtones, it also had one of the earliest songs on Tamil revivalism, written by Ayyamuthu. It was released as a disc and large numbers were sold and was broadcast simultaneously by Tiruchi, Madras and Colombo radio stations. There was also another song in praise of Tamil Nadu. All the songs in the film were based on Hindustani or Carnatic tunes.

Servant Maid/ Velaikari

B&W 1949
Producer: Jupiter Pictures
Director: A S A Swamy
Photography: M Masthan
Music: C R Subbaraman and S M Subbaiya Naidu
Cast: V N Janaki, M V Rajamma, K R Ramasamy, M N Nambiar, T S Balaiya

The film version of a popular play by C N Annadurai, the leader of the Dravida Munnetra Kazhagam or DMK (the founding of the party coincided with the release of the film) it is the story of a rapacious landlord and how he is brought to heel by the hero. Anandan returns home after a two-year stint as a worker in a tea garden in Sri Lanka only to find his father hanging from a tree, harassed into this desperate move by the landlord. Anandan's piety leads him nowhere. Disillusioned, he follows the advice of his rationalist friend Mani. Anandan's revenge, which is pegged on props like look-alikes and coincidences, forms the rather tortuous and contrived plot, which shows strong influences of *The Count of Monte Cristo,* a novel by Alexander Dumas.[10] The subplot of the landlord's son in love with the servant maid provides a context for egalitarian ideas and supplies the film's title.

The film is laced with anti-caste, anti-religious and socialistic rhetoric. The character Harihara Das, a criminal who masquerades as a "godman" and runs an ashram (based on the real-life Bhowal Sanyasi case), is used to lampoon religiosity. The trend of long monologues and flowery dialogues began with such films and remained very aural resulting in poor visual quality.

Velaikari was very much like a filmed drama. A S A Swamy, the director, was a playwright and therefore there is no outdoor shots in the film and much of the story is carried on through verbal narration and mid-shots. We are merely told that Anandan had worked in a tea estate in Ceylon and had saved money. The film leaves you with a claustrophobic feeling. Characters turn towards the camera to speak their lines, rather than the camera turning towards them. However, it was a commercial success and paved the way for more dialogue-oriented films.

What stood out was a dance number by the Travancore sisters, Lalitha and Padmini, a popular feature of films in the 1950s. On the 100th day's run of the film in a Coimbatore cinema house, Tamil writer Va Ramasamy (Va Ra) presided over the celebrations. The dialogue writer of the film, Annadurai later became the chief minister of Tamil Nadu and V N Janaki, who played the vamp, was briefly the interim chief minister in 1987 after the passing of her husband or ex-chief minister and renowned actor, M G Ramachandran.

The Plight of the Poor/ Ezhai Padum Padu

B&W 1950
Producer: Pakshiraja Films
Director: K Ramnoth
Photography: N Prakasam
Music: S M Subbaiya Naidu
Cast: Lalitha, Padmini, V Nagaiya, Javert Seetharaman, T S Durairaj, T S Balaiya, V Gopalakrishnan

Based on *Ezhai Padum Padu,* a Tamil translation by Suddhanandha Bharathi of Victor Hugo's classic *Les Miserables,* the film opens with Kandhan serving a ten-year sentence in jail. When released, he realizes that the stigma attached to a jail-bird is difficult to shake off. He has a brief but significant encounter with a Christian priest, who remains nameless in the film. The priest gifts valuable silver, including two candlesticks, to Kandhan which, in

The Eye of the Serpent

fact, he had tried to steal. A transformed Kandhan assumes a different name, sets up a glass factory and prospers. He becomes the mayor of the town. He assumes custody of the daughter of his niece, the only member of the family to have survived. She is in love with Umakanth, an activist during India's struggle for freedom. Javert, the Police Inspector who had arrested Kandhan earlier, is posted to the same town. (This is the only instance of the original name of a character from Hugo's novel being retained in this film). Javert is bent upon exposing Kandhan.

The film is set in the last decade of British rule in India. India's nationalistic struggle replaces the French Revolution as the backdrop for the story. Period flavour is provided by props like Queen Victoria's portrait in the court room, horse-drawn coaches, and costumes, particularly those of the policemen. The story stretches over a period of forty to forty-five years and the ageing of Kandhan and Javert is made evident through effective make-up. The film is well photographed; its visuals bring out the bleakness of a life of poverty, imprisonment and of Kandhan's life as a fugitive. The camera movements are dynamic and tight close-ups are used aptly and intensely. Though the shots are longish, they are quite fluid. The filmmaker resorts to verbal narration of events in one or two places. But the basic economy of words heightens the impact of the film. The music of the film is subdued and appropriate. For instance, the sound of the inspector's stomping boots is used to convey a premonition of trouble.

The highlight of the film was Seetharaman's portrayal of Javert, the loner who builds a wall around himself and single mindedly pursues Kandhan. After this film, this actor came to be known as "Javert Seetharaman". Nagaiya's performance as Kandhan was equally poignant and powerful. He was at the peak of his career at that time.

The Minister's Daughter/ Mandhirikumari

B&W 1950
Producer: Modern Theatres
Director: Ellis R Dungan
Photography: K G Vijayan
Music: G Ramanathan
Cast: Madhuri Devi, G Shakunthala,
M G Ramachandran, S A Natarajan,
A Karunanidhi

The film was an adaptation of one of the five Tamil classics, *Kundalakesi*. Parthiban, son of the royal priest, is disappointed at not being made the commandant of the king's army. To discredit the new commandant Veeramohan, he takes to looting and robbing. The imbecile king is not in control of the situation. His daughter Jeeva is in love with Veeramohan. The minister's daughter Amudavalli grows fond of Parthiban, unaware of his evil ways. When she learns the truth, she makes futile attempts to change him. To get her out of the way, Parthiban takes her to a mountain peak and threatens to push her down. She outwits him, and then takes his life. She announces his death in the royal court, only to be killed by the enraged priest.

This was one of the most popular films of the decade.

The Eye of the Serpent

The dialogues by M Karunanidhi, who later became the chief minister of Tamil Nadu, was one of the reasons for its popularity. His barbs against the royal priest had a distinct anti-priesthood edge which was part of the Dravidian movement. The songs were another reason for the movie's success, particularly *Varai! Nee Varai* (Come O! Come) sung by Tiruchi Loganathan and Jikki. For T M Soundararajan, the playback singer whose career lasted more than three decades, this film was a landmark. Master Subbaiya, a teenage prodigy who died young, also sang a song in a cameo appearance as a cowherd. These songs are still popular and are featured in film music concerts. A long-playing disc of these songs was released in the late Seventies.

M G Ramachandran played the role of the commandant. However, the character that stood out was that of Amudavalli, played well by Madhuri Devi. She portrayed an assertive and confident woman who could handle a sword with dexterity and could kill her husband when necessary. Such an independent female character was a rarity in films.

The film shows little respect for period detail and costume authenticity. Parthiban, as a dacoit, wears a 'Batman' mask (Batman comics were popular in the Forties); his men wear Greek theatre masks; and modern fencing style is used by the soldiers. One refreshing feature was that many sequences had been shot outdoors, mainly in and out of Yercaud, a hill resort near Salem. Lalitha and Padmini, whose dance number was a sine qua non for any film that aspired to succeed in those days, had a number in this film as well.

The Films

The Mysterious Sage/ Marmayogi

B&W 1951
Producer: Jupiter Pictures
Director: K Ramnoth
Music: C R Subbaraman and S M Subbaiya Naidu
Photography: M Masthan
Cast: Madhuri Devi, Anjali Devi, M G Ramachandran, Serukalathur Sama

Stories of kings and queens, set in historical and geographical unspecified periods and locations, formed a common genre in the early decades of Tamil cinema. In such films, the costume designer and the art director had the license to do as they pleased. *Marmayogi* belongs to this genre. It even features a tournament contested in the manner of the Knights of the Round Table.

The story is a mix of a legend and a novel—that of Robin Hood of Sherwood forest and Marie Corelli's *Vendetta*. A courtesan gets intimate with the king; soon she plots to kill him and usurp his throne. He survives the assassination attempt and returns disguised as a sage and earns a place in her court. His son, the prince, who has been saved by the commandant, grows up in the forest as a do-gooder on the lines of Robin Hood, complete with bows and arrows. As the protector of the oppressed, he organizes them against the cruel imposter, the courtesan. He even makes a daring appearance in the court to caution her about her misdeeds—a scene very reminiscent of Robinhood's (Errol Flynn) dramatic appearance in the royal court, in the film *The Adventures of*

Robinhood (1936). After many sword fights and chases, the sage exposes the courtesan before the citizens; she dies of shock. The prince marries the commandant's daughter and rules his subjects with a benign hand.

The film was scripted by A S A Swamy, with his friend, M G Ramachandran, in mind; the film made the latter a star. Ramachandran was heavily influenced by Errol Flynn and Douglas Fairbanks. In this film, he fences, swings from chandeliers and creepers, leaps from the ramparts of the fort directly atop a saddled mare and shoots arrows with amazing dexterity. All this brought him tremendous popularity amongst film-goers. His name in the film, Karikalan, was borrowed from a legendary Chola king. This synchronized with Tamil revivalism, the spirit of the times.

However, the film showed total disregard for plausibility of events. The sage disguises himself as a ghost and frightens the queen; and he walks on air. There is no explanation as to why he waited for twenty years to expose the courtesan even as the people suffered under her tyranny. The film also had a few derogatory comments against women, a persistent feature of Tamil films till the late Seventies. The "tide" sequence was inspired by *Ivan the Terrible* (Russian, 1942). The silhouette of Ivan, with his flowing and pointed beard, was even featured on the title cards. For some paradoxical reason, most probably due to the innocuous ghost scenes, this film was given an 'Adults Only' certificate by the censors.

The Films

The Goddess/ Parasakthi
B&W 1952
Producer: National Pictures
Director: Krishnan-Panju
Music: R Sudarsanam
Photography: S Maruthi Rao
Cast: Sriranjani, Pandari Bai, Sivaji Ganesan, S S Rajendran, S V Sahasranamam

One of the most controversial films in the history of Tamil cinema, *Parasakthi* is important for more than one reason. It owed its success in large part to its dialogues and enhanced the value placed on dialogue writers. It spawned more such films, each one replete with similar assonant monologues. M Karunanidhi, who wrote the dialogues for *Parasakthi* used this film to express his ideas on religion, god and priesthood. Sivaji Ganesan, who was still working with drama companies, made his debut in this film as the lead actor. He later went on to act in more than 200 films in a career that lasted fifty-two years.

Adapted from a successful play by Pavalar Balasundaram, the film's story, set against the backdrop of the Second World War, is about three brothers in Rangoon and their sister in Madras. The brothers are separated in the chaos of war; Gunasekaran, the youngest, travels to Madras in search of his sister and finds she is a destitute widow. He does not reveal his own identity as he is powerless and cannot offer her any help. He sets himself up as her protector; when the priest tries to molest her inside a temple, he inflicts grievous injuries on the

The Eye of the Serpent

priest. Driven to despair, his sister tries to kill herself, along with her infant child. All end up in court where matters are sorted out and the family is united.

The emphasis on family ties and kinship roles formed the fabric of the plot. Black-marketing and the unseemly conduct of priests was also given considerable significance and rationalist ideas permeated every scene. But the film remains predominantly aural, with the characters delivering long monologues, which were entertaining in themselves. Gramophone records and later, audio cassettes of these dialogues were released. The story was told mostly through static mid-shots. The film also retained much of its character as a stage play. The songs in the film, popular as they were, added to its aural character. Some of the tunes were based on songs from Hindi films, including *Sunehre Din* (1949) and *Babul* (1950). Two songs were rehashes from two Urdu films made in Lahore, *Dopatta* (1951) and *Akeli* (1952) for which the music was composed by the legendary Ghulam Haider.[11]

The DMK was launched as a political party in 1949 and M Karunanidhi, as one of its leading ideologues, used the characters in this film as mouthpieces for his rationalist ideas, with digs at mythological episodes and rigid, inflexible casteism. The film opens with a song on the glories of Dravidian heritage. As it ran into difficulties with the censors, a special committee of the Film Censor Board was asked to view and clear *Parasakthi*.

The Films

The Prisoner of Andaman/ Andaman Kaithi

B&W 1952
Producer: Radhakrishnan Films
Director: V Krishnan
Cast: , M S Draupathi, Santhanalakshmi, M G Ramachandran, T S Balaiya, K Sarangapani

This was adapted from a play written by Ku Sa Krishnamurthy which was later staged by T K S Brothers Drama Company, a popular theatre company of the Forties. The film tells the story of a prisoner in the notorious cellular jail in the Andaman Islands. It also has a reformist slant.

Ponnambalam swindles his sister's property and kills her husband. She, along with her son, Nataraj, and daughter, Leela, escape the communal holocaust in Karachi during Partition and arrive in Madras on the eve of Independence. Ponnambalam gets Nataraj out of the way by implicating him in a criminal case, and marries Leela who pretends to be insane. When he comes out of jail, Nataraj kills Ponnambalam and is sent back to the prison. The making of this film was supervised by K. Subrahmanyam.[12]

The story is told in flashback as Nataraj narrates it to a fellow-prisoner. The film opens with newsreel footage of Independence Day celebrations and cuts to communal riots in Karachi showing people running in panic. Nataraj's flight is shown by interweaving enacted sequences with real footage. Trains arrive loaded with refugees in Nilokheri station and you see Nataraj scrambling into the train with his mother and sister.

The Eye of the Serpent

The film was made at a time when the labour movement was starting to gain ground in India. Nataraj joins the trade union movement and becomes an office bearer. Though he talks of "the fire of revolution"', he dissuades workers from striking because it would affect the growth of the movement.

The story was bowdlerized to suit the film version and it was prudent to jettison much of the radicalism when plays were adapted for the screen because the stakes in a film were much higher. Leela, a widow, is remarried but care is taken to tell the audience that she had remained a virgin by pretending insanity. Nataraj marries a rape victim but the child dies, which makes it convenient for everyone. Nationalistic overtones, a hangover from the Forties, was amply evident in the film. The villain, a British loyalist, contributes to the war fund and is awarded the title of Diwan Bahadur. The film also touches upon unemployment and laments the shortage of food. The song, *Anju ruba nottu* (Five rupee note) was quite a hit and so was poet Bharathi's *Kaani nilam vendum* (I want a piece of land) which was also featured. However a lengthy dance sequence, quite unconnected with the film, hampers the flow of events.

M G Ramachandran as Nataraj does not dominate the film. Contrary to his saint-like image in later films, Nataraj even commits a murder in this film.

Devadas

B &W 1953
Producer: Vinodha Pictures
Director: Vedantham Ragavaiya
Photography: B S Ranga
Music: C R Subbaraman
Cast: Savithri, Lalitha, Nageswara Rao

One of the most enduring Tamil films, *Devadas* was based on a novel by the Bengali writer, Sarat Chandra Chatterjee. It is a story of unrequited love and human frailty. Devadas and Parvathi are childhood friends; when they grow up, they discover they are in love. He leaves the village and goes to the city for higher studies. On his return, he finds his hopes dashed: to stave off poverty and destitution, Parvathi has been married off to an old man. To overcome his disappointment, Devadas takes to drink and Parvathi's efforts to change his ways prove fruitless. Soon he becomes an alcoholic. His brief affair with a prostitute, Chandramukhi, does not help matters. He dies of alcohol abuse and Parvathi also dies soon after.

One factor that sustains the popularity of this film to this day is the songs, eleven in number, all written by Udumalai Narayana Kavi. Songs like O...*Devadas* proved very popular. However, C R Subbaraman, who composed the music, could not enjoy the fruits of his success and died before the film was released. The film was dedicated to his memory. The songs, however, dominated the visuals as the sequences were static. The film was shot mostly indoors at Narasu Studios, Madras.

Another factor that contributed to the film's success was its casting. Nageswara Rao as the tragic hero and Savithri as the innocent village girl in love with her childhood sweetheart, were near perfect. This film was a remake of an earlier version made in 1937 which starred P V Rao—who also directed the film—and G R Rajayi in the lead roles. The film's tragic ending was new to Tamil cinema but it proved acceptable to film-goers. This story was later filmed in Telugu also, and a few years later in Hindi. All the versions were highly popular, making a film historian comment, 'And virtually a generation wept over Devadas.'

He is Immortal/ Avan Amaran

B&W 1955
Producer: The People's Films
Director: S Balachandar
Music: T M Ibrahim
Photography: Nemai Ghosh
Cast: Rajasulochana, Kannamba, K R Ramasamy, T S Balaiya

This was a film which espoused Leftist ideology and with distinct propagandist overtones. The script was by S Nagarajan, a communal idealogue. Arul, the son of mill hand Mariamma, works as a paper boy and a shoeblack but also manages to do well in college. Lily, the mill owner's daughter, studies in the same college and falls in love with him. Arul goes to England for higher studies and returns as a barrister. Instead of practising law, he decides to organize the workers. He declares that workers in India should be united. He deprecates the multiplicity of trade unions and the infighting that goes on. He manages to unite all the four unions in the mill and also gets elected as secretary of the new union. When workers are retrenched due to the installation of modern machines, Arul leads a strike, is prosecuted and is eventually acquitted by the court. The mill owner tries to blow up the bridge on which the labourers are marching in protest. Arul foils the attempt but is shot in the process. He dies, leaving behind his wife and son.

This film stood apart both in content and form. S Balachandar, the veena maestro, was in the limelight as a filmmaker after his successful, *Andha Naal* (1954). With Nemai Ghosh at the camera, *Avan Amaran* was a visually-oriented work, particularly the protest march scene shot on a bridge near Fort St.George in Madras.Later, the film was subjected to severe cuts by the Film Censor Board: several sentences were excised from Arul's deposition before the court; his references to class struggle, economic inequality and landless tillers were removed. Though it had a progressive political stance, the film also stuck to the usual screen conventions of a Tamil film, like, women prostrating before the hero. Here, Lily falls at Arul's feet and begs for his affection.

The logo of the producers, the People's Films, featured two factory workers, a woman and a man, with raised hands, inspired by the famous statue at the Red Square in Moscow.

The Pay Day/ Mudhal Thedhi

B&W 1955
Producer: Padmini Pictures
Director: P Neelakantan
Photography: V Ramamurthy
Music: T G Lingappa
Cast: Anjali Devi, T A Mathuram, Sivaji Ganesan, N S Krishnan, R Balasubramaniam

This film had an unusual plot which dealt with the financial problems of salaried, lower-middle class families. It broke away from the filmic traditions of the times by eschewing romantic sequences, duets and fights.

Although he handles a lot of cash as a bank clerk, Sivagnanam's pay is meager but he and his devoted wife, Lakshmi, can just about manage to get by. Their daughter's marriage is being negotiated and two other children are at school. The bank where he works crashes; so he starts looking for a job but can find no opening. Dejected, he decides to kill himself, hoping to make the insurance money available to the family. His soul reaches the court of Yama, the lord of death, in the netherworld. Angered by his irresponsible act, Yama sends him back to earth to see for himself whether the purpose for which he took his own life has been fulfilled.

He is able to observe the goings on but cannot participate as he cannot be seen or heard. He watches, helplessly, his son being taken away by the police for stealing food, his daughter molested and his wife drowning herself in a well after murdering the molester. Sivagnanam realizes his folly in abandoning his family and screams, only to find that the whole series of dreadful events has been a mere dream.

Though the content of this film was refreshingly new, its form was quite conventional. It was shot mostly indoors, with painted backdrops and rudimentary sets. The shots were mostly mid and close-up. Iris was used as a device to change shots. The most notable feature was Sivaji Ganesan's convincing portrayal of the harassed bank clerk. Featuring gods and goddesses in a film with a contemporary setting gives *Mudhal Thedhi* a unique flavour. In one sequence, Brahma, the god of creation, explains to the bewildered Sivagnanam the perceived injustices in the world.

N S Krishnan, in a sub-plot, plays the role of a carefree clerk, a colleague of Sivagnanam. He, along with T A Mathuram, fill the slot of the *kattiyakaran* of traditional Tamil drama who provided comic relief and social comments. N S Krishnan deals with unemployment, economic inequality and hypocrisy in high places and sings a song on the plight of salaried class, a song that proved enduring. Noted Carnatic musician, Dandabani Desikar, then a professor of music at Annamalai University, sang two songs in this film.

Alibaba and 40 Thieves/ Alibabavum 40 Thirudargalum

1955	Colour
Producer:	Modern Theatres
Director:	T R Sundaram
Music:	S Dakshinamurthy
Cast:	P Bhanumathi, M N Rajam, M G Ramachandran, P S Veerappa, K A Thangavelu, M G Chakrapani

Many fantastic stories—like this one from Arabian folklore—find their place in Tamil cinema. This film was a remake of the Hindi film of the same title made by Basant Wadia. Alibaba, a poor woodcutter in Baghdad, chances upon the hideout of Abu Hussain, a notorious dacoit. He overhears the password to the hideout, and helps himself liberally to the loot hidden there. Alibaba's brother, Kasim, finds out the password from Alibaba and enters the cave. He is caught by the dacoits; they kill him and keep his body inside the cave. Alibaba manages to retrieve the body. Abu Hussain realizes that the password has leaked out and Alibaba is the culprit. He comes to Alibaba's house, disguised as an oil merchant. Each of the thirty-nine barrels he brings with him contains a dacoit who is to come out on cue, so that together they can take over the house. However, Alibaba's wife outwits and kills the dacoits.

Modern Theatres specialized in entertainers, without any pretensions to social comment and their films made no demands on the minds of the audience. This film was typical, with many songs that were popular hits, group dances, fencing, chases and a cliffhanger finish. The film's cast of M G Ramachandran as the swash-buckling Alibaba, Bhanumathi as the singing-heroine—two of the most popular artistes of the Fifties—and Thangavelu as the comedian contributed to its huge success. That it was the first colour film of South India was another significant factor. The screen villain of the Fifties, P S Veerappa's portrayal of the heartless Abu Hussain was also memorable. Waheeda Rehman, who later rose to be a star in Hindi cinema, made her debut in this film in a dance number.

Except for the riding sequences, the whole film was shot on indoor sets. Though there are incongruities like Alibaba's wife referring to Yama, the Hindu god of death, the costumes were middle-eastern. For changes of scene, irises and wipes were used, a hangover from the early talkie days. In 1941, an earlier version of this film was made with N S Krishnan as Alibaba, which was a full length comedy.

The Eternal Flame/ Amaradeepam

B&W 1956
Producer: Venus Pictures
Director: T Prakash Rao
Photography: A Vincent
Music: T Chalapathi Rao
Cast: Savithri, Padmini, Sivaji Ganesan,
M N Nambiar, Thangavelu

When Ashok tries to rescue Aruna, the girl he fancies, from her kidnappers, he is hit by a car and loses his memory. He

The Eye of the Serpent

wanders around and joins a group of nomads. Rupa the gypsy in the group falls in love with him. Her love and songs have a therapeutic effect on Ashok who is given to bouts of depression whenever he tries to recollect his past. Eventually, Ashok is cured of amnesia and is reunited with Aruna. Rupa is shot while trying to save Ashok as the bad guy tries to kill him, and dies. It is revealed that Rupa is, in fact, Aruna's sister who had been kidnapped as an infant.

This film had all the ingredients of an entertainer—group dances, songs, drama and a climactic ending. The story and script was written by C V Sridhar, who later emerged as a successful director and made the "eternal triangle" his favourite theme. He later wrote and directed many films based on the same motif, with all the characteristic conventions of such stories.

An interesting feature was that more than one person composed the music for this film. G N Balasubramaniam, the Carnatic music maestro composed one and the other was composed by G Ramanathan. The popularity of the lead actors, Sivaji Ganesan as Ashok, Savithri as Aruna and Padmini as Rupa, all three at the peak of their careers, was another reason for the success of the film. There was also a comic sub-plot, with Thangavelu in the lead. The cinematography of the film stood out as well as A Vincent made his mark in this film and particularly the scene where the villain smashes a radio, recalling a similar sequence in *A Street Car Named Desire* (English, 1951).

Anti-capitalist sentiments and vague radical ideas are mouthed by the hero, who works for a brief time, in a factory and as proof of his ideology, one of the songs makes a reference to the landowner and tiller conflict in the Thanjavur area.

The Soldier of Madurai/ Madurai Veeran

B&W 1956
Producer: Krishna Pictures
Director: Yoganand
Photography: M A Rahman
Music: G Ramanathan
Cast: M G Ramachandran, O A K Thevar, N S Krishnan, Bhanumathi, Padmini, E V Saroja, T A Mathuram

Madurai Veeran is a popular folk deity of Southern Tamil Nadu and his legend has been the subject of ballads and plays. This was the second filmed version of the story; the first appeared in 1938.

The story is set in seventeenth century Tamil Nadu when the Poligars ruled the Madurai region. A prince is born with the umbilical cord around his neck. The court astrologer predicts that this would spell disaster for the royal family and persuades the king to abandon the infant in the forest. A cobbler rescues the infant; Veeran grows up to become the commandant of the army and marries a princess. The king of Madurai requests Veeran to come and put down dacoit gangs in his kingdom. While on that commission, Veeran falls in love with the court dancer who is also the object of the king's attention. Enraged, the king executes Veeran. The two women die of grief. The three attain godhood and rise up to heaven.

In the traditional ballad version of the legend, Veeran is, in fact, a dalit (cobbler); he abducts the princess and has an affair with the courtesan, who is the king's mistress. But, in the film, he is a prince, who grows up in a cobbler household. The audience knows that he is really a prince while the characters in the film do not. This is the typical manner in which conflicts are resolved in Tamil films.

In the film, the costumes and sets have no relation to any known period in history. In one scene, even the guillotine makes an appearance! Sword fight sequences, songs—solo and duets—and dances made the film a mass entertainer. M G Ramachandran's popularity as an actor and a leader increased tremendously with this film in which he played the role of a folk deity. The enormous takings of this film made it a precursor for many more movies of this type, but none as big a hit as *Madurai Veeran*.

Though the background of the story was feudal, the dialogue writer, Kannadasan of the DMK, made the characters utter some progressive ideas, including anti-caste sentiments. There is a reference to the practice of untouchability in the court of the Chola king when it is discovered that Veeran is of the cobbler caste.

The Films

The Land of Sivagangai/ Sivagangai Seemai

B&W 1959
Producer: Kannadasan Productions
Director: K Shankar
Photography: Thambu
Music: Viswanathan-Ramamurthy
Cast: S Varalakshmi, M N Rajam, S S Rajendran,
T K Bhagavathi, M K Mustafa, P S Veerappa

During the last decades of the eighteenth century, the British East India Company was busy annexing the small kingdoms. This is the story of a kingdom which resisted the Company's attempts to conquer it.

The two Marudu brothers from Sivagangai steered clear of any confrontation with the British even as Col Welsh bided his time. In 1798, Oomaithurai, brother of Kattabomman who fought valiantly against the British, is given refuge at Sivagangai. The Company forces storm the fort and execute the Marudu brothers.

Though the film was based largely on actual events in history, the introduction of fictional characters and events detracted from its historical authenticity. Muthazhagu and his love for Chittu also occupied a sizable portion of the film. The scriptwriter, Kannadasan of the DMK, loaded the film with propaganda, further diluting its quality as a historical. However, his use of ballads and folk songs endowed the film with a distinct regional flavour.

There was little effort at creating a period ambience of this momentous phase in Indian history. Though some of the costumes were authentic, they were often gaudy and extravagant. The two British officers in the film appeared in the same costumes throughout the film. Col Welsh is shown drinking all the time, even while at work. Overall, the film was more akin to a theatre production, with the characters speaking the written, literary form of Tamil and delivering the lines looking directly into the camera, as though they were making a speech.

Although the place names in the film were authentic, like Kalaiyarkovil and Panjalankurichi, no attempt was made to establish any sense of topography which is so essential in a story such as this. Much of the background of the story and many events were narrated verbally. The film was verbose and totally lacked visual quality. The gravity of certain situations was established through loud background music and Russian angle shots.

There were however two interesting episodes. A villager and his daughter tend two Marudam trees and when the axemen come to fell them for making a temple chariot, they hug the trees, very much like the latter day activists of the Chipko movement. In another scene, when the husband is killed by robbers, his wife commits Sati (self-immolation) and the Marudu brothers declare that she should be worshipped as a deity. In fact, two other women in the film, Kannathal and Chittu, die, apparently of no cause, after their husbands are killed.

The Wedding Gift/ Kalyanaparisu

B&W 1959
Producer: Venus Pictures
Director: C V Sridhar
Photography: A Vincent
Music: A M Raja
Cast: Saroja Devi, Vijayakumari, M Saroja, Gemini Ganesh, Nageswara Rao, Thangavelu

Playwright Sridhar's directorial debut, as mentioned earlier, this film set the pattern for his later works in which he repeated the motif of the eternal triangle and unrequited love.

College mates, Baskar and Vasanthi, are in love, but their affair is kept a secret. Geetha, Vasanthi's elder sister, supports the family by toiling at her sewing machine. Baskar rents the room upstairs in their house. When he is down with fever, Geetha nurses him back to health and, in the process, falls in love with him. She confides her love to Vasanthi who decides to give up Baskar and persuades him to marry Geetha. A few years later, Geetha dies leaving him to bring up their child. When Baskar learns of Vasanthi's proposed marriage to her former boss, Raghu, he rushes but by the time he arrives, the marriage ceremony is over. He hands over his child as a wedding gift to Vasanthi and walks out into the grey mist.

The film brought in a great deal of money; its songs were stupendous hits. It owed its phenomenal success in large part to its music composed by A M Raja, who was at his peak as a playback singer. The filmic convention of singing the same song twice, once in joy and once in sorrow, is followed. In fact, there are two such happy-sad songs.

The film is very much within the framework of traditional conduct, though the filmmaker tried to accommodate romantic love into this scheme of things. The concept of one man-one woman for a lifetime is emphasized. Vasanthi makes it clear that she marries Raghu only to avoid a scandal about her relationship with Baskar, not even for the sake of a marital life for herself. In an earlier sequence, she falls at Baskar's feet, a recurring event in Tamil films. And in another scene, Baskar beats up his wife Geetha. Therefore, the man-woman relationship is treated in a very superficial way. The filmmaker treats romantic love in a relentlessly maudlin manner, with much weeping and wailing.

The film depends on quite a few contrived coincidences to bring about the turn of events. Baskar and Vasanthi fall in love after they collide with each other at a college function. She learns about a job opening from a piece of a newspaper in which the grocery comes wrapped.

The separate sub-plot for comic relief neither fits into the main story nor is it cinematic. However, these episodes were a major point of attraction and audio cassettes of this kind of humour are still sold. The film won a certificate of merit from the Government of India.

The Films

Parthiban's Dream/ Parthiban Kanavu

B&W 1960
Producer: Jubilee Films
Director: Yoganand
Music: Veda
Photography: Selvaraj
Cast: Ragini, Vijayanthimala, Kumari Kamala, S V Ranga Rao, Gemini Ganesh, P S Veerappa

Based on a novel by Kalki who was known for historical fiction on the model of Walter Scott's novels, this film is set against the background of the conflict between the Pallavas, the Chalukyas and the Cholas in seventh century AD. Parthiban, the Chola king, who yearns to be free from the yoke of the Pallavas, dies in battle. His son Vikraman, while attempting to fulfil his father's dream, is arrested by the Pallava monarch, Narasimhavarman. He is exiled to an island, where he is chosen king. This, in fact, had been plotted by the Pallava king who wishes the Chola prince well, since he knows of Vikraman's love for his daughter Kundhavi. When Vikraman returns to the mainland to see his mother, he is waylaid by robbers. Narasimhavarman, who in the guise of a sage had been helping the prince, comes to his rescue. Vikraman is married to Kundhavi and rules over the Chola kingdom as a sovereign monarch, fulfilling his father Parthiban's dream.

Though some of the film's characters like Narasimhavarman I and Siruthondar are historically authentic, it comes through as a mere fictional story. The ethos of Tamil revivalism is wrongly projected back in time, and come across as an anachronism. For instance, Narasimhavarman talks about reuniting the kingdoms of the Tamil region under one flag; he cites the Ashokan and Gupta empires as models fit for emulation; the costumes are not at all authentic; Marapaboopathi, the Chola commandant, sports a nineteenth century Maharashtrian turban; scenes of the royal court are stagy and unconvincing.

The only Pallava monuments featured in the film are the Mamallapuram monoliths, though there are many others not far from Chennai. Other than this, most of the shots are indoors, on sets with painted backdrops: the impact of a well-made historical is hardly achieved. An abridged version of *Sivakamiyin Sabatham* (The Vow of Sivakami), another novel by Kalki, was incorporated, as a dance drama, in a contrived manner; a tedious intrusion.

The soundtrack was continuously filled with jarring background music. What could have been a worthwhile visual experience was instead reduced to a film in which much of the story was narrated verbally. The script was expository; for instance, Hiuen Tsang's historic visit to Kanchipuram was merely mentioned.

The film was however awarded a silver medal by the Government of India.

The Films

Forgiveness of Sins/ Pavamannippu

B&W 1961
Producer: Buddha Pictures
Director: A Bhimsingh
Photography: G Vittal Rao
Music: Viswanathan-Ramamurthy
Cast: Savithri, Devika, Sivaji Ganesan, Gemini Ganesh, Kothamangalam Subbu, M R Radha

Communal harmony is ostensibly the main thrust of this film: it has three characters representing the three major religions of Tamil Nadu—a Hindu diamond merchant, a Muslim village doctor and a Christian do-gooder—around whom the melodramatic story revolves. The greedy merchant has two sons and his driver has two daughters. Both families are Hindus and of high caste. The children get separated; one boy grows up as a Muslim and one girl as a Christian. The Muslim boy falls in love with the Christian girl, and the Hindu boy with the Hindu girl, who is now growing up in a slum. After a number of twists and turns, the evil diamond merchant is arrested; the young lovers are united. The social and religious antecedents of each character are revealed, amidst much hugging and crying. The audience knows all along that everyone belongs to what is considered as a high caste, though they grow up in different religious backgrounds. Thus, though seemingly reformist, the film confirmed to existing social norms.

Muslims and Hindus live together in a ghetto under the leadership of a Muslim and a Brahmin who addresses the former as *annan* (elder brother). Religious symbols like the cap and beard for Muslims and forehead marks for the Hindus are liberally used. This facilitates showing, visually, the harmonious intermingling of the two communities. Symbols like the crucifix and figurine of the Buddha are also used. Pedagogic lines on the unity of all religions and on the equality of all human beings are spouted by the characters.

The songwriter, Kannadasan, then of the DMK, had quite a few lines lampooning religion. In a well-known song of the period, the main protagonist, Rahim (Sivaji Ganesan), wonders why man invented religion at all.

The galaxy of stars, the eight songs (all of them major hits), a riotous performance by M R Radha and the theme of communal harmony made *Pavamannippu* a successful and memorable film of the Sixties. The director, Bhimsingh, went on to make more films with the same combination of actors and similar preachy themes, and established himself as a successful filmmaker of the times.

This film won the All India Certificate of Merit, a Government of India award.

The Tamil Who Launched a Ship/Kappalotiya Thamizhan

B&W 1961
Producer: Padmini Pictures
Director: B R Banthulu
Cast: Sivaji Ganesan, Gemini Ganesh,
T K Shanmugam, Savithri, Rukmani

The Films

This film is based on the life story of freedom fighter Va Vu Chidambaram Pillai, who launched the Swadeshi Steam Navigation Company to break the British monopoly over maritime trade out of India and earned the title "Kappalotiya Thamizhan".

It is one of those rare Tamil films set in the recent past and is based on historical events. Its backdrop is the momentous era of the Swadeshi movement at the turn of the century when nationalist awakening was just beginning. The Tirunelveli district saw intense political activity and Chidambaram was its leading spirit. His friends, poet Bharathi and Subramania Siva, are major characters in the film. Other leaders featured include Tilak, Salem Vijayaraghavachariar and Pandithurai Thevar. At the time, a group of nationalists of the extremist faction were operating near Tirunelveli and their activity culminated in the murder of the district collector, Col Ashe. This bit of history was also woven into the film.

However, the flavour of this interesting period in Indian history was not captured authentically.[14] There is no evidence of any research undertaken for making this film. There are no props either, other than the costumes and distended ear-lobes on some female characters, to create a period effect. Some characters spoke the Tirunelveli dialect, but only occasionally; most of the time, they spoke the chaste, written form of Tamil, which lent the film a certain staginess. Though Sivaji Ganesan's portrayal of Chidambaram was affected in the earlier part of the film, in the prison sequences and during the trauma of disillusionment later, his acting was intense and natural.

The format of the film remains traditional with duets, songs and fight sequences. A romantic theme involving Madasamy, an authentic character, was also introduced. Several coincidences as a ploy to move the story forward persist in the film. Most of the shots were indoors without any efforts to visually delineate the period. Scenes of making a bonfire of foreign textiles and Chidambaram's encounter with British officers were flat and unconvincing. However, riots in Tuticorin, following the attempt to celebrate the release of Bipin Chandra Pal, the strike at Harvey Mills and the launching of Chidambaram's ship, feature in the film as well. All the songs were by Bharathi and became very popular.

The film was adjudged the best Tamil film of the year by the Government of India.

Server Sundaram

B & W   1964
Producer: Guhan Films
Director: Krishnan-Panju
Music: Viswanathan-Ramamurthy
Photography: S Maruthi Rao
Cast: K R Vijaya, S N Lakshmi, Nagesh, Muthuraman, Major Sundararajan

Sundaram who comes to Chennai with dreams of making it big in the movies ends up as a waiter (server) in a coffee shop. While catering at a picnic party, he meets Radha, a wealthy girl and imagines that she has fallen in love with him. Through his friend Raghavan, Sundaram gets a break in the movies and rises steadily to become a star. He proposes to Radha who discloses that she is engaged to Raghavan. Sundaram accepts his disappointment in good spirit and continues to work in films. This film is a tribute to the persona of Nagesh, who plays the role of Sundaram. Nagesh was at the peak of his career when this film was made. It has autobiographical resonances of his rise to stardom.

Filming a popular play was a tried and tested method during the Fifties and Sixties. K Balachandar, who wrote the dialogues for *Server Sundaram*, specialized in films with an urban, middle-class ambience. Nagesh, through his portrayal of the bungling waiter, introduced the anti-hero to Tamil filmgoers. Long monologues of the Fifties had given way to short, witty exchanges, a style which was K Balachandar's forte.

Departing from the practice of having a separate character for comedy, the entire film was laced with humour, emanating from the main protagonist, Sundaram himself. It has a distinct Chaplinesque flavour, with scenes of pathos and humour intermingling. A poor waiter pining for the attention of the woman he fancies was reminiscent of similar scenes from films like Chaplin's *City Lights* (English, 1931). A persistent theme in Tamil cinema, the bond between the mother and son, is emphasized in this film.

In the process of adapting the play for filming, a number of songs and group dances were introduced. The songs were written by Kannadasan who was then at his productive best. The processes during the making of a film—shooting sequences, interiors of a studio and song recordings—were shown as part of the film, giving the viewers a peep into the world of make-believe.

Danseuse Mohanambal/ Thillana Mohanambal

Colour 1968
Producer: Vijayalakshmi Pictures
Director: A P Nagarajan
Photography: K S Prasad
Music: K V Mahadevan
Cast: Padmini, Manorama, Sivaji Ganesan, M N Nambiar

The story was adapted from a popular serial in a magazine by Kothamangalam Subbu. The Cauvery delta has long been the nursery of performing arts. Set in that area, this story revolves around danseuse Mohanambal and nagaswaram player Shanmugasundaram. The two meet at a festival and in an ensuing argument, Sundaram challenges her to dance to his music, even as he loses his heart to her. But there are hurdles in the way of their relationship. A wealthy playboy pursues Mohanambal. A "toughie" who is spurned by her knifes Sundaram. After a few incidents, the lovers are united and, in the last scene, bid goodbye to the audience from the wedding dais.

The director, A P Nagarajan, was from the world of theatre and its influence can be seen in his emphasis on dance, music and frontal shots. For instance, he lined up his characters to face the camera during their delivery of lines. He also paid tribute to Sankaradas Swamigal, a major figure in the history of commercial drama, by naming a drama company in the film after him. Nagarajan's work was steeped in the Tamil artistic tradition, imbued with religious sentiment. He sprinkled his narration with humour and cast the right set of actors and this resulted in most of his films gaining popularity.

The courtesan tradition, zamindars in horse-drawn coaches and palaces in the movie suggest the period to be the last century, but contemporary Madurai and Thanjavur railway junctions were also the venue of some scenes. This ambiguity with respect to period is common in Tamil cinema. There were also geographical anomalies. While the story moves around Madurai, Thanjavur and Tiruvarur, the scene suddenly shifts to a fictional town, Madanpur, which boasts of an *achkan*-clad king with a western wife. Therefore, although the story is conventional, with predictable twists and turns; it relies heavily on coincidences.

Understandably, nagaswaram music and Bharatanatyam are given prominence in the film. Leading pundits, Sethuraman and Ponnusamy played the nagaswaram for Sundaram, the character enacted by Sivaji Ganesan. Padmini plays the danseuse Mohanambal. In keeping with Nagarajan's fondness for featuring a large number of old-time actors, T S Balaiya, K Sarangapani, V Nagaiya, M N Nambiar, S V Sahasranamam, E R Sahadevan, P T Sambandam, K A Thangavelu and A Karunanidhi formed part of the cast.

The film was chosen as the best Tamil film of the year and won the country's best cinematography award also.

The Eye of the Serpent

The Guardian Deity/ Kaval Deivam
B & W 1969
Producer: Ambal Productions
Director: K Vijayan
Photography: R Vijayan
Music: G Devarajan
Cast: Lakshmi, Sowkar Janaki, S V Subbaya, Sivaji Ganesan, Nagesh, Sivakumar

This story was based on a novelette titled *Kai Vilangu* (Handcuff) by the noted Tamil writer, Jayakanthan, and is one of those occasional interactions between literature and cinema in Tamil film history. The central character is the jail superintendent, Raghavan, played memorably by S V Subbaiya. The Raghavans, who are childless, treat the prisoners as their own children and take care of them; they are cast in a very different mould from the archetypal jail official. The filmmaker equates Raghavan with Ayyanar, the guardian deity of villages in Tamil Nadu.

Manikam, the sharecropper who cultivates Raghavan's land in the village, is in love with the girl next door. A rival attacks him while he is with her. Enraged, Manikam pulls the sword from the hands of the gigantic terracotta statue of Ayyanar and injures him. He is sent to Raghavan's jail for a five-year term. One day, Raghavan allows Manikam to go out to visit his ailing mother on the promise that he will return before sunrise. Manikam returns, eventually. This is the main plot of the story. There is an unrelated sub-plot of a toddy-tapper, played rather theatrically by Sivaji Ganesan. He kills the two ruffians who rape his teenage daughter and is hanged. The director had made quite a few changes in the original story.

The performing arts of rural Tamil Nadu, like Therukoothu, Karagam dance and Villupaatu, were featured in the film very authentically. In fact, the leading exponent of Therukoothu, Purisai Natesa Thambiran, performed the piece "The Extermination of Hiranyan"; shots of Narasimha killing Hiranyan are inter-cut with the toddy-tapper killing the rapists. Tamil films usually depict only classical art forms and rarely focus attention on folk art forms. This was one of the first films to do so. Village life is also portrayed convincingly, though in some scenes, the painted curtains stand out like sore thumbs. Scenes of an actual village fair and worship of village deities add to the convincing portrayal of rural life in the film. Routine life inside a prison was also depicted authentically. There were only two songs in the film. All in all, both in form and content, this film was quite different from the run-of-the-mill film of the Sixties.

Our Darling/ Engal Thangam

Colour   1970
Producer: Mekala Pictures
Director: Krishnan-Panju
Photography: S Maruthi Rao
Music: M S Viswanathan
Cast: Jayalalithaa, S R Janaki, M G Ramachandran, Cho Ramasamy, A V M Rajan

This film, made at the height of his popularity, can be considered a good example of an MGR film. Thangam, a truck driver played by MGR, has his own driving ethics — he drives carefully, follows the rules strictly and is concerned about the safety of pedestrians. His blind sister, Sumathi, is raped by his friend, Murthy, under the influence of liquor, and Thangam vows revenge. When Sumathi tries to kill herself, she is saved by an old lady. The old woman extracts a promise from a grateful Thangam that he will find her wastrel son and make him mend his ways. Thangam learns that this son is none other than Murthy. He locates Murthy, who is repentant, and gets him married to Sumathi. Thangam falls in love with a police officer's daughter, Kala, whom he saves from the hands of some goons. He later busts a robber gang and marries Kala.

This film was made when M G Ramachandran was a member of the Legislature of Tamil Nadu and deputy chairman of Small Savings. In the opening scene, MGR plays himself at a Small Savings function. Thangam meanwhile is in the audience and opens a savings bank account. He refers to MGR as *vathiyar* (teacher), the honorific by which he was known to his innumerable fans. C N Annadurai, former chief minister of Tamil Nadu, represented in the film through a look-alike, makes a speech and presents a cheque to Thangam, a prize winner in the state-run lottery scheme.

All the characteristics of a MGR film can be seen in *Engal Thangam*.[15] Thangam fights, sings, cares for the poor and preaches against smoking and drinking, vices that MGR shunned in his private life. The colours of the DMK party,

The Films

red and black are frequently featured in the clothes the hero wears. There is a humorous sequence in which Thangam, dressed as a traditional religious minstrel, complete with a tuft, sacred thread and forehead marks, conducts a musical discourse (*kalakshepam*) on man's first trip to the moon. In another scene, he leans on a pole, with a bamboo stick on his shoulders and a shot of his shadow appears like the crucifixion. He is also featured in a song which says that he has risen from the dead, a reference to a real-life attempt on MGR's life in 1967.

Vietnam House/ Vietnam Veedu

B & W 1970
Producer: Sivaji Productions
Director: P Madhavan
Photography: A Somasundaram
Music: K V Mahadevan
Cast: Padmini, Ramaprabha, Sivaji Ganesan, Srikanth, Thangavelu

This is an unusual film in which the main protagonist is an elderly man and the story ends with his death. It is also the first Tamil film to handle the subject of retirement, along with the pain and puzzlement of ageing.

The story revolves around a company executive, Padmanabhan Aiyar, who has come up the hard way from his origins as the son of a humble cook. For him, honour, integrity and prestige are all-important and he is therefore called "Prestige" Padmanabhan Aiyar. In his typical Brahmin household, which consists of two sons, a daughter and a widowed sister, there is constant squabbling. So, when he buys back his ancestral house, he names it "Vietnam Veedu".

Padmanabhan suffers a heart attack when he is suddenly informed that he has to retire that day. He is unable to come to terms with retirement, the loss of identity and fall in income. His children and servants grow indifferent to him. His elder son and his daughter-in-law turn hostile. Padmanabhan watches helplessly as his children flout the values he holds so dear. He clings to his wife and realizes how precious her love and concern is. When his firm wants him to return and serve for a few more years, he has another heart attack which proves fatal.

The film opens with a housewarming ceremony where Padmanabhan introduces the members of his family to the camera, much like a play. In fact, this film was an adaptation of a successful play staged by Sivaji Ganesan's drama troupe. The costumes in the film were incongruous; college-going girls wear mini-skirts while office-goers are in three-piece suits. Characters, particularly Padmanabhan, are often preachy and pedagogic. There are two long soliloquies as also a group dance, reminiscent of Busby Berkeley.

The travails of retirement and the bond between the aged couple, a rare motif in Tamil films, were however touchingly portrayed. Even the subtle eroticism between the two was depicted well. In one of the film's most moving moments, the old couple lie together in each others' arms: he sings about his love for her and what she means to him. But much of

The Films

the impact of the film was lost by extraneous and irrelevant comedy situations and group dances.

Thirst/ Dhakam

B&W 1972
Producer: Kavya Chithra
Director: Babu Nandancode
Photography: T Vaiyadurai
Music: M B Srinivasan
Cast: Nanditha Bose, Muthuraman, Major Sundararajan

A band of young professionals from the Institute of Film Technology, Madras made this film centred on a blind man and the manner in which he comes to terms with life. Sekhar, a blind boy, is brought up in a Gandhian ashram whose inmates are orphans, destitutes and women who have been rescued from whorehouses. In his rambles around the ashram lands, his constant companion is a little girl called Sarada. When they grow into adulthood, Sekhar is not able to conceive of a life without Sarada who is now an employee of the ashram. They get married with the blessings of the ashram elders and move to Chennai where Sarada gets a job as a door-to-door salesperson. Used to the simple and straight-forward life of the ashram, the couple is unable to cope with the brutality of city life and return to the ashram.

Babu Nandancode and T Vaiyadurai were on the staff of the film institute when they conceived the idea for this film. The story was by Vaiyadurai and the script was written by

K K Raman. The freshness of their approach was evident in the film as the characters were portrayed realistically. The film was shot in Gandhigram near Madurai and Vaiyadurai captured the beauty of the region with the backdrop of the Sirumalai hills effectively. Child actors in the film were handled deftly and their performance was realistic. The bond between the blind boy and the little girl Sarada was depicted through a song sequence set in a field of sunflowers. The sequences in the city were also picturized in a manner that brought out the alienation of life in a metropolis. The shot of blind Sekhar running scared along the Marina beach in Chennai was also shot convincingly. It was a very visual and cinematic film.

The music was well integrated into the main theme of the film. Choral music was music director M B Srinivasan's forte and the songs *Vanam namadhu thandhai* (The sky is our father) and Bharathi's song *Bharatha samudayam* (The people of India) were popular favourites for a long time.

The portrayal of a blind person as incapable of any work or fending for himself was however, not helpful to the cause of visually handicapped people. The Year of the Handicapped and the awakening it created about the blind was to come years later.

The Light of Wisdom/ Gnanavoli

B&W 1972
Producer: Jayaar Movies
Director: P Madhavan
Photography: P N Sundaram
Music: M S Viswanathan
Cast: Sharada, Sivaji Ganesan, M R R Vasu, Srikanth

The plot is woven around Antony, a fugitive, a Christian priest and a police inspector who is out to get Antony. Though the basic idea of the story, complete with a pair of candlesticks, is from Victor Hugo's *Les Miserables* (not acknowledged), there is wide variation in details.

Antony, a sexton, is an orphan who was cared for by the priest. His wife dies during childbirth; he has a brush with the law and is sent to jail. Years later, he flees to Singapore after committing a murder. He returns a wealthy man under a different name and becomes a philanthropist. Lawrence, the police inspector, suspects his real identity; he makes many attempts to expose him. When Antony's granddaughter and Lawrence's son fall in love, the inspector sees this as an opportunity to expose Antony. He finally manages to reveal Antony's identity at the marriage altar and arrests him. Antony is happy because his responsibility towards his granddaughter is over.

Antony is depicted as an impulsive character. In fact, he hits his daughter's lover in a rage and kills him. The idea was to show him as innocent of evil motives and still as a jail bird. Lawrence is conveniently made a childhood friend of Antony.

He is a far cry from the ruthless Javert of the original. The portrayal of the priest is weak and he goes about as if stricken by a dreadful disease. Excessive make-up is employed, to make Antony's disguise credible.

The screen convention of a character wearing a cross to announce one's Christian identity is scrupulously followed. Though there are ludicrous scenes, such as the one which has Antony and his girlfriend gambolling on a rooftop in the night, the photography was decidedly better than in most of the Tamil films of the time as there was a sense of depth in the images. A critic had once commented that this is one of the few films in which the ceiling can be seen. The film had all the ingredients of a box office movie— duets, fisticuffs and comedy that had nothing to do with the main story. A song by Antony, *En thevane ennai parungal* (O God look at me) turned out to be one of the most popular songs of the year.

The film was shot around the Church of Immaculate Lady at Poondi near Thanjavur and was released to coincide with the twentieth centenary of the arrival of St Thomas in India.

She too is a Woman/ Avalum Penthane

B&W 1975
Producer: Panduranga Productions
Director: Durai
Music: V Kumar
Cast: Sumithra, Pandari Bai, Kutti Padmini, Muthuraman, Thengai Srinivasan

This story, unusual in Tamil filmic tradition, revolved

around a destitute woman and her attempts to escape from a brothel and lead a normal life. Sita is brought to Madras by a confidence trickster and is sold off to a whorehouse. Muthu, a young man from a small town on a business trip to Madras, visits the brothel with his friends. He is shocked by what he sees and takes pity on Sita. Later, he proposes marriage to Sita; she agrees after some initial hesitation. Muthu brings her home where Sita wins the love of Muthu's mother. The pimp who first sold her to the brothel shows up in this small town and life gets complicated for Sita. He exposes Sita's past and the film ends with her suicide.

This was Durai's first film. Restricting the number of songs to just two and avoiding dances and comedy sub-plots, he maintained the film's dramatic tension. The money-lender and his young wife with a penchant for pornography, and the housewife who dreams of getting her daughter a break in the movies as a singer, all supported the narration. Even minor characters like Kanagu, the vegetable vendor and Sambandam, the cycle mechanic, were sharply etched; a refreshing break from the archetypal characters of Tamil cinema. The Tamil spoken by characters, like the merchant and the mechanic, had a definite regional flavour which gave the film a certain authenticity; so did their caste identities which were made explicit. The filmmaker's compassion came through in the non-judgmental manner in which he portrayed characters like Kanagu who waits patiently for Sambandam to marry her and Sita, the prostitute, who falls in love with Muthu. The filmmaker named his heroine Sita, after the legendary symbol of Indian womanhood from the epic, Ramayana.

Except for the events that took place indoors, much of the film was shot outdoors. Durai's style of narration was direct and straightforward. By giving music a secondary place, he emphasized on the story: the film's content gets priority in the presentation. In the climax, he used melodrama rather effectively, though he also relied on usual props like coincidence and fistfights in the sequence.

Annam the Parrot/ Annakili

B&W 1976
Producer: SPT Films
Director: Devaraj-Mohan
Photography: A Somasundaram
Music: Ilayaraja
Cast: Sujatha, Jayalakshmi, Sivakumar, S V Subbaiya, Srikanth

The film tells the story of Annam, a village midwife, and her love for the schoolmaster. When he arrives to take care of the primary school, Annam falls in love with him. But a rich landlord wants the schoolmaster to marry his daughter, Sumathi, who is a friend of Annam. The schoolmaster's mother favours this idea because she can get her daughter (the teacher's sister) married with the dowry he would bring. So, the teacher marries Sumathi and leaves the village. Annam extracts a promise from him that he will love and protect Sumathi. The owner of the village cinema house, an inveterate womaniser, has his eye on Annam. He kidnaps Sumathi's infant son when she is on a visit to the village and blackmails Annam. Annam dies in a fire accident while trying to rescue the child. The ending is in conformity with the screen convention of killing one of the three characters involved in a love triangle.

The film, otherwise conventional, with a predictable turn of events, is noteworthy on two counts. First, it was one of the very few films to be shot entirely in one village, Thengumarada, located in a picturesque valley near Sathyamangalam. There were hardly any sets used, thus endowing it with a certain plausibility and geographical specificity. The film therefore succeeded in bringing out the tenor of life in a village. Second, it launched music director, Ilayaraja, who went on to build a phenomenal career in Tamil cinema. The song *Annakili unnai theduthu* (Annakili is searching for you) reverberated all over Tamil Nadu in a matter of weeks, and the popularity of the songs from this film lasted for a long time.

One of the screen conventions in Tamil cinema was to have a short play or a dance drama within the film. This was a hangover from the silent era when extra entertainment was packed into the bill for the evening as added attraction. In this film, two long sequences from two other films were added, as part of the film show at the village cinema house. One sequence from the film *Sendhamarai* (Lotus, 1962) showed actress Padmini dancing as Andal, a devotee who offered flowers from her braid to the Lord, like Annam who gifts the man she loves to her friend. And the second was a clip from the film *Kannagi* in which Kannamba as Kannagi, sets the city of Madurai afire after establishing her husband's innocence. In a similar fashion, the cinema house owned by the villain goes up in flames.

A Donkey in the Brahmin Enclave/Agraharathil Oru Kazhuthai

B&W 1977
Producer: Nirmadhi Films
Director: John Abraham
Music: M B Srinivasan
Cast: R Savithiri, M B Srinivasan

The story, inspired by Robert Bresson's *Au Hasard Balthazar* (French, 1965) revolves around a donkey which strays into the Brahmin quarter (agraharam) of a village. A college professor, Narayanaswami, adopts the donkey as his pet. When he is ridiculed for this peculiar choice of a pet, he asks Usha, a mute servant-maid in the village, to take care of the donkey. The Brahmins object to the presence of a donkey in the agraharam. A series of problems follow. The mute girl is seduced by someone from the village and the dead body of her infant is found outside the temple. The residents of the agraharam blame the donkey; they drag it out of the village and kill it in cold blood. Several miracles follow. The villagers are now convinced that the donkey is actually a holy spirit. They dance around the dead donkey in celebration and set fire to it. In a symbolic sequence, the fire spreads and the village is swallowed by the flames. Only the professor and the dumb girl survive.

The film instantly became controversial. Some Brahmin

organizations branded the film anti-Brahmin and called for a ban. Commercially, it was not well received and the reviews in Tamil magazines were not favourable. Elsewhere, the film won critical acclaim and went on to win the President's silver medal for the best regional film of the year. But controversy dogged the film. In December 1989, it was scheduled to be telecast on national television but was cancelled at the eleventh hour, to avoid controversy.

This is the only Tamil film made by John Abraham, a gold medallist from the Film and Television Institute of Pune. Famous as an iconoclast, he held that any film which dealt with people and society was political, including this one. In the surrealistic sequences of this film, his indebtedness to Bresson is evident. The film was shot in thirty days around Kunrathur near Chinglepet and in Loyola College, Madras.

Some People at Some Moments/Sila Nerangalil Sila Manithargal

B&W 1977
Producer: A B S Productions
Director : A Bhimsingh
Photography: D S Pandian
Music: M S Viswanathan
Cast: Lakshmi, Srikanth, Sundaribai, Y G Parthasarathy, Nagesh

Jayakanthan's short story, *Agnipravesam* (Ordeal by Fire), first published in 1966 provoked a raging controversy; he wrote the novel *Sila Nerangalil Sila Manithargal* later, giving a

The Eye of the Serpent

different ending to the earlier story by taking it further. This film was based on the novel; it also incorporated the first story which had preceded the novel.

Ganga, a teenager, is raped by a man who gives her a lift on a rainy evening. Her widowed mother, on hearing the matter rouses the household and bewails her fate. Ganga is blamed by her family for what has occurred; the news spreads, and she remains single due to the stigma. She works in a firm and lives with her mother. Her uncle, who helped to see her through college, makes passes at her, hinting that she might as well become his mistress, since it will be impossible for her to get married. Ganga spurns his advances.

Years later, Ganga is able to make contact with Prabhu, the man who had raped her. He is a wealthy businessman, married, with a daughter. Ganga starts a relationship with him 'He is my man,' she declares. The pain of sustaining such a relationship in the Indian cultural milieu is rendered truthfully. The Brahmin identity of Ganga's family is clearly established; though Prabhu's caste is not indicated, he is shown as a non-Brahmin. However there was no suggestion of any sexual relations between them. The frequent shots of Mother Sharada's (the saintly wife of Ramakrishna Paramahamsa) portrait, served to confirm this. When Ganga's marriage to a forty-year old man is proposed, Prabhu is sure that it will be the best course for her; he refuses to meet her till she assents to this marriage proposal. Ganga however remains firm in her decision to stay single.

The manner in which this film was photographed did not do justice to the depth of the subject. Long conversations, one prominent feature of Jayakanthan's stories, was retained in this film as well. Two characters who dominated the film by the sheer brilliance of their performances were Ganga's mother (played by Sundaribai) and Ganga, the woman in conflict, played by Lakshmi who won the National award for best actress for her role. Srikanth's portrayal of the chain-smoking, hard-drinking businessman pales beside their performances. (The image of smoking, wayward heroes persisted till the late Seventies, but not later.)

However the sincerity and integrity of the novel was diluted by certain visuals in the film. When Ganga is being raped inside the car, nagaswaram music, which by tradition signifies auspicious moments such as marriage, comes on the soundtrack. In the last scene, Ganga is shown dressed in a white sari, a symbol of widowhood, and the offscreen voice intones pompously that she keeps on flowing, pure and serene, like the river Ganga.

That's The Way She is/ Aval Appadithan

B&W 1978
Producer: Ragamanjari
Director: Rudhraiya
Photography: Nallisamy and Gnanasekaran
Music: Ilayaraja
Cast: Sri Priya, Kamalahasan, Rajnikanth

Made at a time of nascent awareness of feminist issues in India, this film was ahead of its time. The story is about Manju and her search for a meaningful relationship highlighting her

The Eye of the Serpent

strength and independence. Manju, an advertising executive, her boss, and Arun, whom she assists in making a film on the status of women, are the main characters. She warms up to the sensitive and understanding Arun, who is in sharp contrast to her chauvinist boss. She unburdens herself to Arun and tells him about her traumatic childhood and earlier affairs – how her first affair with a college mate had ended abruptly when he decided to marry another girl for the sake of a job, making her turn cynical and wary of people.

She hesitates to commit herself emotionally to Arun. Meanwhile, weary of waiting, he agrees to marry a girl his father has chosen. When Manju eventually makes her move, it is too late. In a poignant last scene, the car in which she has been travelling with Arun, his wife and her boss, drops her at the Marina beach in Chennai and leaves. Her lonely figure recedes, getting smaller and smaller as the car speeds away.

The story was conceived by Rudhraiya (original name, Arumugam), an alumnus of the Institue of Film Technology, Chennai and scripted by Vannanilavan, an avant-garde writer, and Someswar. It was a very visual film, impressively photographed with balanced dialogue and unobtrusive music. The lighting brought out Manju's loneliness and her conflicts effectively. Snatches of cinema verite are seen in the sequence showing Arun interviewing students and women workers for his documentary. No artifical sets were used in the film; this made the film's action more credible to the viewer. Part of the story was told in flashback, through images with Manju's offscreen voice and interspersed with shots of the actual events. Camera movements were fluid and in one sequence the camera lingers on a poster of Jonathan Livingstone Seagull which exhorts one to be independent.

The three main characters stand out and their portrayal is natural and convincing. Sri Priya plays Manju, with Rajnikanth as the boss and Kamalahasan as Arun, the filmmaker. This film was placed in the second best feature-film category at the state level.

Hunger/ Pasi

Colour 1979
Producer: Sunitha Cine Arts
Director: Durai
Photography: V Ranga
Music: Shankar-Ganesh
Cast: Shoba, Sathya, Delhi Ganesh, Vijayan, Tambaram Lalitha

In the city of Chennai, millions live in shacks along sewage canals and under flyovers. Their lifestyle forms a separate sub-culture and they speak a heavily accented Tamil, practically an urban dialect, referred to contemptuously as "Madras Tamil". In Tamil filmic tradition, characters from this world are featured for comic relief or as bad characters and, often, their way of speaking is ridiculed. *Pasi* was the first film to approach their life dispassionately, without patronizing, and record the sordidness of their lives. What emerged was a powerful human drama that raised many disturbing social and political questions.

The story is structured around teenager Kuppamma, a rag-picker and her father Muniyandi, who plies a cycle-rickshaw. In the course of her wanderings, Kuppamma meets a truck driver who gets her pregnant. When her mother learns of this, she dies of a broken heart. Kuppamma is shocked to learn that the driver is already married and has a family. She soon regains her poise but dies during childbirth.

The film, shot in the streets and slums of Chennai, beautifully captured the flavour of the sub-culture of the slum-dwellers. Concealed camera positions yielded some very convincing footage of life in the city. Most of the scenes were shot outdoors and there was hardly any constructed set, except for the interior of the hut. The "Madras Tamil" spoken by the characters was authentic and much study had evidently gone into this aspect.[17] The fact that there was no song or dance, which intrudes upon the narrative, lent a certain tightness to the film. Music came in at the appropriate contexts to support the visuals. Even minor characters like the prostitute, the tea shop owner and the food vendor—all stand out sharply and add verisimilitude to the whole story. The filmmaker resisted the temptation to be either judgmental or sermonizing.

The portrayal of the rickshawala by Delhi Ganesh was very realistic. However, the highlight of the film was the intense and impeccable performance by Shoba as the rag-picker which won her the National award for best actress that year, the youngest artiste to have won the honour. Sad to record that Shoba killed herself the following year.

The Films

New Moulds/ Puthiya Varpukal
Colour   1979
Producer: Manoj Creations
Director: Bharathiraaja
Photography: P S Srinivas
Music: Ilayaraja
Cast: Rathi Agnihotri, K Bagyaraj, Koundamani, Chandrasekaran

Shanmugamani, a primary school teacher, arrives in a village to take up a new assignment and promptly falls in love with Jothi, the daughter of the temple musician. The village elder, an archetypal feudal bully, has his eyes on her. His factotum, Amavasai, is also keen on marrying Jothi. The village elder frames the teacher on a murder charge and gets Jothi married to Amavasai, with the idea of setting her up as his own mistress. When the elder approaches Jothi one night, she inveigles him and knifes him. The teacher and Amavasai appear on the scene at the same moment. Amavasai gets rid of the body by flinging it into the festival bonfire which is ceremonially lit by the son of the elder. Amavasai releases Jothi from the marriage and unites her with the teacher. All of them leave the village in search of a new life.

The film is typical of Bharathiraaja's work. Set in an authentic rural locale, it tries to capture the flavour of life in a Tamil village. Like in his other films, the story in this film also revolves around a newcomer to a village, the impact of his arrival, love at first sight, the villain desiring the heroine and the final denouement with a village ritual in the background.

The Eye of the Serpent

This film was shot in lush outdoor locales; the use of actual village houses lent credibility to events in the film. Some of the minor characters, like the woman who comes to the village as a social worker, stand out in their true to life portrayal. However, there is an incongruous group dance by women clad in white gowns; the children in the film were precocious and often behaved like adults. The conflicts in a rural society were hardly touched upon and particularly caste as a significant factor in village life, did not figure in the film. The police does not show up after the rape and murder and the story moves forward on coincidences; the ultimate one being when the teacher and Amavasai appear simultaneously on the scene of the elder's murder. Amavasai's sudden metamorphosis into a "character" is a well-worn Tamil filmic cliche pressed into service for winding up a story.

Family Life Is Like Electricity/Samsaram Adhu Minsaram

Colour   1980
Producer: AVM Productions
Director: Visu
Photography: N Balakrishnan
Music: Shankar-Ganesh
Cast: Manorama, Lakshmi, Kamala Kamesh, Visu, Raghuvaran

This story, an apology for joint family and kinship roles, was woven around Ammaiyappa Mudaliar, his three sons and a daughter. Counting him and his wife, there were four couples

The Films

in the household. The daughter falls in love with a Christian and marries him. The eldest son is a miser and the youngest son, a teenager does not do well in school. The conflicts that arise in relationships within the family and the manner in which they are resolved form the burden of this film, which has the maudlin sentimental character of a soap opera.

Visu, the director and scriptwriter of this film, played the main role himself. He came to films after a long stint in amateur drama companies. His plays reiterated traditional beliefs and social behaviour of the Tamil urban middle class. The draw in his dramas was his combination of humour and tear-jerking scenes which were set around family ties. He successfully brought this genre into films.

His films would routinely attract sharp criticism from women's organizations. In this film, Visu contrasts the daughter, who tries to be liberated, with a tradition-bound daughter-in-law, who marries the man chosen by the father without demur. In one sequence, Visu inter-cuts between scenes of the daughter arguing with her husband and the daughter-in-law with hers. Both the wives get slapped during the argument and both leave their husbands in anger. But the daughter-in-law is sent back by her father. Eventually, both the women get back to their husbands. While other filmmakers try and appear progressive but betray their hand-me-down prejudices in the way they resolve conflicts, Visu does not even try to hide his regressive views on women. However, in the film, he approves an inter-religious marriage between his Hindu daughter and her Christian lover and also accepts the elder son's decision to quit the joint family.

Visu's characters are true-to-life mortals and not larger-than-life filmic characters. In the film, caste identities are featured clearly, lending authenticity to the characters. The servant maid, played brilliantly by Manorama, fulfils the role of a trouble-shooter. The dialogue is often pedagogic and is studded with trite metaphors, like the title of the film itself. Visu used music and songs with great restraint and relied more on human drama to sustain the film's momentum.

Water...Water/ Thanneer...Thanneer

Colour 1981
Producer: Kavithalaya
Director: K Balachandar
Photography: B S Lokanathan
Music: M S Viswanathan
Cast: Saritha, Veerasami, Radha Ravi

This film was based on a play by Komal Swaminathan, a playwright with Leftist leanings. The story was set in Athipattu, a hamlet in the arid region of southern Tamil Nadu, which does not have access to any source of water. The villagers have to struggle for even a bucket of water. A fugitive seeks refuge in the village and Sevanthi, wife of a policeman, protects him. Meanwhile, elections to the legislative assembly of the State are announced. Candidates from different political parties visit the village and promise many projects. But the villagers boycott the elections to drive home their unfulfilled demand for water. Their own effort to dig a canal from the rarest water source, which is miles away, is thwarted by government officers. The film ends with police action against the villagers for defying orders. The fugitive dies while attempting to flee the police.

The main thrust of the film was its expose of caste dynamics in politics and the insensitivity of the bureaucracy to the needs of the rural poor. The film portrayed the total helplessness of the villagers when faced with the inexorable government machinery. There is a telling sequence in which the villagers hand over a petition to the minister, who passes it on to his personal assistant, who, in turn, hands it over to the district collector, who gives it to his orderly, who then casually shoves it into his pocket.

The movie, shot predominantly outdoors, was filmed authentically in a village in southern Tamil Nadu, in a drought-prone area which receives practically no rainfall. The actors, most of them from a theatre background and hence new to cinema, were cast appropriately. The dialect of southern Tamil Nadu was used effectively. The canal digging sequence recalled a similar situation in King Vidor's *Our Daily Bread* (English, 1934) and *Kalam Mari Pochu*.

Many contemporary issues were effectively handled: the neglect of education in rural areas, exploitation of unorganized labour and the ineffectiveness of the press. The novel method of protest in the film—of the villagers boycotting the elections—was adopted in real life later by a village in Thanjavur in 1982.

The film was chosen as the best Tamil film and also won the award for best screenplay, for 'translating the sufferings of the people in drought-affected areas into a gripping visual narrative.'

The Eye of the Serpent

The Prison/ Sirai
Colour 1984
Producer: Anandhi Films
Director : R C Sakthi
Photography: Viswam-Nataraj
Music: M S Viswanathan
Cast: Lakshmi, Rajesh, V Gopalakrishnan, Pandian

Based on a short story by Anuradha Ramanan, a popular writer in Tamil, this film was about the priest of a Hindu temple and his wife. It had created quite a controversy with Brahmin organizations clamouring for a ban. Antony, a landlord and a hard-drinking bully, fancies the priest's wife Bhagirathi, and under the influence of liquor, rapes her. The priest refuses to live with her. As she wanders around aimlessly, a policeman tells her that she should not meekly accept her circumstances when the guilty man goes about as though nothing has happened. Convinced by his argument, Bhagirathi walks into Antony's house and declares that she intends to stay there. Antony takes care of her and over the years, she develops a secret respect for him. But they do not have any physical relationship. When Antony dies, she realizes what he had meant to her. On the same day, the priest returns and implores Bhagirathi to come back to him. She spurns his offer and declares that she would rather be known as Antony's widow than be the wife of the man who rejected her.

Though iconoclastic in theme, the film had all the trappings of a run-of-the-mill commercial movie—a cabaret type dance, duets, and a fight sequence along with cliched devices like using obesity for comic effect. These diluted much of the film's impact. A totally irrelevant, parallel story—of a farmhand, courting the daughter of a local politician—served as an intrusion. The music was unobtrusive and appropriate, with ambient sounds woven in. Much of the film was shot in authentic locales, keeping sets to the minimum and the lush, outdoor shots brought out the tenor of village life quite well. The manifestation of corrupt political practices at the village level, particularly the nexus between the police and the politician was ably depicted. Antony's shotgun, through the barrel of which he first sights Bhagirathi, was used as a symbol of his manhood. But neither the metamorphosis of his character nor his death was convincingly explained. Also, the passage of years, that Bhagirathi spent in Antony's house was not depicted visually at all.

The high point of the film was the powerful and convincing portrayal of the wronged woman by Lakshmi; her Brahmin accent was very authentic. The fact that she spoke the lines herself (different from the now common practice of having another artiste dub for the actors) added to this effect.

The Mute Eyes/ Oomai Vizhigal

Colour 1986
Producer: Thirai Chirpi
Director: Aravindaraj
Photography: A Rameshkumar
Music: Manoj Gyan
Cast: Vijayakanth, Jaishankar, Saritha, Ilavarasi

The Eye of the Serpent

PRK, a man jilted by a doe-eyed beauty, goes about killing beautiful girls who come to picnic near his mansion. Reminiscent of Hitchcock's *Psycho* (English, 1960), the film has other motifs also woven into it. The woman-killer has links with a local politician who heads a mafia-like gang. A doctor helps him in his nefarious deeds—different from the usual screen depiction of doctors as ministering angels. An archetypal police officer—invincible, honest and a tireless defender of the rule of law—is after them. The editor of a daily, who talks about the role played by *The Washington Post* in the Watergate scandal, vows to expose the truth behind the murders. His band of men support the police officer. After much bloodshed and killing, the evil man is shot and the gang is arrested.

The thriller as a genre is uncommon in Tamil cinema and the difference between a detective story and a thriller is often blurred. Though this film was a thriller, the conventional songs and dances were included, serving as interruptions and thus destroying the momentum of the narrative. Visual narration in a thriller has to be precise and clear; otherwise the audience is left guessing. Here, the filmmaker often fell back on verbal narration; for instance, when PRK tells the editor at the end why he turned a maniac.

The film focusses on violence in political life. The sequences in which the politician's gang storm the daily's office is an allusion to similar real-life incidents in Tamil Nadu. The song the editor sings after the attack, to inspire confidence among his workers, is often used in political and trade union processions.

This cinemoscope film is described in the credits as "A film by film students". This was a rare occasion when a group of qualified film technologists came together to make a film. Though this is evident in the use of ambience sound, silence on the sound track, hand-held camera and sophisticated lighting techniques, the content of the film was very much conventional, with crutches like semi-nude dances and composed fight sequences.

In fact, the basic tenor of the film was violent, with many gory scenes. There were eight murders, shown in graphic detail. In the last scene, the police officer, using his pistol for the first time in the film, slugs four bullets into PRK, in a stylized slowmotion action and therefore, the emergence of stylized fights as an ingredient of filmic entertainment is very evident in this film.

The Hero/ Nayakan

Colour   1987
Producer: Muktha Films
Director: Mani Ratnam
Photography: P C Sriram
Music: Ilayaraja
Cast: Kamalahasan, Saranya, Nizhalgal Ravi, Janakaraj

This is a tale about a chief of the underworld in Mumbai, believed to be based on the real-life story of a smuggler from Chennai, who made it big in Mumbai as a don.

When a political activist is killed by the police, his son

attacks a cop and runs away to Mumbai. He grows up to become Velu Naicker who operates from a ghetto. When he kills an unpopular police inspector during a fight, he finds himself instantly becoming the hero among the slum dwellers. Naicker soon becomes a ganglord, engages in smuggling on a big scale and also acts as a protector of the oppressed. On one of his visits to a brothel, he takes a fancy to a girl and marries her. When a real estate shark buys up the land on which the ghetto is situated, Naicker raids his house and destroys the title deed. He wipes out rival smugglers and extends his empire in the underworld. As he reigns supreme, even police officers seek his help. But a series of tragedies strike his personal life. His wife is killed by an enemy gang, his daughter walks out on him and marries a police officer, and his son dies in an accident. In the end, Naicker himself is shot dead by a mentally challenged youth whom he had earlier taken under his care. Ironically, this occurs right after he is acquitted by a court of justice.

The film is noteworthy for the way it had been crafted and not so much for the content. It had all the ingredients of a commercial film made with an eye on the box office— songs, a raunchy dance number, and gore In many ways the film recalls Francis Ford Coppola's *Godfather* (English, 1972).

The film belonged to the cinematographer, Sriram and art director, Thottaa Tharani. For Tamil cinema this was a new development. They both endowed the film with cinematic qualities that were rarely seen in an Indian film. Their attempts to evoke period flavour through automobiles and furniture pieces were new to Tamil filmic tradition. Sriram won the national award for cinematography and Tharani for art direction. It was selected as the Best Film of the Year by the National Awards Committee. The film won other honours also. Kamalahasan's screen portrayal of the ruthless don received much favourable notice and won him the country's best actor award for the year.

The House/ Veedu

Colour 1988
Producer: Kala Das
Director: Balu Mahendra
Music: Ilayaraja
Photography: Balu Mahendra
Cast: Archana, Bhanuchandar, M A Chokkalinga Bhagavathar

Housing is a major problem faced by the average urban middle class Indian, and this film was rightly released in 1988, the International Year of Shelter.

The owner of the house rented by Sudha, a clerk in Chennai, her sister and her grandfather, a retired music teacher, wants them to vacate the house. Her colleagues advise her to build her own house. When Sudha starts on this venture, she runs into numerous hurdles. Helped by Gopi, her friend and colleague (at the time maybe aspiring to be her fiancè), she goes from one office to another, trying to get the project going. The contractor cheats her, government officials demand bribes and her boss propositions her for the favour of sanctioning a loan. As the house is nearing completion, the grandfather dies and the Metropolitan Water Authority appropriates the house. The film ends with Sudha seeking justice in a court of law.

The film was a striking departure from the earlier works of Balu Mahendra. He said that *Veedu* was inspired by his mother, who started building a house and in the process underwent a personality change. This made a big impact on young Balu Mahendra; the incident formed the seed for this movie project. While at one level the film dealt with the problem of housing, at another it probed the changes in human behaviour, corruption in government and the predicament of the middle class in India. The only optimistic note was struck by Mangamma, a construction worker. One of the screen conventions of Balu Mahendra was to portray his women characters as strong personalities.

Balu Mahendra, who photographed the film himself, made it look extremely visual, taking great care about lighting. Much of the story was told in jump-cuts. He also used montage 'to bring about an undercurrent of emotion.' In the house-hunting sequences, the hand-held camera was effectively employed. Devoid of any song or dance, the film was chosen as the best Tamil film of the year.

Archana, as Sudha, the harassed clerk, won the best actress award of the country. But the most striking feature of the film was the portrayal of the grandfather by M A Chokkalinga Bhagavathar, a one-time commercial drama artiste.

The house he started building in Chennai as a set for the film, now houses the training centre that Balu Mahendra runs for aspiring filmmakers.

The Films

Once Upon A Time in A Village/ Ore Oru Gramathile

Colour   1988
Producer: Aries Pictures
Director: K Jyothipandian
Photography: Ranga
Music: Ilayaraja
Cast: Lakshmi, Poornam Viswanathan, Vinu Chakravarthi, Manorama

The film was a critique of the policy of reserving a percentage of government jobs for certain castes, officially referred to as Scheduled Castes. During its impending release, the film created such a furore that the government had to ban the film. The producers then sought legal remedy and the film was cleared for screening by the Supreme Court of India.

A poor Brahmin finds it difficult to educate his daughter, who is quite bright in her studies. His friend, a Christian working as an officer in the government, takes charge of the girl, certifies that she is a Harijan (officially of the Scheduled Caste) and changes her name from Gayathri to Karupayi. The girl grows up and enters the civil service, under a certain quota reserved for Harijans. While working in a cyclone-ravaged area, Karupayi wins the love and loyalty of the villagers. A man from her native village turns up, threatening to reveal her secret. The matter is taken to court and both the girl and the father are convicted.

The courtroom scene was used to argue a case against reservations for jobs. It was this sequence which came in for attack from pro-reservationists.

The film opens with scenes of a raging cyclone, very reminiscent of *Thyagabhoomi* which also protested against caste discrimination, though of a different kind, and was also banned. *Ore Oru Gramathile* is a very visual picture, with the camera moving quite dynamically in tracking, crane and hand-held shots to bring the story alive. Lakshmi's intense portrayal of the tormented officer Karupayi is another strong point. Feminist ideas get expressed through Karupayi, who is single and talks about single life and the way men exploit women.

Characters like the head clerk and the village cobbler were true to life and added verisimilitude to the story. The village scenes and the houses in it were convincingly portrayed. The songs, set to folk tunes, did not intrude on the narrative. This was the first film to handle the constantly debated subject of reservations.

High Noon/Uchi Veyil

Colour 1990
Producer: Jwala
Director: Jayabharathi
Photography: Ramesh Vyas
Music: L Vaidhyanathan
Cast: Kuppusamy, Uma, Vijay, Srividya, Usha, Preetha

This film revolved around a working class family and had no well known actors as part of its cast. The central character, Doraisamy, is a freedom fighter in his Seventies who lives with

The Films

his son. When the family's finances are strained, he agrees to rent out his room to Shankar, a young executive.

The old man is weak and ill; his son is concerned that he might lose the benefit of his father's pension if he dies. He persuades his father to sign a letter of authorization to receive the pension amount. This shocks Mallika, the granddaughter, who has a close bond with her grandfather. Meanwhile, an organization plans to honour Doraisamy for his contribution to India's freedom struggle. Shankar and Mallika escort him to the function. On the way, they stop for a drink, leaving the old man in the car. When they return, they find him missing. They wonder where he had gone and why?

The film was unusual in conception and treatment. It had a tightly woven narrative without unnecessary interruptions like songs. The story is told through the deft use of the camera. The fact of Shankar occupying the room upstairs is brought home by a series of high and low angle shots.

The music was unobtrusive, coming in only occasionally to emphasize certain scenes. Further, ambient noises in the form of muted street sounds and voices helped to recreate the tenor of life in a Madras street. Jayabharathi, the director, had etched his characters sharply and handled his artistes very well. Kuppusamy, who plays the grandfather, delivers a convincing performance as a dejected old man. In Mallika, the filmmaker transcends gender and treats her first as a human being, a rare feature in Tamil films. Even minor characters like the lift-operator, live up to their roles.

The scriptwriter brought out the dynamics of relationships in a family through the interaction between different members. The undercurrent of hostility between the mother and the daughter surfaces ever so subtly when they talk about Shankar.[19] The film was screened at the International Film Festival in Calcutta and the Toronto Film Festival, both in 1990.

Subramaniapuram

Colour	2008
Producer:	M Sasikumar
Director:	M Sasikumar
Music:	James Vasanthan
Cast:	Swathi, Jai, Sasikumar, Samuthrakari, Ganja Karuppu

Subramaniapuram, set in the 1980s in Madurai city is about five young men used by a crooked politician. One of them Azhagar, is fond of Thulasi, the niece of the local politician which complicates matters. The opening scene sets the mood for the film. A convict who walks out of the prison at the end of his sentence is stabbed and killed. The establishing shots of Madurai at night – the silhouette of the temple towers, the bus stand and the fish market – create the ambience of Madurai as the filmmaker begins his taut narrative. The film has a series of murders in the background of deceit and betrayals. The violence in Subramaniapuram is not the choreographed variety of earlier Tamil films; there are murders but revenge is not valorized. The flavour of the period is captured meticulously through props like cars, dial telephone, Lambretta scooters and film posters. The four songs are pictured in such a way that there is a fine balance between the visual and the aural, achieved by sprinkling the songs with visual gags. For the music director this was his first film. The debutant director, Sasikumar, himself plays the second main character, Pamaran. The secondary characters are all etched minutely. The scenes showing the police station, the court room and the prison are realistic and grim. The film marked the beginning of a trend in Tamil cinema in which violent scenes were featured in great detail. Some critics named these films "Cruel Cinema". The film was a hit at the box office.

Notes

1. *Anandavikatan,* 16 December 1931.
2. "The Secret of Success", interview with Dungan in *Anandavikatan, 7* February 1937.
3. K C Dey had also acted in a Tamil film *Miss Sundari* (1937).
4. Guy, Randor, "M.R.Santhanalakshmi: The Daring Heroine of *Ambikapathi",* in *Indian Express,* 15 September 1990. A number of Shakespearean plays have been made into films in Tamil: *Merchant of Venice* as *Shylock* (1940), *Twelfth Night* as *Kanniyin Kathali, Hamlet* as *Manohara, King Lear* as *Gunasundari* and *As You Like It* as *Sollu Thambi Sollu* (1959).
5. P S Srinivasa Rao interviewed by the author in Madras, 13 July 1975. Review of the film in *Anandavikatan,* 21 November 1937. Arandhai, Narayanan, "*Thamizh Cinemavin Veeramanigal", Thinamani Kadir,* 26 August 1984.
6. Vai Mu Kothainayaki Ammal, one of the early women novelists of Tamil Nadu. Quite a few of her works were made into films, including Jupiters' *Anadhaipenn* (silent, 1931) directed by Raja Sandow, and *Rajamohan* directed

by Fram Sethna. Her novel *Dayanidhi* was filmed as *Aunt/ Chithi* (1968) directed by K S Gopalakrishnan. She gave the commentary for A K Chettiar's *Mahatma Gandhi,* a long documentary released in 1940. Born on 1 December 1901, she was married to Parthasarathy when she was just seven. She was one of the very few women writers to get involved in cinema in the early decades. She died on 20 February 1960.

7. Double-acting as a cinematic device was first employed in *Dhuruva.* The artiste to appear first in a double role in a Tamil film was Sivapackiam, who appeared as the queen and the gypsy who reads her palm. (Review of the film in *Anandavikatan,* 5 May 1935).

8. *"Mathrubhoomi:* An Unforgettable Film", *Bommai* (Tamil), May 1977.

9. Kovai Ayyamuthu interviewed by the author at Singarampalayam, 21 October 1974.
Narasimhabharathi, interviewed by the author in Madras, 26 April 1975.

10. Guy, Randor, "Dumas in Tamil", *Aside,* 16-30 June 1989. There were four film versions of this story and the first one was in 1934.

11. Jayaraman, S, "The Music of Ghulam Haider", Sangeet *Natak,* No. 100, April-June 1991.

12. Ku Sa Krishnamurthy interviewed by the author in Madras, 20 February 1975.

13. Guy, Randor, "Colour" *Aside,* 1-15 March 1990. There had been earlier attempts at colour. Filmmaker S Soundararajan of Tamil Nadu Talkies had done hand-tinting for a 3-minute dance sequence in his film *Mohini Rukmangatha* in 1935. There was hand-tinted footage in *Haridas* and *Salivahanan* (1945). *Burma Rani* had some colour sequences. *Avan* (1952)

was a dubbed version of the Hindi film *Aan,* a full-length colour film.

14. Zaidi, Shama, "Historical Genre in Indian Cinema: Past Bypassed", in *Cinema In India,* April-June 1988.
15. Pandian, M S S, *The Image Trap: M.G.Ramachandran in Film and Politics* (New Delhi, Sage Publications, 1992).
16. "The Movement is Spreading", interview with John Abraham by Amrit Gangar in *Indian Cinema* (New Delhi, Directorate of Film Festivals, 1987).
17. See chapter on dialogue.
18. Hariharan, K, "The Face of Feeling" in *Cinema In India,* Mumbai, July-Sept 1988.
19. Baskaran, Theodore S, "Rare Bloom in a Cine Desert" in *The Economic Times,* 14 January 1992.

Chapter Eight
The Filmmakers

K Bagyaraj (born.1953)

BAGYARAJ STARTED HIS CAREER AS AN ASSISTANT DIRECTOR to G Ramakrishnan and then to Bharathiraaja when the latter was making his first film, *At The Age of Sixteen/16 Vayathinile* in 1977; Bagyaraj even played a small role in the film. He wrote the dialogues for *The East Bound Train/ Kizhake Pogum Rayil* (1978), Bharathiraaja's second film and made his directorial debut with the film *Murals Without Walls/Suvarillatha Chithirangal* in 1979. Encouraged by its moderate success, he started his own concern, Ammu Productions, and made a series of highly popular films. Most of his films were set in a rural background and the protagonist was invariably cast in an anti-hero mould. He packs his films with all the ingredients typical of a Tamil film entertainment—songs, group dances, fights, eroticism and a story that revolves around marital relationships and has a happy end. Bagyaraj laces his storytelling with ribald humour which is very popular with his audiences.

M G Ramachandran, the matinee idol-turned-chief minister, declared Bagyaraj his heir in the film world. In 1989, a year after MGR's demise, Bagyaraj founded a political party – M G R Makkal Munnetra Kazhagam; but it folded up less than a year later. In addition to the films he has directed, including a film in Hindi, he has acted in twenty-five films and scripted twenty-six.

Select Filmography
The Sound Of One Hand/Oru Kai Osai (1980), *Silent Songs/ Mouna Geethangal* (1981), *Wait Until Dawn/ Vidiyumvarai Kathiru* (1981), *Those 7 Days/Andha 7 Natkal* (1981), *Mundhanai Mudichu* (1983), *Sari Dreams/ Thavanikanavugal* (1984), *Sundarakandam* (1991), *Rasukutty* (1992).

P Bala (b.1966)
Born in Narayanathevanpatti near Kambam in Tamil Nadu, he grew up, with seven siblings, in Vadipatti and Periyakulam. After his schooling in Theni , Bala joined American college in Madurai for a degree in Tamil literature. While in college, he developed a passion for literature particularly the writings of Jayakanthan and Nanjil Nadan.

Through poet Arivumathi's recommendation, who was in Chennai, Bala joined Balu Mahendra's film crew as a set assistant and worked his way up. He joined the team when the director was making the film, *Veedu* in which he made a cameo appearance as a postman. Balu Mahendra's team became a school for Bala where he learnt elements of filmmaking. He says of his mentor 'He is the spark that ignited my passion for cinema' and talks of him as the major influence in his life. He got his first screen credit as an Assistant Director for the film, *Sunset Melody/Sandhyaragam*. In the film *Flowers of many hues/Vanna Vanna Pookkal*, Bala got credited as the co-director.

He made his debut as a director with *Sethu* in 1999. The film, centering around a mentally deranged character, proved to be a critical and commercial success. He later went on to make memorable films like *The Doyen/Pithamagan*. He won the National Award for Best Director in 2009 for the film *I am God/Nan Kadavul*, about a devotee of the Aghori cult and beggar mafia. One of the reasons why Bala's film making style caught the fancy of Tamil audience was because his films were raw and riveting and included scenes of gore and violence. He engaged renowned writer B Jeyamohan to write the dialogues but kept spoken words to the essential minimum, preferring visuals to narrate the story and retaining the primacy of images. He once said, 'Cinema is a visual medium. So I keep dialogue to minimum. There is so much a character can convey through their facial expression and body language.'

Select Filmography.
Avan Ivan (2011), *Paradesi* (2013).

K Balachandar (b.1930)
Balachandar, after a long gestation period in the world of amateur drama units, came to cinema while he was still working in the Accountant General's office in Madras. Earlier, he founded his own drama unit, Ragini Recreations,

The Filmmakers

and staged a number of successful plays. Through M G Ramachandran, he got a break as scriptwriter for *The Divine Mother/Deivathai* (1964) and made his debut as a director in 1964, with the help of filmmaker A K Velan. The film, *Bubble/ Neerkumizhi* (1965) was based on one of his successful plays. He founded his own concern, Kavithalaya, and produced a string of successful movies. Balachandar wrote the story and dialogues for many of his film and elevated the image of a director in the eyes of filmgoers in Tamil Nadu. As a director, he excercised total command over his films, consciously avoiding the undue pressure exerted by stars on the filmmaker. This greatly enabled his development as a filmmaker with a unique style.

His films are set in contemporary times and deal mostly with urban middle class issues and, in the process, reinforce the value systems and beliefs held by this class. The endings of his films in particular, conform to existing middle class mores and a sense of morality. His audience consists mainly of urbanites and he often describes himself as a "middle-of-the-road filmmaker". His early films retained quite a few features of the theatrical convention, but in later works like *We Are Not Afraid/Achamillai... Achamillai* (1984) he used outdoor locales effectively and also began to handle political issues. He has so far directed sixty-five films, most of them in Tamil, but also some in Kannada and Hindi. At one point of his career, after he had made *Fence of Yarn/Noolveli* (1979), he began making Telugu films. He is credited with having introduced a number of artistes who later made their mark in Indian cinema. They include Kamalahasan, Rajnikanth, Sujatha and S V Shekhar. He was awarded the Padma Shri by the Government of India in 1987. Four of his films *Two Lines/Iru Kodugal* (1969), *Rare Tunes/Aboorva Ragangal* (1975), *Thanneer...Thanneer* and *Achamillai*. .*Achamillai* won awards from the Government of India as best regional films. In 2010, he was awarded the prestigious Dada Saheb Phalke award.

Select Filmography
Reed/Nanal (1965), *Swimming Against The Current/ Edhirneechal* (1968), *Echo/Ethiroli* (1970), *Smile/Punnagai* (1971), *The Debut/Arangetram* (1973), *Three Knots/Moonru Mudichu* (1976), *The Colour Of Poverty is Red/ Jarumaiyin Niram Sivappu* (1980), *47 Days/47Natkal* (1981), *Refugees of Marriage/Kalyana Agathigal* (1985), *One House Two Entrances/ Oru Veedu Iru Vasal* (1990). *They Sky is the Limit/Vaname Ellai* (1992).

S Balachandar (1927-1990)
S Balachandar's career in films, as producer, director, music director and actor is overshadowed by his image as a Carnatic musician and a veena maestro. Making his debut as a child actor in *Sita Kalyanam* (Tamil, 1933) he enacted child-roles in a number of films. At twenty-one, he played the role of twins in the film, *Is this Real? / Idhu Nijama?* (1948) for which he also composed the music. He made his debut as a director in the film, *My Husband/En Kanavar* (1948). Three years later, he directed and acted in *Prisoner/Kaithi* (1951), a

suspense drama. This was followed by films like *Devaki* and *Rajambal* (Aruna Films), both in 1951.

However the film that brought him fame as a director was *That Day/Andha Naal*. A story about espionage in war years, the film was modelled on Kurosawa's *The Main Gate/Rashomon* (Japanese, 1950). That this film had no songs was considered a revolutionary step in Tamil cinema.

S Balachandar was a very innovative filmmaker whose works were remarkable more for their form than the content. The influence of American films was very evident in his work; his film, *Is he the same Person? /Avana Ivan?* (1962) was based on George Stevens' *A Place in the Sun* (English, 1951). His debt to Alfred Hitchcock can be seen in *The Doll/Bommai* (1963; *What is Truth/Edhu Nijam* (1958) was an adaptation of the Italian film *Il Tradimento* (1949.) Although he was a Carnatic musician, his music for films showed heavy western influences. It was a blend of musical styles: jazz, Latin American, western and Indian classical.

In the 1960s, he began producing films under the banner S B Creations and specialized in thrillers and suspense stories. The film, *At Midnight/Nadu Iravil* (1966) was based on Agatha Christie's famous thriller, *Ten Little Niggers*. [1]

Select Filmography
My *Husband/En Kanavar* (1948), *Avan Amaran* (1958), *At Midnight/Nadu Iravil* (1966).

Balu Mahendra (b.1946)
Born in Sri Lanka, Balu Mahendra (given name Benjamin

Mahendra) is a graduate in cinematography and a gold medallist from the Film and Television Institute of India, Pune, in 1969. He began his career as a cameraman for the Malaylam film *Paddy/Nellu* (1974) which got him the best cinematographer award from the Government of India. He has been chosen the best cinematographer for as many as ten films and has worked as a cinematographer with directors like J Mahendran. His first film as director was *Kokila* (Kannada, 1976) which earned him a National Award and in 1979 he directed his first Tamil film, *The Enduring Pattems/Azhiyatha Kolangal* and went on to make a series of award-winning films. Many of his films are inspired by American movies, like *Turin-tailed Sparrow/Rettaival Kuruvi* (1987) based on *Micky and Maude* (1984). In his later films he began handling social issues like bureaucratic corruption *(Veedu)* and problems like old age in *The Sunset Melody/Sandhyaragam* (1991). Professionally competent, he crafts his films with great care and is one of the very few filmmakers in Tamil who can tell a story visually. The music in his films is well integrated with other elements. He describes himself as belonging to the realistic school of Satyajit Ray and Vittorio De Sica. In most of his films, women emerge as stronger characters, as was evident in *Veedu*. Balu Mahendra writes the script for his films, handles the camera and edits the films himself, thus retaining firm control over his works.[2] In Chennai he runs a training centre for aspiring filmmakers with Tamil as medium of instruction.

Select Filmography
Azhiyatha Kolangal (1979), *Third Day Crescent/Moonrampirai* (1982), *Listeners' Choice/Neengal Kettavai* (1984), *Veedu* (1988).

Bharathiraaja (b.1944)

Bharathiraaja (born Chinnasamy), a self-taught filmmaker, started his career in 1968 as an assistant to director P Pullaiya and Kannada filmmaker Puttanna Kanagal. It was the latter who left a lasting influence on him. His first film *16 Vayathinile,* for which he wrote the story and the script, made a big impact on filmgoers. The music for the film by his childhood friend, Ilayaraja, was one of the major factors behind the film's success. His first six films proved to be remarkably successful at the box office, and started the trend of films set in a rural backdrop. With authentic rural locales, outdoor sequences, melodrama, romantic love and songs as the main ingredients, his films tend to glamourize village life where the rituals involving folk deities and rural performing arts are often depicted. A complex story structure and multiplicity of characters are the other features of his films. His techniques of using "quick-cutting" in his editing and flash-forwards added to his overall filmic narration and one of the thrillers he made, like *Red Roses/Sigappu Rojakkal* (1978), which is still recalled, however lacked the tight structure of that genre. By abandoning film studios for the countryside and by casting new faces in lead roles, he retains control over his work. Many artistes introduced by him rose to be stars; the best known among them are Radha, Revathi, Karthick and Bagyaraj. His *Prime Honour/Mudhal Mariyadhai* (1985) in Tamil won the best regional film award although he has made films in Malayalam, Telugu and Hindi also. His film *Karuthamma* (1994) on the theme of female infanticide won him an award for the best film with a social message.

Select Filmography
The East Bound Train/Kizhake Pogum Rayil (1978), *Moisture In The Stone/Kallukul Eeram* (1980), *The Smell Of Earth/ Manvasanai* (1983), *Diary Of A Prisoner/Oru Kaithiyin Diary* (1985), *A New Veda/Vedham Puthithu* (1986), *New Paddy New Seedling/Pudu Nellu Pudu Nathu* (1992).

A Bhimsingh (1924-1978)
Hailing from Chitoor in Andhra Pradesh, Bhimsingh started as a proofreader for the Telugu daily *Andhra Prabha;* he began his career in films as an assistant editor with the filmmaking duo, Krishnan-Panju, in the late Forties. An opportunity to direct a film came to him in the early Fifties with *Ammaiyappan* (1954) which was soon followed by a few others. Encouraged by their success at the box office, he started his own production concern, Buddha Pictures and directed *Pathi Bakthi* which established him as a director of popular films. Interestingly, in many of his films he made it a point to feature a statue of the Buddha. He made a series of films, the tides of all of which began with the Tamil syllable "pa". Thus came *Pavamannippu* and *Blossom of Affection/ Pasamalar* (1961) and all of them did very well commercially. Bhimsingh relied on his star cast (eighteen of his films had

Sivaji Ganesan in the lead), songs and maudlin sentimental plots woven around family relationships. The music for his films was composed by the duo, Viswanathan-Ramamurthy; this was another factor that contributed to their success. In his work, he never expressed anything contrary to the prevalent beliefs and traditions of his audience. Bhimsingh also made films in Hindi, like *Man/Admi* (1963) a remake of the Tamil film *The Temple Bell/Alayamani* (1962).

Select Filmography
Ammaiyappan (1954), *Rajarani* (1956), *Kalathur Kannamma* (1960), *Green Lamp/Pachai Vilakku* (1964), *Pazhani* (1964), *Husband and Wife/Kanavan Manaivi* (1976).

Cheran (b.1966)
Cheran (given name P Ilancheran) was born in Pazhyurpatti village near Madurai in Southern India. His introduction to the world of images began when he started his career as a photographer in Chennai and later joined films as an assistant to K S Ravikumar and later Santhana Bharathy. By closely observing the two successful directors at work, he picked up the nuances of cinema. His debut film, *Bharathi Kannamma* (1997; in which he handled the sensitive subject of caste divisions in Tamil society) received critical acclaim and won him the Filmfare Best Director award. In the same year he made his next film *Porkalam* (*The Golden Era*) on disability. This film also won him accolades such as the Best Film award from the Government of Tamil Nadu in 1997. *Desiya Geetham* (The National Anthem) came next which was on political

corruption and fetched him the Filmfare Best Director award yet again. In the film *Autograph,* he once again touched upon the subject of disability and the film was screened at the Montreal film festival. With *Solla Marandhe Kathai (The Untold Story)* directed by Thangar Bachan, Cheran turned an actor and has acted in a few films.

Some of the discussions that followed in the press on his films proved how social messages can be packaged in an entertaining film and provoke a discourse. Cheran retains tight control over his creation and although he writes the script himself, he is not bound by words and creates powerful and riveting images. One reason for his popularity is that he works with a cinematic language which is familiar with the Tamil audiences.

Select Filmography
Hoist the Flag /Vetri Kodi Kattu (2000), *The Land of the Pandavas/Pandavar Bhoomi* (2001), *Autograph* (2004), *After the Penance/Thavamai Thavamirundhu* (2005), *The Magic Mirror/ Mayakkannadi* (2007).

Durai
Durai (given name Chelladurai) entered cinema after a stint in the world of theatre. He started his career in films as a sound recordist and then as an assistant to director Yoganand and later worked with G V Aiyar in the latter's award-winning *Swan's Song/Hamsageethe* (Kannada, 1975). Determined to break new ground, he made his first film *Avalum Penthane.* This film, unusual in theme and structure, established him as

a director of merit. From then on, he made a series of films, mostly in Tamil, but also in Kannada, Telugu, Malayalam and Hindi. In his later films he continued to handle social issues. *One Home, One World/Oru Veedu, Oru Ulagam* (1985) looked at the plight of a young Brahmin widow and the rituals connected with widowhood. A number of his films won awards; the best known among them is *Pasi* which remains the highest watermark in his career. It was adjudged the best Tamil film of the year by the Government of India; the heroine, Shoba, was chosen the Best Actress of the year. He however later quit films and now runs a grocery store in Madras.

Select Filmography

The Story Of A Family/Oru Kudumbathin Kathai (1975), *The Wages Of Sin/Pavathin Sambalam* (1977), *Jungle/Kadu* (1979), *Maria My Darling* (1979), *Help/Thunai* (1982), *Sacred Flower/Punitha Malar* (1982), *One Man, One Wife/Oru Manithan Oru Manaivi* (1985), *A Butterfly In A Desert/Palaivanathil Pattamboochi* (1988).

Ellis R Dungan (1909-2002)

An American who came to India to sell cinema equipment, Ellis Roderick Dungan stayed on for seventeen years and made a number of films. Trained as a cameraman in Hollywood, he was signed on to direct *Sathi Leelavathi* while he was on a visit to Madras. This work brought in more contracts like *Seemandhini* (1936) but the film that established his reputation as a filmmaker was *Iru Sakodharargal*. With this film, he began to edit his films himself in order to gain more control over the structure. He reduced the number of songs, avoided separate comedy plots and went outdoors for filming. As a result, his films were distinctly more cinematic and raised the level of Tamil films from being mere photographed dramas. Unfortunately, this trend did not catch on. Dungan directed the lead stars of his times like M K Thyagaraja Bhagavathar in *Ambikapathi* (1937) a film which showed the influence of *Romeo and Juliet*. He also made the lead pair— Bhagavathar and Santhanalakshmi—see this film a number of times. Though he did not know Tamil, he hired interpreters (known as "rush directors") to help him, and filmed classics like *Sakunthala*. Musical luminaries like G N Balasubramaniam, M S Subbulakshmi and Rajarathinam Pillai played the lead roles in some of his films. His last Tamil film was *Mandhirikumari* for Modern Theatres. During the Second World War, he was engaged to make war propaganda films; he made *Returning Soldier*, a short film in Tamil with T S Balaiya in the lead, in support of the war effort. The Government of India commissioned him to film the transfer of power proceedings when India attained independence. Shortly thereafter, he left India. His book, *A Guide to Adventure: An Autobiography* (2001) contains valuable information on early Tamil cinema. A Mumbai-based filmmaker, Karan Bali is making a documentary on Dungan titled "An American in Madras".

Select Filmography
Sathi Leelavathi (1936), *Sakunthala* (1940), *Kalamegam*

(1940), *Dasipenn/Courtesan* (1943), *Meera* (1945), *Ponmudi* (1949).

K S Gopalakrishnan (b.1926)

K S Gopalakrishnan, born in Sakkottai near Kumbakonam, lost his parents in an epidemic and joined as a child actor in Nawab Rajamanikkam Drama Company and later grew up to became a playwright. He made his entry into films when he wrote a song for the film, *The Unexpected /Ethirparathathu* (1954) and later dialogues for *The Illiterate Genius/Padikatha Medhai* (1960). After scripting a few successful films, he directed *Sarada* (1961), the story of an impotent husband. The film did well at the box office and he began making a series of films on similar lines. AVM's *Mother/Annai* (1962) established him as a successful director. His films were very popular in the Sixties. When his film *Karpagam* (1964) did exceptionally well, he opened a studio and named it Karpagam. One of his films, *Money or Affection/Panama Pasama* (1968), was screened at the Tashkent Film Festival.

His films had maudlin, sentimental scenes, and were often verbose and theatrical. They centred on kinship roles and traditional social mores. Much of the action was set inside the house (or the set). Inspired by the phenomenal success of director A P Nagarajan's mythological films, Goplakrishnan also tried his hand in that genre: he made successful films like *Adhiparasakthi* (1971).

(This filmmaker is not to be confused with his namesake, K S Gopalakrishnan, actor and filmmaker of the 1930s who directed films like *Jalaja* (1938) and *Chakradhari* (1948) and acted in *Progress of the Nation/Desamunnetram* (1938). He was instrumental in organizing trade unions for workers in film studios.)

Select Filmography
Sarada (1961), *Deivathin Deivam/God Of Gods* (1962), *A Small World/Chinnanchiru Ulagam* (1966), *Postman's Sister/ Thabalkaran Thangai* (1970), *Gypsy's Son/Kurathi Magan* (1972), *The Ten Avatars/Dasavatharam* (1976).

Jayabharathi (b.1946)

A self-taught filmmaker, Jayabharathi came into films from the world of literature. He is a short story writer, as were his parents, Saroja and Ramamurthy. In order to finance his first venture, *The Hut/Kudisai* (1978) a neo-realistic work, he collected contributions, even as small as one rupee, from the public. This film was screened in the film society circuit and in some festivals as well. His second film, *The Mute Masses/ Oomai Janangal* (1980) was based on a novel *Theneer* (Tea) by D Selvaraj and dealt with the plight of bonded labourers and the exploitation of tea garden workers during the British Raj. His third film *Two plus Two is Five/Rendum Rendum Anju* (1982) was about the superstitions of a woman. His fourth film *Uchi Veyil* centered on an old and ailing freedom fighter. This film was screened at the International Film Festival at Calcutta and also at the Toronto Film Festival, both in 1990. His literary background does not bind him to words. He understands the power of images and handles them effectively in his filmic narrations.

Select Filmography
Kudisai (1978), *Oomai Janangal* (1980), *Rendum Rendum Anju* (1982), *Uchi Veyil* (1990).

J Mahendran (b.1939)
Mahendran (given name J Alexander), a graduate from Madurai, started his career as a writer for the magazine *Porwaal* edited by DMK ideologue, C P Chittrarasu. He later joined as an assistant to film director, A Kasilingam. One of his stories, *Son of Sivagami/Sivagamiyin Selvan* (1973), was filmed when he was still working as a sub-editor in the weekly *Tughlak*. He first established his reputation as a playwright with *The Origins of a Sage/Rishimoolam*, a play he wrote and directed, which brought him critical acclaim. He later made his mark as a scriptwriter when he wrote the dialogues for the film *The Gold Medal/Thangapathakkam* (1974). He worked for some time as an assistant director before he directed his first film *Thorn and Flower/Mullum Malarum* (1978). With Balu Mahendra at the camera, he made an immediate impact as a filmmaker. His next work, *Scattered Flowers/ Udhiripookal* (1979), based on a short story by writer Pudumaipithan, firmly established him as a filmmaker of importance. His *Unlockable Locks/Pootatha Pootukkal* (1980) centred on Kanniamma, whose husband accepts her even though she conceives a child by her lover. His work stood apart stylistically, with a penchant for realism and sincerity of approach. In his films, he dealt with issues like the aridity of loveless marriages or a woman's search for her identity, but the promise he showed in his earlier films was absent in *Johnny* (1981), a story about

two look-alikes, a filmic cliche. For a brief while it looked as though, he, along with other filmmakers like Durai, was ushering in a new movement in Tamil cinema. But that did not come to pass.

Select Filmography
Mullum Malarum (1978), *Udhiri Pookal* (1979), *Pootatha Pootukkal* (1980), *Nenjathai Killathe* (1982), *Nandu* (1981), *Sasanam* (2005).

Mani Ratnam (b.1956)
With a Masters degreee in Business Administration, Mani Ratnam (given name Gopalarathinam Subramanian) made his entry into the world of films in 1983 with a Kannada film *Pallavi Anupallavi*. In 1986 he made *The Silent Tune/Mouna Ragam* in Tamil which won him the national award as the Best Tamil film of the year. *Hero/Nayagan* (1987) a story about a youngster from Tamil Nadu who grows to be a powerful don in Bombay, closely resembled *Godfather*, including the sub plot about a girl who is molested by politically connected youngsters and the manner in which the don organizes vendetta. *Anjali* (1990) the story around a mentally challenged child, had a scene reminiscent of the fantasy scene in *ET* when the kids fly into the sky. *Rose/Roja* (1992) while it brought him money and fame, created controversy about its ideology. The film, about a cryptologist who gets kidnapped while on his honeymoon in Kashmir was set in the backdrop of the insurgency. The film, made in Tamil and Hindi, created a debate in the media about its ideological position. His films

often have the backdrop of struggle, such as in Kashmir, Sri Lanka, the North East but avoided engaging with everyday basic issues. Mani Ratnam often writes the script and dialogues for his films. In his films *Nayagan* and *Iruvar* he made serious attempts to create a period flavour through relevant props, with the help of art director Thotta Tharani, and showed that he did have an eye for detail.

Captivating music has been one of the high points of his films. It was he who introduced A R Rehman as the music director in the film *Roja* and transformed the Indian film music scene. He retains the basic ingredients of Tamil filmic entertainment like song-dance, choreographed violence and melodrama.

The group dance sequences in his films display a strong influence of music videos. His films have been screened in many film festivals, including Cannes and Locarno. Mani Ratnam is known for treating his crew kindly and for being one of the most professional directors in the industry today.

His last film *The Ocean/Kadal* (2013) was not a commercial success although it was written by the renowned writer B Jeyamohan. He has been awarded the Padma Shri by the Government of India.

Select Filmography
Rose/Roja (1992), *Thiruda Thiruda* (1995), *A Peck on the Cheek/ Kannathil Muthamittal* (1996), *Thalapathi, The Duo/ Iruvar* (1998), *Ravanan* (2011).

Murugadasa (b. 1900- ?)

Murugadasa (original name K Muthusamy Aiyar) graduated from St Joseph's College, Tiruchi, and joined the Madras-based daily, *The Mail*. After ten years with the newspaper, he entered films through journalism, as the editor of *Sound and Shadow*, a film magazine in English. His filmmaking career began when he worked as an assistant to director Baburao Pendharkar in his Tamil film *Sita Kalyanam* (1933), which was made in Prabhat studios at Kolhapur. In this film, Murugadasa introduced two men who were to become famous later—Papanasam Sivan who wrote the songs and S Balachandar who played the role of a musician. Then, along with cinematographer K Ramnoth and art director A Shekhar, he founded Vel Pictures at Adyar, Madras. This team played an important role in establishing filmmaking as an industry in Madras and many films including *The Crowning/Padhuka Pattabishekam* (1937) were made, In 1937, Murugadasa established another studio, Karthikeya Films, on Greenways Road and directed *Sundaramurthy Nayanar* (1937). Later when this studio was destroyed in a fire, Murugadasa went back to journalism and ran the journal *Chithravani*, in which he was assisted by *Manikodi* writer B S Ramaiya, and the duo through their articles, spread awareness of cinema as an art form.

He was called back to direct *Divine Music/Venuganam* (1941), the dialogues for which was written by the famous Tamil writer, Va Ra. This film is remembered for its songs which were sung by the lead actress, N C Vasanthakokilam and by V V Sadagopan. The film that brought great fame to Murugadasa was Gemini Studios' *Nandanar* (1942) which dealt with untouchability. Carnatic musician M M Dandapani Desikar played the lead in the film. For several years, Murugadasa was the secretary of the Cine Technicians Association of Madras.

Select Filmography
Baktha Ramdas (1935), *Markandeya, Gnanasoundari* (*Gemini Studios,* 1948).

A P Nagarajan (1928-1977)
Akkammapettai Paramasivam Nagarajan started as a *vathiyar* (playwright-composer-director) in a drama company and came into films as a dialogue writer for *The Foursome/Nalvar* (1953), in which he also acted. He soon began writing scripts, at a time when dialogue dominated Tamil cinema. When anti-religious and rationalistic films by writers belonging to the Dravidian movement enjoyed great popularity, Nagarajan tried to counter this trend through his scripts. This was particularly evident in the film *Nalvar*. He later founded a production company with actor V K Ramasamy and made *The Good Alliance/ Nalla Idathu Sambandham* in 1958. In the same year he wrote the dialogues for the film *Sampoorna Ramayanam* which became a hit, thus reviving the era of mythologicals. When he started directing, his first few films were based on contemporary themes, like the one on a boy guide working in Mamallapuram *(Come Raja Come/Vaa Raja Vaa,* 1969). However by the mid-Sixties he began directing

a series of films on religious subjects, and thereby started a trend. His films were stagy and had scant respect for appropriateness of costumes. In *The Vow of Saraswathi/ Saraswathiyin Sabatham* (1966), Siva appears dressed like an ancient Greek warrior! Flowery dialogues, garish sets, semi-classical music, dance, glorification of Tamil, a star cast and religious mythology were the ingredients of his films and Sivaji Ganesan played the lead in many of his films.

On another note, Nagarajan was instrumental in organizing junior artistes into a union. He often patronized retired stage actors and associates from his drama days by engaging them to act in his films. So far as his political leanings were concerned, he identified himself with the Thamizharasu party led by Ma Po Sivagnanam, his political mentor. Nagarajan was for sometime the editor of *Saattai,* which served as the mouthpiece of this party, in which he bitterly attacked the Dravidian movement.

Select Filmography
Virtuous Woman/Kulamagal Radhai (1963), *God's Ways/ Thiruvilaryadal* (1965), *From Tirupathi to Cape Comerin/ Thirumalai Thenkumari* (1970), *The Exhibition/ Kankatchi* (1971), *Rajarajachozhan* (1973), *The Western Daughter-in-Law/Melnattu Marumagal* (1975).

A Narayanan (1900-1939)
Narayanan was the man who laid the foundation for cinema in South India, and was a prolific filmmaker during the silent

era. He started his career in a film distribution company in Mumbai and later set up his own unit, Exhibitor Film Services in 1927 in Madras. He toured western countries to promote Indian films and also visited the Universal City Studios in the US. In August 1929, he founded the General Pictures Corporation (GPC) in Tondiarpet in Madras as a public limited company and linked it to a network for film distribution and exhibition. GPC played a major role as a production centre and as a training ground for many individuals who later shaped cinema in this region. These included Y V Rao, R Prakasa and C Pullaiya. Beginning with *Dharmapathini* (1929), GPC produced eighteen films which were also screened in Burma (now Myanmar) and Singapore.

In 1934, he founded the first sound studio in Madras, Srinivasa Cinetone; the same year, he made *The Wedding of Srinivasa/Srinivasa Kalyanam,* the first talkie that was made in South India. He made a series of successful films till his death in 1939.

Narayanan supported the nationalist struggle and advocated propaganda through films. Va Ra, of the *Manikodi* group of writers, was a major influence on Narayanan and he was also associated with Rajaji and S Satyamurthi and made bonfires of foreign textiles as part of the Swadeshi movement. He wrote articles on cinema in *The Hindu* and for a while edited a film magazine, *Movie Mirror.* He also made documentaries and assisted Robert Flaherty in making *The Elephant Boy* (English, 1937).[3]

Select Filmography

Silent: *Nandanar* or *The Elevation of the Downtrodden* (1929), *Gnanasoundari* (1930), *Destruction of the Pride of Garuda/Garuda Garva Bangam* (1930).

Talkies: *Rajambal* (Coimbatore Talkies, 1935), *Viswamithra* (1936), *Rajasekaran* (1938), *Sri Ramanujar* (1938).

Documentaries: Indian National Congress At Guwahati (1927), Unfurling the National Flag, The Spirit of Agriculture, Venereal Diseases.

R Nataraja Mudaliar (1885-1972)

Credited as the man who made the first feature film in South India, Nataraja Mudaliar, was in the bicycle business, and recognized the possibility of making films in Madras when he saw the silent films from the West. He travelled to Pune, where he met cinematographer Stewart Smith who taught him how to handle a movie camera. The aspiring filmmaker's first efforts were screened after dinner at Smith's Pune residence. Mudaliar returned to Madras and with the help of business associate, S M Dharmalingam Mudaliar, formed the India Film Company.

They set up South India's first studio with a second hand Williamson camera, in a bungalow called Tower House in Millers Road, in Kilpauk, Madras. Nataraja Mudaliar directed while Narayanasamy, trained in processing, was in charge of the laboratory established in Bangalore, a city which had a climate suitable for such work. Exposed film rolls were rushed daily to Bangalore; Mudaliar visited the city once a week. C Rangavadivelu, an actor from Suguna

Vilas Sabha was engaged to train actors. Within thirty-five days, Mudaliar brought out the first film to be made in South India, *Keechakavatham* (1916). The company's second film, *Draupathi Vasthirabaranam* was released in 1917. The title cards in his films were in Tamil, Hindi and English. Madan of Calcutta and Ardeshir Irani of Mumbai, renowned in their respective fields, distributed Mudaliar's films throughout India. Later, he left the company to start his independent production and travelled to Vellore, his native town, to set up a studio in Sathuvachari and single handedly produced *Mahiravanan* and *Markandeya,* both in 1919. These films were shot in and around the hills of Vellore. In 1923, when his studio was burnt in a fire accident and his son died, Mudaliar gave up films. He died in 1972 in Madras.

Select Filmography

Silent: *Keechakavatham* (1936), *Draupathi Vasthirabaranam* (1917) *Maitreyi Vijayam* (1918), *Lava and Kusa/Lava Kusa* (1919), *Vanquishing Kalinga / Kalinganarthanam* (1920), *The Wedding of Rukmani/ Rukmani Kalyanam* (1921).

P Neelakantan (1916-1992)

Born in Villupuram, Neelakantan began his career as a journalist with the magazine called *Jeevamani*, in Tiruchi. He later worked for the journal, *Kumaran* and began writing plays for radio. His play *Rose among Thorns/Mullil Roja* staged by TKS Brothers brought him fame. His other play, *Nam Iruvar* was bought by the movie Moghul, A V Meyyappa Chettiar and made into a film in 1947. Then, Neelakantan wrote the dialogues for films like, *The Demon World/Vedala Ulagam* (1948) and *Life/Vazhkai* (1949). The first film he directed was *One Night/Oor Iravu* (1951), the dialogues for which were written by C N Annadurai. From then on, his fortunes rose steadily; he directed many films in Tamil, Kannada and even Sinhalese *(Suneetha)*. Two films in particular brought him fame: ALS Productions' *Ambikapathi* (1957), starring Sivaji Ganesan and *Do Not Steal/Thirudathe* (1961) with M G Ramachandran. He later directed a large number of films with MGR in the lead, including *My Brother/En Annan* (1970) and *The Globetrotting Young Man/Ulagam Sutrum Valiban* (1973). In 1979 he was appointed principal of the Institute of Film Technology in Madras, when M G Ramachandran was the chief minister of Tamil Nadu.

Select Filmography
Oor Iravu (1951), *Mudhal Thedhi* (1955), *Poompuhar* (1964), *The Watchman/Kavalkaran* (1967), *Enclave of Maidens/Kumarikottam* (1970), *Yesterday, Today, Tomorrow/ Netru Inru Nalai* (1974), *Divine Marriages/Deiva Thirumanangal* (1981).

R Padmanabhan (1896 - ?)
Padmanabhan was one of the pioneers in the South Indian film industry and his innings lasted long into the era of talkies. He began his career in 1926 as a film distributor and dealer in cinema equipment. In 1928, he started Associated Films, with financial backing from a lawyer from Nagapatinam, K S Venkataraman (father-in-law of film

director, KSubrahmanyam), and set up a studio in Saidapet in Madras. K Subrahmanyam and Raja Sandow joined him and they made a series of films like *The Pride of Hindustan* (1931). In the silent era, this was the second biggest production centre in South India, next only to GPC and Padmanabhan even recruited technicians from Mumbai like K P Bhave and G G Gogate. After the advent of sound, he entered filmmaking under the banner of Oriental Films, in partnership with Ramalinga Mudaliar, and produced a number of films including *The Illusory Market/Maya Bazaar* (1935). He was active in the industry till the end of the Fifties.

Select Filmography

The Illusory Market/Maya Bazaar (1935), *Construction of the Bridge/Sethubandhanam* (1937), *The Illusory Light/ Mayajothi* (1941), *Baktha Kalathi* (1945), *Changing Fortune/Sakata Yogam* (1946), *The Maiden/Kumari* (1952), *Everything is Delightful/Ellam Inba Mayam* (1955).

R Prakasa (1901-1956)

Son of pioneer film distributor, R Venkiah, Prakasa was a major force in the South Indian film industry during its formative years. He was trained for a year in filmmaking in England and returned to India after visiting Metro Studios in the US, Pathe in France, and Milano Film Company in Italy. In Madras, he set up the Star of the East Film Company, behind Roxy theatre. Equipped with a laboratory, work began in this glass-roofed studio with *Bhishma Pratignai*. Encouraged by its success, he made a number of films; yet the company ran into financial difficulties and was attached by the court in 1924. Then he joined Narayanan in the General Pictures Corporation. When GPC folded up, Prakasa took to film distribution. He built three cinema houses in Madras. Later when Narayanan founded his Srinivasa Cinetone studio, Prakasa joined him as technical adviser and directed a few films. Later, he freelanced and made *Krishna Arjuna* (1935) in Calcutta. His film *Anadhaipenn* (1938) is remembered for the sequences containing nationalist propaganda. But most of his works were mythological and his favourite locale was Gingee fort near Madras. His last completed film was *Three Girls/ Moonru Pengal* (1956). He made Telugu films also; when he died in 1956, he was in the midst of directing a Telugu film, *The Celestial Beauty/Devasundari,* which was released in 1960.

Prakasa saw a bright future for cinema in this country. Apart from regular features, he made a number of short films as well. He also had plans to run a regular newsreel service. To begin with he covered some important happenings in the city and made shorts like *The Inauguration of the Royal Bath*. He even assisted in the production of a film titled *The Catechist of Killarney* for T G Duffy, an Irish missionary, which was shot in a village near Tiruvannamalai. The film was exhibited widely in England; however in India, there were protests against its screening. He is also well known for his film on the prevention of cholera for the government of India.[4]

Select Filmography
Silent: *Deliverance of the Elephant/Gajendra Mokskam* (1923), *Mahatma Kabirdas* (1923), *Stage Girl* (1926), *Kovalan* (1929),

The Rose of Rajasthan (1931), *The Coral Queen* (1931), *Leila or the Star of Mangrelia* (1931).

Talkies: *Indra's Court/Indra Sabha* (1936), *The Attendant/ Thookuthooki* (Royal Talkies, 1935), *Soldier's Wife/Porveeran Manaivi* (1937), *The Wedding of Andal/Andal Thirukalyanam* (1937), *Bhoja* (1948).

T R Raghunath (1912-1990)

A leading filmmaker of the Fifties and Sixties, Raghunath started as an assistant to his brother, Raja Chandrasekhar, when the latter directed Srinivasa Cinetone's *Gnanasoundari* (1935). He worked with A Narayanan of Srinivasa Cinetone in films like *Tarasasankam* (1936). Raghunath's first effort at filmmaking was a 3-reeler titled *The Aged Bridegroom/ Kizhattu Mappillai* in 1936. He then went on to make his first feature film *Jothi alladhu Srimath Ramalinga Swamigal* in Calcutta in 1939. However the film that brought him fame was *Kannagi* with Kannamba and P U Chinnappa in the lead. In a number of his films, he gave MGR minor roles. His best years were the Fifties, when he made a series of very successful films like *Husband is a Palpable God/Kanavane Kan Kanda Deivam* (1955). He cast top stars and told folk tales, packed with fencing, songs and dances, without any regard to period or plausibility. Most of the stars of the Fifties and Sixties made films with him. He later worked for some years as a technical adviser in Karpagam Studios in Madras. When M G Ramachandran became the chief minister, Raghunath was appointed the president of the Films Division of the Government of Tamil Nadu.

Select Filmography

The Birth of Sita/Sita Jananam (1940), *The God Who Had Mastered Tamil/Tamizhariyum Perumal* (1942), *Jungle Beauty/ Vanasundari* (1951), *Whose Boy/Yar Paiyan* (1957), *Allavudin And His Wonderful Lamp/Allavudinum Arputha Vilakkum* (1957), *Welcoming The Bridegroom/Mappillai Azhaippu* (1972).

Raja Chandrasekhar (1904-1971)

A pioneer filmmaker, Raja Chandrasekhar was born in Tiruchi and trained in Mumbai to be a textile engineer. But his primary interest was in movie making. He started his career in films as an assitant to Fatima Begum, probably the first woman film director in India, in 1929. Later, he joined General Pictures Corporation. His first film was *Mohini Rukmangatha* which was followed by a few more. He made about twelve silent films, the most well-known among them being *Pandava Nirvahan* (1930). After the advent of sound, he made *Raja Desingu* and *Chandramohan* (1936) in Mumbai Film City. At East India Films Studio in Calcutta, he made *Baktha Thulasidas* (1937) for Murugan Talkies of Madurai. In his films like *Ashokumar* he, similar to T R Raghunath, gave M G Ramachandran, then a struggling actor, small roles and helped him to build his career. When MGR made his *Vagabond King/Nadodi Mannan* (1958), he engaged Raja Chandrasekhar as technical adviser.

Select Filmography

Silent: *Milan Dinar* (1930), *Pandava Nirvahan* (1930).

Talkies: *Gnanasoundari* (Srinivasa Cinetone, 1935), *Chandramohan* (1936), *The Fire Sacrifice of Daksha/ Dakshayagnam* (1938), *Maya Machindra* (1939), *Royal Deliverance/Rajamukthi* (1948), *My Daughter/En Magal* (1954).

Raja Sandow (1894-1943)

Raja Sandow (given name P K Nagalingam) was born in Pollachi. While he was growing up in Pudukottai, he trained to be a gymnast. He later went to Mumbai and after a short stint there as an actor, started directing films in Ranjit Studios, and worked for a monthly salary. When R Padmanabhan founded Associated Films, Raja moved to Madras and directed many movies. When sound came, he went back to Mumbai and shone as an actor, pairing with stars like Gohar. In Mumbai, he was commissioned to direct his first Tamil film, *Menaka*. Enthused by the reception to this film, he came to Madras and established his credentials as a filmmaker. As a director, actor, scriptwriter and producer, his contribution to Tamil cinema is significant. Many of the stars of the Forties and Fifties have worked with him. He was very competent at coaching actors and maintained complete control over his films. He was a martinet on the sets and was often compared to a ringmaster in a circus. In his films, the emphasis shifted from songs to the spoken word. He directed and acted in *Vasanthasena* (1936), made in Pune. When Orr's Gramophone and Talkies Limited made *Vishnu Leela* (1938), they chose Raja Sandow to direct and act in the film, which was also shot in Pune. He was fluent in

Marathi, Hindi, Gujarati and Telugu and had directed a few Hindi films while at Mumbai. He was one of the earliest to establish a link between the world of Hindi and Tamil cinemas and left his mark on both. In 1941 he started his own film company, Janaki Pictures and made *Choodamani* (Telugu, 1941). He died on 24 November 1943 of a heart attack in Coimbatore.

The Government of Tamil Nadu has instituted an award in his memory, the Raja Sandow Award, which is given to veterans in Tamil cinema. Unfortunately, none of his films have been preserved.

Select Filmography

Silent: *Devil and the Damsel* (1930), *Rajeswari* (1931), *Usha Sundari* (1931), *Bakthavathsala* (1931).

Talkies: *Menaka* (1935), *Chandrakantha* (1936), *Minor Rajamani* (1937), *Thiruneelakantar* (1939), *The Bell Of Justice/Araichimani* (1942).

T Rajendar (b.1955)

Hailing from a family of musicians, Rajendar graduated from Annamalai University and entered films with *(Unrequited Love/Oruthalai Ragam* (1980) as the dialogue-writer and lyricist. His first directorial venture was *The Call of Spring/ Vasanthathin Azhaipugal (*1980) for which he wrote the dialogues and songs, and also composed the music. This became a pattern in his subsequent films, in which he assumed responsibility for nearly all the major departments; they did extremely well at the box office. Soon he started handling the camera himself and came to be referred to as "the one man production unit". His films are a combination of melodrama, implausible situations, fights, dances and songs. He rarely goes outdoors for shooting, preferring the studio sets. With garish decor, psychedelic lighting and group dances, his films provide heavy doses of cinematic kitsch. The dialogue is replete with unnecessary rhymes, which are often contrived and meaningless. The stories usually revolve around the travails of a woman and a large majority of his fans are women. He introduced many new artistes who rose to be stars, like Amala and Anand Babu. He featured his five-year-old son in a major role and fan clubs were started in the latter's name. In 1984, at the height of his popularity, Rajendar joined politics and allied himself with the DMK, then an opposition party. He was sought after as a speaker at political meetings and rallies. When he fell out with the DMK, he started his own party, Thainadu Marumalarchi Kazhagam (Motherland Renaissance Party). Under this banner, his wife Usha contested for a seat in the national parliament from Palani and lost. He himself stood against Jayalalithaa in the Kangeyam constituency during the elections to the Tamil Nadu Legislative Assembly in 1991 and lost.

Select Filmography

During Train Journeys/Rayil Payanangalil (1981), *A Melody In The Heart/Nenjil Oru Ragam* (1982), *A Song For The Sister/Thangaikor Geetham* (1983), *Love Me, Maithili/Maithili Ennai Kathali* (1986), *My Sister Kalyani/En Thangai Kalyani* (1988).

K Ramnoth (1912-56)

A significant figure in South Indian film history, Ramnoth started as an assistant with Kodak, Madras. When Vel Pictures was founded in 1934, he joined as a technician, along with A Sekhar and Murugadasa, who were to make a mark later, respectively as an art director and filmmaker. It was Ramnoth who was responsible for all the technical aspects in this studio. It was here that he blossomed into a cinematographer when he filmed *Sita Kalyanam* (Telugu, 1934). He later worked with the famous filmmaker B N Reddy and filmed *Vandematharam* (1939) and *Baktha Pothanna* (1942) both in Telugu. He worked in Gemini Studios as production chief and was the cinematographer for many films produced by them, including *The Vow of Mangamma/Mangamma Sabatham* (1943). He shot a good part of *Chandraleka* also—notably the circus sequences and the drum dance. The acme of his work as a cameraman was *Kalpana* (Hindi, 1948) made by dancer Uday Shankar. When he switched over to directing films, he proved so successful that he was sought after by many companies. He worked for big banners like AVM and Jupiter and made important films like *Ezhai Padum Padu*. He later turned producer, founded New Era Films and made *Freedom/ Viduthalai* (1954) which got enmeshed in legal tangles and ruined him financially.

Ramnoth was versatile; he could handle the camera expertly, edit effectively and also proved his mettle as a director. A graduate, he was deeply interested in English literature and adapted Shakespeare's *Twelfth Night* as *Kanniyin Kathali*. It was in this film that Kannadasan was introduced as a songwriter. He and art director Shekhar worked as a team in many films of the Forties and early Fifties. He was aware of the creative potential of cinema at a time when filmmaking was seen merely as a commercial proposition. He founded the Cine Technicians Association in Madras in 1940, which is still going strong. M G Ramachandran desired that he direct his film *Nadodi Mannan;* but before work on the film could begin, Ramnoth died at the age of forty-five in Hyderabad in 1956.[5]

Select Filmography

Mohini (1948, only partly), *Kanniyin Kathali* (1949), *Ezhai Padum Padu* (1950), *Marmayogi* (1951), *Mother's Heart/ Thai Ullam* (1952), *Where Is Comfort/Sugam Enge* (1954), *Viduthalai* (1954), *The Man/Manithan* (1954), *The Heroine/ Kathanayaki* (1955), *Boolokarambai* (1958, only partly).

C V Sridhar (1932-2008)

While working in a government office in Chinglepet, Sridhar made his mark as a playwright, with the successful play *The Bond of Blood/Ratha Pasam* (1954) which was staged by TKS Brothers Drama Company. He entered films as a dialogue writer when this play was adapted as a film. He wrote the dialogues for *The Unexpected Turn/ Ethirparathathu* (1954) and established a reputation through *Amaradeepam.* His directorial debut *Kalyanaparisu* was a blockbuster. Based on the eternal triangle—which was to be a recurrent leitmotif in his work—it was a mix of romance and melodrama. Sridhar founded his own production concern, Chithralaya, in 1961 and made a series of commercially successful films, including the memorable *A Temple in the Heart/Nenjil Oor Alayam* (1962), a story around three people in a hospital, which he scripted and directed. He planned his shooting schedules meticulously and worked on a tight budget. He could thus make his films in record time. In all his films, he used the stars-melodrama-and-songs combination. The work of cinematographer, A Vincent, who was his business partner and who later emerged as a filmmaker in his own right, and music by the Viswanathan-Ramamurthy duo, were important features of his early films. Some of the stars of the Sixties like Jayalalithaa, Ravichandran and Kanchana were introduced by him as lead characters in his films. Sridhar, who said that his guru in cinema was V Shantaram, made films in Hindi, Kannada and Telugu also. In 1962 he started a film fortnightly, *Chithralaya* in a newspaper format. It carried a lot of serious matter, including news of the industry.

Select Filmography
The Morning Star/Vidivelli (1960), *The Honeymoon/Thenilavu* (1961), *Constable's Daughter/ Policekaran Magal* (1962), *No Time To Love/Kathalika Neramillai* (1964), *The Riotous Wedding/Gallatakalyanam* (1968), *The Voice Of Right/ Urimaikural* (1974), *Youth Swings / Ilamai Oonjaladukiradhu* (1978).

K Subrahmanyam (1904-1971)
Trained to be a lawyer, Subrahmanyam joined Associated Films as a scriptwriter in 1928. In 1934, he produced *Pavalakodi*

under the banner Meenakshi Cinetone, in which he introduced M K Thyagaraja Bhagavathar. He started his own concern in 1935, the Madras United Artistes Corporation, and made *New Satharam /Naveena Satharam* (1935) in just nineteen days. He shot his first few films in Calcutta and later set up his own studio, the Motion Picture Combines in Madras, in which he employed well-known technicians from Calcutta. A votary of the nationalist movement, he used cinema to further its cause; criticized caste oppression in *Balayogini*, advocated a better deal for women in *Sevasadan* and attacked untouchability in *Baktha Chetha* (1940). *Thyagabhoomi* was undoubtedly the best of his films. Subrahmanyam believed in organizing the film industry on more professional grounds and worked for setting up the South Indian Film Chamber of Commerce, of which he was president for four terms. He founded the South Indian Artistes Association and the Film Producers Guild of South India as well. He pleaded for an insurance scheme for the industry, a common bank and a school for acting. A number of artistes who were introduced by him rose to great heights and the best known among them were T R Rajakumari and M K Thyagaraja Bhagavathar. He introduced Papanasam Sivan in a lead role in *Baktha Kuchela*. Subrahmanyam himself played a role in *Ananthasayanam* (1942).[6]

In 1942, he founded a school for dancing, Nrityodaya, one of the earliest of its kind in the country. For some years he was also the president of the Indian Peoples Theatre Association.[7] In 2005, a commemorative postage stamp was released in his honour.

Select Filmography
The Wedding of Usha/Usha Kalyanam (1936), *Balayogini* (1936), *Kachadevayani* (1937), *Thyagabhoomi* (1939), *Ocean of Love/Premsagar* (Hindi, 1949), *Manasamrakshanam* (1944), *Vichithravanitha* (1947), *Geethagandhi* (1949), *Pandithevan* (1957), *The Journey/Yatra* (Hindi, children's film, 1960).

T R Sundaram (1907-1963)

A pioneer of the studio system in India, Sundaram came from a wealthy family of yarn merchants and began his career as a textile engineer, with a degree from Leeds. Back in India, he started Angel Films in Salem, along with S S Velayudham Pillai, and made two films in Calcutta. With the money he earned, he set up his own studio, Modern Theatres, in Salem. His first film was *Sathi Akalya* (1937) and soon there was a steady stream of films from Modern Theatres, averaging three a year. The films were mostly in Tamil but sometimes also in Telugu, Hindi, Kannada, Malayalam (the first ever called *Balan* in 1938) and Sinhalese. There was even an English film titled, *The Jungle* (1952).

It was in Modern Theatres that Sundaram directed the first colour film of South India, *Alibaba and the Forty Thieves/Alibabavum 40 Thirudargalum*. His films were geared at entertainment, without any pretensions to social or political comment. Some famous stars of Tamil cinema were introduced by Sundaram such as M R Radha in *Santhanathevan* (1939). Sundaram had himself acted in two films, *Burma Rani* and *Sulochana* (1946). He later directed *Manonmani* and *Valaiyapathi* (1952), films based on two of the five great Tamil epics and was instrumental in hiring poet Bharathidasan as a writer and produced his story *Ponmudi*. Sundaram also ran a Tamil film magazine, *Chandamarutham,* for a few years, with lyricist Kannadasan as the editor.

Sundaram ran Modern Theatres like a factory and he was strict with his employees, who were about 250 in number. He was the president of the South Indian Film Chamber of Commerce twice, during 1949-50 and 1956-59 and was instrumental in acquiring the land in Madras on which the Chamber building now stands. The road has been named after him.

Select Filmography
Burma Rani (1944), *Sulochana* (1946), *Athithan Kanavu* (1948), *The Phantom Woman/Mayavathi* (1949), *Digambara Samiyar* (1950), *The Dictator/Sarvadhikari* (1951), *Thief of Baghdad/Baghdad Thirudan* (1960).

A S A Swamy (1917-1998)
Born in Ceylon, in Sri Lanka, Swamy developed an interest in drama through his father who was engaged in organizing shows by drama companies from the Madras presidency. Swamy came to India where his play *Bilhana* was staged by the TKS Brothers Drama Company. He was then hired to script a war effort film, My *Son/En Magan* (1945) and later found regular employment with Jupiter Pictures of Coimbatore and directed his first film, *Sri Murugan* in 1946 and followed it up with *The Princess/Rajakumari* (1947). This was also M G Ramachandran's first film as a hero. Swamy was

also associated with the film careers of other DMK leaders of the time. For instance, the film that brought Swamy fame as a director, *Velaikari,* was written by C N Annadurai. Riding on its success, Swamy was engaged to direct a number of films and was one of the leading filmmakers of the Fifties. He was also instrumental in introducing M Karunanidhi, who later became the chief minister of Tamil Nadu for three terms, as a dialogue writer. Swamy relied on established stars; his films followed all the filmic conventions of the times. They were theatrical, with songs, dances and melodrama. Spoken words and indoor sets predominated and many of his films were based on folklore. He later served on the faculty of the Institute of Film Technology, Madras.

Select Filmography
Vijayakumari (1950), *A Drop of Poison/Thulivisham* (1954), *The Judge/Neethipathi* (1955), *The Golden Statue/Thangapadumai* (1958), *Kalyani is Getting Married/Kalyaniku Kalyanam* (1960).

S S Vasan (1903-1969)
Subramanyan Srinivasan came from Tiruthuraipoondi to Madras to study and started an advertising agency. With the money he earned, he bought a small press and a magazine and established *Anandavikatan* which is still a very popular weekly in Tamil Nadu. His entry into films was with his novel *Sathi Leelavathi* in 1936. Three years later, he started a film distribution company in 1939, Gemini Studios, and also financed films. He spent a lot of time in National Movietone

The Filmmakers

studios in Madras learning filmmaking techniques. When the Motion Picture Combines studio came up for auction, Vasan bought the facility. Here, he set up Gemini Studios and produced his first film, *Madanakamarajan,* in 1941; it earned him a lot of money. He established Gemini as a major production centre in the country and also started directing films and his most memorable work was *Chandraleka,* which was made in Tamil and Hindi, of which 603 prints were made. It was also released in the United States as *Chandra* with English sub-titles.[9]

Vasan believed that films were meant to entertain and that filmic narration should be structured to enable even the most ordinary man to follow it. Songs, dances, fencing, small skits, humour and spectacular sets were featured in every film and as a result, his films were akin more to variety entertainment programmes than cinema. He also relied on elaborate, and often innovative, promotion strategies. Even when nationalist fervour was at its peak in the mid-Forties, his films did not deal with political issues. In 1958, he started Gemini Colour Laboratories, a premier processing laboratory in the country today. He believed in establishing the film trade on professional lines and his contribution was more in the realm of organizing the industry than in the development of cinema. He was the president of the Film Federation of India for two terms and was also nominated as Member of Parliament (Rajya Sabha). He was honoured with the Padma Bhushan by the Government of India in 1969.[10]

Select Filmography

Chandraleka (1948), *The Strange Brothers/Aboorva Sakodharargal* (1949), *Family Life/Samsaram* (1951), *Avvaiyar* (1953), *Iron Curtain/Irumbu Thirai* (1960).

Notes

1. Guy, Randor, "Innovative Filmmaker Too". *The Hindu*, 6 May 1990.
2. Hariharan, K, "The Face of Feeling", *Cinema in India*, July-September 1988.
3. Meena Narayanan, wife of filmmaker A Narayanan, was the first woman sound-recordist of India. When her husband founded Srinivasa Cinetone, he engaged Poddar as a sound-recordist and Meena who was proficient in Carnatic music, assisted him in recording music; in the process, she learnt the technique of recording. When Poddar left the company suddenly, Meena took his place. The first film she worked in was *Visvamithra* (1936), followed by *Worshipping Krishna/Krishna Tulabaram* (1937). She worked in six films made by her husband. For all these films the recording was done on a BTH sound system. She also made a short film on the Eucharistic Congress held in the Island grounds in Madras.
   Dr N Kalavathy (daughter of A Narayanan) interviewed by the author in Madras, 26 April 1976.
4. Prakasa's witness before the ICC., Vol III, 1927.
5. Information given by Randor Guy.
6. S Krishnaswamy, son of K Subrahmanyam, interviewed by the author in Madras, 3 March 1975.
7. Padma Subrahmanyam interviewed in *Puthiya Parvai*, 16-31 November 1994.

8. ASA Swamy interviewed by the author in Madras, 6 April 1975.
9. Ashokamitran, "The Great Dream Bazar", *The Illustrated Weekly of India,* 28 July 1985.
10. Guy, Randor, "The Making of Gemini", *Aside,* 1-15 October 1988.

Chapter Nine
The Songwriters

Baskara Das (1892-1952)

BASKARA DAS (ORIGINALLY VELLAISAMY THEVAR) FROM Madurai was one of the earliest song writers. He wrote for the first ever Tamil talkie, *Kalidas* and later for many films. By the time sound appeared, he was already famous as a writer of nationalist songs, of which many were sung by famous vocalists like K B Sundarambal and M S Subbulakshmi and released as discs. He worked closely with Madurai Manoranjani Sangeetha Sabha and produced many successful dramas. He began writing patriotic songs, some in ballad style, during the Khilafat agitation of 1919. One song for which he is still remembered was about the Jallianwala Bagh massacre. This made him the best known among writers of patriotic songs. Some plays which featured his songs were banned by the British government.

Baskara Das also wrote a number of musical plays like *Usha Parinayam* and wrote for recording companies like

Broadcast Gramophone Company. It was common practice in those days to release a complete musical play as a set of 78 rpm discs; Baskara Das authored quite a few "musical" record sets. With the arrival of sound in films, successful dramas were taken up for filming and Baskara Das was the natural choice as song writer for the films. In *Kalidas,* which was a mythological, he introduced nationalistic songs on the glories of hand-spinning. He wrote for films like *Prahalada* and *Valli,* both released in 1933. It was a period when songs were more important as an element of cinema than the spoken word. Even K L Saigal sang some Tamil songs written by Baskara Das in *Devadas* (1937) as did K C Dey, from Bengal, in *Miss. Sundari.* Many of his songs had reformist themes like temperance and anti-child marriage. His songs from films such as *Raja Desingu* and *Rajasekaran* were highly popular, though only a few of these have survived. In 1952, he died in Nagalapuram, where he was buried.

A residential colony—Baskara Das Nagar—in Madurai is named after him.[1]

Kambadasan (1916 -1973)

Kambadasan (original name C S Rajappa) was from Villayanur near Puducheri. Through his association with P Sambanda Mudaliar, he developed an interest in drama—he acted on stage, worked as a musician and then started writing songs for plays. He blossomed into a leading song writer for films during the Forties and Fifties. Kambadasan made his debut through the film *Vamana Avatharam* (1940) and wrote the songs and dialogue for the film, *Salivahanan.* But it was his work in *Mangaiyarkarasi* (1949), particularly the song *Parthal pasi theerum* (My hunger will vanish if I look at you), sung by P U Chinnappa, and in *Gnanasoundari* (1948), including the song *Arul tharum deva mathave* (Mother Mary, have mercy), that established his position as a song writer. His work contributed to the emergence of the film song as an independent entertainment form. They were direct and simple, and displayed an awareness of social issues. He also wrote many songs for successful films that were dubbed from Hindi into Tamil: like *The Celestial Chariot / Vaanaratham* (1956), from the Hindi *Udan Khatola,* released in the same year. He made a cameo appearance as poet Vidyapathi in *Mangaiyarkarasi*. Kambadasan also published a few anthologies of his poems and was active in the Socialist party led by Jayaprakash Narayan.

Kannadasan (1927-1981)

Kannadasan (original name Muthaiya), born in Sirukatalapatti in Ramanathapuram district in a merchant family, dominated Tamil cinema as a songwriter in the Sixties and Seventies. A school dropout, at the age of seventeen he became the editor of a Tamil monthly from Pudukottai, in which he published his first poem.

Filmmaker K Ramnoth introduced him to cinema and Kannadasan wrote his first song for *Kanniyin Kathali,* which featured six of his songs. Ramnoth engaged him for his next film, *Marmayogi,* also. Later, he came to be associated with Modern Theatres in Salem and consolidated his position as a songwriter. When the DMK leaders entered films,

The Songwriters

Kannadasan also wrote a number of propagandist songs for their films like *Money/Panam* (1952) and *Look Back/Thirumbipaar* (1953). Later, he wrote a large number of songs for films starring M G Ramachandran. Kannadasan also wrote the dialogues for one of MGR's more famous films, *Madurai Veeran*. He founded his own concern, Kannadasan Films, in 1957 and made *Sivagangai Seemai* and other films with many propagandist songs.

He began his political career as a staunch supporter of the Dravidian movement. Then he came under the influence of Jalakantapuram Pa Kannan and took the name Kannadasan ("Follower of Kannan"). When the DMK was formed, Kannadasan joined the party and stayed on till 1964, when he moved to the Congress. After he left the DMK, he grew increasingly religious and wrote many essays and booklets on Hinduism. The range of his film songs was wide—from the devotional to the erotic. His ability to compose a song, within a few minutes, for any given tune, made him the most sought after lyricist. He was instrumental in conferring a literary status to film songs. Some of his songs, set to music by the Viswanathan-Ramamurthy duo, proved enduring: for instance *Ponal pogattum poda* (Let it be so), from the film *Milk and Fruit/Palum Pazhamum* (1961). He wrote prodigiously; his works totalling 109 volumes include 5,000 film songs, 4,000 poems, dialogues for a few films, twenty-one novels and ten volumes of religious essays, in addition to numerous columns in journals. His novel, *Cheramaan Kathali* (Cheramaan's Lover) won the Sahitya Akademi award. The last film to feature one of his songs was *Moonrampirai*. He died in 1981 while on a visit to the US.[2]

A Marudakasi (1920-1989)

Born in a farming family at Melakudikadu near Tiruchi, Marudakasi was interested in theatre even as a student and came under the influence of musician Rajagopala Aiyar, brother of Papanasam Sivan. Dropping out of college, Marudakasi worked for a while as a village official and later joined theatre companies and acted in the troupes of TKS Brothers and Nawab Rajamanikkam. He wrote his first song for a play staged by Devi Nataka Sabha and made his debut in films with a song in *Mayavathi*. His songs in the film, *Mandhirikumari*, particularly the number *Vaarai... nee... vaarai* (Won't you come) ensured his place in Tamil cinema. In writing songs for films, he was deeply influenced by Udumalai Narayana Kavi, who dominated Tamil cinema as a lyricist in the 1950s. Marudakasi had a steady career during which he wrote nearly 3,000 songs featured in more than 320 films. Some of the most popular songs of the Fifties were authored by him.

Playback singer the late T M Soundararajan and music director M S Viswanathan made Marudakasi's songs immensely popular. He was an archetypal film lyricist as he would deftly write the words for tunes composed by music directors; his songs were simple and often colloquial. He wrote many songs for M G Ramachandran in many of his successful films.

The Government of Tamil Nadu honoured him with the

title "Kalaimamani" in his last years. Marudakasi also wrote songs for television and for music groups. His last film as a lyricist was *Bunch of Jasmine/Adukkumalli* (1973).[3]

Papanasam Sivan (1891-1973)

Sivan (original name P R Ramayier) was initiated into music by his mother. He joined Maharaja's Sanskrit College in Thiruvananthapuram and earned the title "Upadhyaya". Noting his talent for music, the court musicians—Noomi Mahadeva Bhagavathar and Samba Bhagavathar—gave him lessons. After his mother died, Sivan roamed around Tamil Nadu on foot, eking out a living by conducting bhajans (devotional group-singing) and came to be called "Sivan". Later, when he stayed in Papanasam for a few years with his brother, he acquired the prefix 'Papanasam'. In Papanasam, he taught music in drama companies and occasionally also acted. He moved to Madras in 1930 where his music was soon noticed, and his first book of devotional lyrics was released in 1934. The world of films, which was then on the lookout for music composers, attracted Sivan who began his career with *Sita Kalyanam* (Tamil, 1933), for which he wrote and composed the songs. Success was instantaneous and he worked in a series of films and soon became a major influence in the formative decades of the Tamil talkie; in some films, he himself sang a few songs. Through his compositions, he brought classical music to the masses as musical giants G N Balasubramaniam and M S Subbulakshmi sang his compositions in films like *Sevasadan* and *Sakunthala*. He himself coached the artistes to sing his songs and some of the biggest stars of the Forties,

M K Thyagaraja Bhagavathar, P U Chinnappa, T R Mahalingam and N C Vasanthakokilam, were trained by him. Two films in particular—*Thyagabhoomi* and *Haridas*—can be considered to be the high watermark of his career. He also acted, and played lead roles in four films—*Baktha Kuchela, Thyagabhoomi, Baktha Chetha* and *Kubera Kuchela* (1943). He wrote and set to music more than a 1,000 songs in about seventy films; many of his songs are still popular. The last film to feature one of his songs was *Sri Krishna Leela* (Tamil, 1971). For him, composing music and writing the lyrics were the expression of a single creative impulse—Sivan did not write words to fit into a tune.—and so his songs truly reflected the mood of the context. They were simple and yet rich in imagination. His contribution to Tamil cinema was only one dimension of his career. His devotional lyrics earned him a place among musical greats like Thyagayya, Shyama Sastri and Muthusamy Dikshithar. In 1962, the Sangeet Natak Akademi made him a Fellow and in 1972, he was awarded the Padma Bhushan by the Government of India.[4] He died in 1973. A road in Santhome, Madras, has been named after him.

Pattukottai Kalyanasundaram (1930-1959)

Kalyanasundaram was born in a farming family in Chengapatuthan village near Pattukottai, and had no formal education. His father, Arunachalam Pillai, was known for his folk songs. Kalyanasundaram tried his hand at many jobs: as a farmer, a dealer in coconuts and a labourer in the salt pans. For a while he was with Madurai Sakthi Nataka

Sabha, a commercial drama company, as an actor. His passion for poetry found expression when he joined the farmers' movement and organized the peasants in the Cauvery delta in Thanjavur. One of his songs was used in the play *The Darlings/Kannin Manigal,* staged at the Tamil Nadu Farmers' Conference in Dindigul in 1954 and his potential as a lyricist was noticed; he was brought into films by A L Narayanan. He made his debut as a lyricist in films with *The Educated Girl/ Paditha Penn* (1954). Immediately thereafter, his songs for *Maheswari* (1955) consolidated his position as a song writer for films. But it was his work in *The Web of Affection/Paasavalai* (1956) which made him truly a top-ranking lyricist. He was active till 1959, the year of his untimely demise, of cerebral haemorrhage, at the age of twenty-nine. *Kalaiyarasi* (1963) was the last film to feature his songs. In a little over nine years, he had written 196 songs for fifty-six films and the romantic songs he wrote for *Kalyanaparisu* (1959) are all-time favourites.

He was greatly influenced by poets Bharathi and Bharathidasan and referred to the latter as his mentor. His political mentor was the leftist leader Pa Jeevanandan; he himself remained a communist throughout. Kalyanasundaram regularly published his poems in leftist papers like *Janasakthi;* some of these were later used in films and several of which had a distinct propagandist flavour. Some of his most popular songs were those written for M G Ramachandran.

Kalyanasundaram carried on the powerful tradition of folk music: the appeal of his songs was simple and direct. By this measure, his songs were better integrated with the films and did not intrude. His work often bore the influence of the philosophical thoughts of ancient *siddhars* (ascetics), who have left behind a body of poetic writing. This is evident in the songs he wrote for *Paasavalai*.[5] He left a lasting impression in the field of popular culture in Tamil Nadu. The Government of Tamil Nadu nationalized his songs in 1995 and freed them of copyright restrictions.

Thanjai Ramaiyadas (1914-1965)

Ramaiyadas started as a Tamil teacher in a school in Thanjavur (Thanjai for short). During his early years, he identified himself with the cause of nationalism and the Congress party. These created problems for him in the school: he resigned his job as a teacher to enter the world of theatre and was engaged by Sudharsana Gana Sabha as a *vathiyar*. Later he launched his own drama company, Jayalakshmi Gana Sabha and wrote his first play titled, *The Mark of a Fish/ Macharekai*. He was introduced to cinema by actor T R Mahalingam with the film, *Chinthamani Who Beheaded A Thousand/Ayiram Thalaivangi Aboorva Chinthamani* (1947). But the film that stabilized his position in the industry was *Pathala Bairavi* (1951) for which he also wrote the dialogues; it was made under the big banner of Vijaya Studios. All the songs in the film were very popular; Ramaiyadas was patronized by leading film concerns. He became the "official song writer" for all Vijaya-Vauhini productions. He dominated the scene in the Fifties, and wrote for very successful films like *Missiamma* (1955), for which he also wrote the dialogues. Many films from the Fifties featuring his songs are still remembered and include Aruna

Films' *Thookuthooki* (1954) and *Amaradeepam*. He believed that film songs were meant to entertain and should have no literary pretensions. Therefore, he pitched his songs at a very populist level, even though he was well versed in traditional poetry. He therefore had the illiterate masses in mind when he wrote his songs. For this he was severely criticized by latter day song-writers.[6] Songs like *Varayo vennilave* (Won't you come...oh...moon) from *Missiamma* and *Kalyana samaiyal sadham* (Wedding feast) from *Maya Bazaar* (1957) were very popular. He later turned a producer and lost all his wealth. In 1962 he wrote the book *Thirukural Isaiyamum*, setting the couplets to music.

Udumalai Narayana Kavi (1899-1981)

Born in a merchant family, Narayanan learnt music from Udumalai Sarabam Muthusamy Kavirayar, who worked in drama companies. Narayanan adopted the prefix "Udumalai" from his mentor's name who was from Udumalaipettai. At the beginning of his career, Narayanan worked for gramophone companies—Taso Phone, Odeon and His Master's Voice—writing funny or comic songs (he wrote comic songs for N S Krishnan in *Sakunthala)* and later as a song writer in Arya Gana Sabha and other drama companies; and at times, he also acted. He entered films and wrote the dialogues and songs for *Krishna Leela* (1933). He joined Angel Films of Salem and worked in their productions *Draupathi Vasthirabaranam* (1934) and Royal Talkies' *Thookuthooki* (1935). In 1937 he campaigned for the Congress party and wrote nationalist songs in *Mayajothi*.

His guru Muthusamy Kavirayar introduced him to the atheistic, Self-respect movement (later known as Dravida Kazhagam); Narayana Kavi became a convert. N S Krishnan invited him to work in his film *Lost Love/Izhanda Kathal* (1941) and more such films followed. Narayana Kavi's atheistic and rationalistic ideas came to be expressed through songs. Through N S Krishnan, he got to know C N Annadurai and other leaders of the Dravidian movement; for over three decades, he was the voice of this movement in Tamil cinema. He believed that film songs could be used to propagate reformist ideas and put them to good use. He also published his songs in magazines of the movement, like *Kudiyarasu* and *Dravidanadu*.

As mentione above, he worked closely with N S Krishnan in a number of films and his humorous, propaganda songs were as much responsible for the growth of his own career as they were for N S Krishnan's popularity. The most famous film in which the two worked together was *Nallathambi*, written by Annadurai. A long opera on temperance and the Kindhanar ballad, a take-off on the legend of Saivite saint Nandanar, are some of their best remembered works. However in the mid-Fifties, the two fell out with each other.

As a lyricist, he was the anti-thesis of Papanasam Sivan, his contemporary. Narayana Kavi's songs were in the tradition of company dramas and were simple and popular. His rationalistic and anti-priesthood songs in *Sorgavasal* can be cited as typical examples of his work. The last film which featured his song was *Kurathi Magan* (1972). When he died in 1981, the Dravida Kazhagam organized a memorial meeting in Madras.

Vairamuthu (b.1953)

Born in Thamaraikulam near Madurai, Vairamuthu graduated from Pachaiyappa's College in Madras and started his career as a translator in a government department. When he started writing poetry, many of his poems were read and broadcast over the radio. He published his first collection of poems in 1972. Though initially he was opposed to modern poetry and favoured only the traditional format, he soon changed his position. He entered films through filmmaker Bharathiraaja: his first song was featured in *The Shadows/Nizhalgal* (1980). Through his association with music director Ilayaraja, he came to write songs for a number of films. His rise as a songwriter was, to a large extent, due to the success of Ilayaraja as music director and Bharathiraaja as a filmmaker. His songs were featured in a number of films in which these two worked together. K Balachandar also engaged Vairamuthu as a songwriter in his successful films like *Thanneer...Thanneer*. Kannadasan's absence from the scene—he died in 1981—was another factor that contributed to his rise. Later, his association with music director A R Rehman also helped in his ascendancy. Vairamuthu does not distinguish between film songs and poetry; so his songs remain very literary and are not helpful as an aid to cinema. Replete with similes, metaphors and imagery, his songs are mostly devoid of ideological content. He won the National award for his songs six times. His book, *Kallikattu ithihasam* won him the Sahitya Akademy Award in 2003.

Vali (1931-2013)

Hailing from Srirangam, T S Rangarajan alias Vali started as an artist under the sculptor Roy Choudhury at the College of Arts and Crafts in Madras. Vali gave up art and went back to Srirangam where he ran a manuscript-magazine under the pen name Netaji. In this role, his skill as an artist came in handy. Later, due to writer Kalki's recommendation, he got a job in All India Radio, Tiruchi, as a daily wage employee. He made a name for himself in the world of drama companies as a dialogue-writer. From then on he tried to make an entry into films with the help of actor V Gopalakrishnan and finally got a break in *The Thief of Azhagar Hill/Azhagarmalai Kallan* in 1958. Music director M S Viswanathan and filmmaker K S Gopalakrishnan engaged him in their films and helped his career rise. But it was the songs he wrote for M G Ramachandran, like *Nan anaiyittal* (If I command) in the film *Son of Our Family/Enga Veetu Pillai*, which contributed to his popularity as much as they did for MGR's. His songs in films like *Nallavan Vazhvan* consolidated his position as a song-writer and from then on his progress was steady.

Vali believed that an ideology and progressive ideas are not essential for achieving success as a song-writer. and didn't attach much importance to literary standards. A large number of his songs were aimed at promoting MGR's image. They were often sung by another character in the film in his praise. He also wrote conventional poetry and published two volumes of his poems.

Vali wrote nearly 10,000 songs; around 2,000 of them were set to music by M S Viswanathan. His songs were featured in sixty films of MGR's and fifty of Sivaji Ganesan's. Some of the most enduring songs of Tamil cinema have indeed been by Vali. He was awarded the Padma Shri in 2007.

Notes

1. Shanmugasundaram, S, *Vairamuthu Varai,* (Bangalore, Kavya publications, 1989) p.20.
2. Vaidyanathan, P S, "Verses for God", *India Today,* 15 November 1981.
3. Alagesan, R K, "*Thamizh Cinemavil Marudakasi*", *Dinamani,* 8 March 1991.
4. Thirumalai, "Papanasam Sivan: Tamil Thyagarajar", *The Illustrated Weekly of India,* 28 December 1975.
   Ramnarayanan, Gowri, "Original Genius of Our Times", *The Hindu,* 21 September 1990.
5. Balakrishnan, B E, (ed.) *Makkal Kavignar Pattukottai Katyanasundaram Padalgal,* (Madras, New Century Book House, 1965). The term *siddhar* denotes one who has attained siddhi or rare achievement through intense meditation and intuition. They were averse to the caste system, condemned idolatry and ritualism. They stressed monotheism and self-realization. The *siddhars* were not only mystics but were great poets also.
6. *Udumalai Narayana Kavi—Thanjai Ramaiya Das Pattu Thiran,* (Madras, Manimekalai publications, 1986).
7. Udumalai Narayana Kavi interviewed by the author at his native village Poolavadi, 11 June 1975. Velavan, Sangai, (ed.) *Udumalai Narayanakaviyin Padalkal,* (Madras, Periyar Suyamariyadhai Prachara Niruvana Veliyeedu, 1986).
   S Shanmugasundaram, *Vairamuthu,* p. 486.

Milestones of Tamil Cinema

1897 The first ever show of movies in South India. M Edwards screens a few shorts in Victoria Public Hall, Madras.

1900 The first cinema house in South India, the Electric Theatre, is built by Warwick Major on Mount Road (the present Anna Salai) Madras.

1902 The second cinema house in Madras, the Lyric, is started by Cohen on Mount Road, on which site Elphinstone Talkies came up later.

1905 Swamikannu Vincent, a railway draughtsman, from Tiruchi, buys touring cinema equipment from Dupont, a Frenchman passing through the town. Vincent forms Edison's Cinematograph, the first touring cinema in South India; travels around showing short films like *Life of Jesus Christ*. Vincent later turned film producer.

Milestones of Tamil Cinema

1907 T H Huffton produces a few shorts, the earliest to be made in South India, and exhibits them at the Electric Theatre. Later he started Peninsular Company and made silent movies like *The Fish Incarnation/ Machavathar* (1927).

1911 Marudamuthu Moopanar of Thanjavur visits London and makes a short film on the coronation of King George V in London on 11 November 1911 and screens it in Madras.

1914 First Indian-owned cinema house in South India, the Gaiety, is built by R Venkiah.

1916 The first film producing concern in South India, the India Film Company, is started in Madras by R Nataraja Mudaliar and S M Dharmalingam Mudaliar. Nataraja Mudaliar makes *Keechakavatham*, the first feature film to be made in South India.

1918 Pre-censorship of films introduced, through the Indian Cinematograph Act of 1918 with the Police Commissioner of Madras as the chief of the committee.

1921 The Evans Report. The British government appoints W Evans, a cinema expert from Britain, to study cinema in India and file a report. He visits Madras.

1927 *Movie Mirror* (English), the first film journal (a monthly) of South India comes out with S K Vasagam as the editor. Later, it was converted into a weekly under the name, *Amusement Weekly.*

1927 Exhibitor Film Services, the first distributing concern in South India, is started by A Narayanan.

1929 With the formation of General Pictures Corporation in Madras, cinema emerges as an entertainment industry in South India.

1929 The Madras Film League, a precursor of the South Indian Film Chamber of Commerce, is set up with Veeranki Rama Rao and V Sundaresan as secretaries.

1931 *Kalidas,* the first Tamil talkie, directed by H M Reddy, is released at Kinema Central, the present day Sri Murugan Talkies, Madras, on 31 October.

1934 The first sound studio in South India, Srinivasa Cinetone, also called Sound City, is founded by A Narayanan on Poonamallee High Road in Madras on 1 April.

1934 *Srinivasa Kalyanam,* the first Tamil talkie to be made in South India and directed by A Narayanan is released.

1935 Sundarabharathi Studio, the first studio outside Madras, is built at Sathuvachari, Vellore by Vajravelu — a small-time soda merchant.

1935 The birth of stardom. K B Sundarambal, receives Rs 1,00,000 for her lead role in the film *Nandanar* produced by Asandas Classical Talkies.

1935 *Kausalya,* the first Tamil talkie, on a contemporary theme ("social"), is made by South India Film Corporation.

1935 *Cinema Ulagam,* the first Tamil film journal, edited and published by P S Chettiar, is launched.

1936 Modern Theatres, the oldest studio in South India, is established at Salem.

Milestones of Tamil Cinema

1936 *Miss Kamala,* the first Tamil talkie to be directed by a woman, T P Rajalakshmi, is released.
1937 *Chinthamani,* the first Tamil film to run for more than one year in a single cinema house, is released.
1937 To discuss ways to improve cinema, the Madras Presidency Film Conference, organized by G Ramaseshan, is held from 19-21 of December at Gokhale Hall. S Satyamurthi and Vai Mu Kothainayaki Ammal participate.
1939 *Ocean of Love/Premsagar,* the first Hindi film made in South India, is directed and produced by K Subrahmanyam.
1939 The South Indian Film Chamber of Commerce comes into being in Madras, with S Satyamurthi as the first president.
1940 The first playback song in Tamil cinema is sung by D K Pattammal for the long documentary *Mahatma Gandhi* by A K Chettiar. The song was *Adu ratte...Adu ratte...suzhandru adu ratte.*
1940 The Cine Technicians Association of South India is formed by K Ramnoth.
1943 *Harishchandra* (Tamil, 1943) is dubbed into Kannada by A V Meyyappa Chettiar, thus becoming the first dubbed film in South India.
1944 The film *Haridas* plays continuously for 110 weeks in Broadway Talkies, Madras (133 weeks in the city of Madras.)
1952 India's first International Film Festival organized in Madras, Delhi, Mumbai and Calcutta.

1952   *The Jungle,* the first English film to be made in South India, is produced by Modern Theatres, with Cesar Romero, Rod Cameron and Mary Windsor in the cast.

1954   *Andha Naal,* the first Tamil film without any songs, is released. Other such films are *Unnaipol Oruvan, Kudisai, Veedu* and *Uchi Veyil.*

1955   *Kanavane Kan Kanda Deivam,* the first Tamil film to have some sequences in Geva colour, released. There had been films with hand-tinted colour sequences earlier.

1955   National awards for films instituted. *Malaikallam* selected the best feature film in Tamil.

1955   *Alibabavum 40 Thirudargalum,* the first full-length colour film, is made in Tamil by Modern Theatres.

1956   The Madras Film Society is formed by Ammu Swaminadhan and Rajammal Anantharaman.

1958   K B Sundarambal, the first film artiste to enter the legislature, is nominated to the Madras Legislative Council.

1959   Thamizh Nadigar Sangam, an association of film artistes, is founded by K Subrahmanyam.

1960   The Institute of Film Technology started in Adyar, Madras.

1967   M G Ramachandran, film star, wins an election, from Parangimalai constituency in Chennai and enters the legislature. S S Rajendran, another film star, wins from Theni constituency.

1967   Film Employees Federation of South India (FEFSI) established.

Milestones of Tamil Cinema

1972	The influence of the Institute of Film Technology, Madras is felt by Tamil cinema. A team of professionals from this institute make the film *Dhakam*.
1973	The first cinemascope film in Tamil, *Rajarajachozhan*, is made.
1985	First 3D film in Tamil, *Motherland/Annai Bhoomi*, is made.
1986	*The Great Soldier/Maveeran*, the first 70mm Tamil film, is released.
1990	*Marupakkam* gets the National award as the Best film in the country. First Tamil film to get this award.
1997	Sivaji Ganesan receives Dada Saheb Phalke award
2008	*Kanchivaram* gets the National award as the Best Film of the Year. Second Tamil film to get it.
2009	A R Rehman gets two Oscars for the Hollywood film *Slumdog Millionaire*.
2010	K Balachandar gets the Dada Saheb Phalke award.

Bibliography

Armes, Roy, *Third World Filmmaking and the West* (Los Angeles, University of California Press, 1987).

Barnouw, Eric, and S Krishnaswamy, *Indian Film* (Madras, Orient Longman, 1963).

Baskaran, Theodore S, *The Message Bearers: The Nationalistic Politics and Entertainment Media in South India 1880-1945* (Madras, Cre-A, 1981).

Burra Rani, *Looking Back 1986-1960* (New Delhi, Directorate of Film Festivals, 1981).

Cinema in Developing Countries, Symposium (New Delhi, Publications Division, Government of India, 1979).

Corliss, Richard, *Talking Pictures: Screen Writers of the American Cinema* (New York, Harper & Row, 1974).

Das Gupta, Chidananda, *Talking About Films* (New Delhi, Orient Longman, 1981).

Bibliography

Dungan, Ellis R with Barbara Smit, *A Guide To Adventure: An Autobiography*, Pittsburgh, 2001.

Gopal, PRS, *Natchathira Malai* (Tamil) (Madras, *Pesumpadum Kariyalayam*, 1949).

Guy, Randor, *History of Tamil Cinema* (Directorate of Information and Public Relations, Government of Tamil Nadu, 1991).

Huntley, John, and Roger Manwell, *The Technique of Film Music* (London, Focal Press, 1957).

The Impact of Film on Society (A Study of Tamil Nadu) (Madras, Centre for Social Research, 1974).

Irschick, Eugene F, *Tamil Revivalism in the 1930s* (Madras, Cre-A, 1986).

Kalki, *Kalaichelvam* (Essays on Tamil Cinema) (Madras, Bharathi Pathippagam, 1956).

Kannadasan, *Vanavasam* (Tamil), (Madras, Kannadasan Noolagam, 1965).

Kurosawa, Akira, *Something Like An Autobiography* (New York, Vintage Books, 1983).

Mahmood, Hameedudin, *The Kaleidoscope of Indian Cinema* (New Delhi, Affliated East-West Press Pvt Ltd., 1974).

Narayanan, Arandhai, *Thamizh Cinemavin Kathai* (Tamil), (Madras, New Century Book House, 1981).

Narayanan, V, *Kalaivanar Vazhvile* (Tamil), (Madras, Parandhaman Pathippagam, 1985).

Nataraja Pillai, T B, *Cinemavin Thennattu Varalaru* (Tamil) (Thanjavur, Published by the author, 1959).

Pandian, MSS, *The Image Trap: M.G.Ramachandran in Film and Politics,* (New Delhi, Sage, 1992).

Ramachandran, T M, (ed.) *Fifty Years of Talkie in India 1931-1981.* Souvenir, South Indian Film Chamber of Commerce (Mumbai, Indian Academy of Motion Picture Arts & Sciences, 1981).

Ramnath, T V , *Raja Sandow* (Kalachuvadu, 2012) Publishing Editor. S Theodore Baskaran

Ramachandran, T M, (ed.) 70 *Years of Indian Cinema* (1931-81) (Mumbai, Cinema -- India International 1985).

Ramaiya, B S, *Cinema?* (Tamil), (Madras, Jothi Nilayam, 1943).

Ramnath, T V, *Raja Sandow* (Tamil), (Madras, *Pesumpadam Kariyalayam*, 1943).

Report of the Indian Cinematograph Committee, 5 Vo.s (Calcutta, Government of India, Central Publiccations Branch, 1928).

Richman, Paula, *Women, Branch Stories and Religious Rhetoric in Tamil Buddhist Text* (New York, Syracuse University, 1988).

Sambanda Mudaliar, P, *Thamizh Pesum Pada Katchi* (Tamil), (Madras, 1937).

Sambanda Mudaliar, P, *Pesum Pada Anubavangal* (Tamil), (Madras, 1938).

Srinivas, N, *Cinema Ulagin Marmangal* (Tamil), (Madras, Talkatone Publishers, 1942).

Bibliography

Sivathamby Karthigesu, *Tamil Film as a Medium of Political Communication* (Madras, New Century Book House, 1981).

Swaminathan, Venkat, *Agraharathil Kazhuthai* (Tamil), (Madras, Sri Mani Pathippagam, 1977).

Articles

Ashokamitran, "The Great Dream Bazar", *The Illustrated Weekly of India* (Mumbai, 21 July 1985, 28 July 1985).

Ashokamitran, "A Case for Experimentalists in Tamil Films", *Indian Films and Film World* (Madras, 1976).

Bahadur, Satish, "The Nehru Years: Indian Filmmakers 1945-65" *Cinewave* No.6 (Mumbai, 1979).

Bahadur, Satish, *The Context of Indian Rim Culture,* Study Material Series, No.2. (Pune, National Film Archives, 1978).

Baskaran, Theodore S, "Cinema and History: The Other Dimension", *Deep Focus,* Vol.11, No.l (Bangalore, September 1989).

Hardgrave, Robert L Jr., and Anthony C Neidhart, "Films and Political Consciousness in Tamil Nadu", *Economic and Political Weekly* (Mumbai, 1 January 1975).

Hardgrave, Robert L Jr., "Politics and the Film in Tamil Nadu: The Stars and the DMK", *Asian Survey,* Vol.13 (1973).

Articles

Hariharan, K, "Writing for the Tamil Screen: Bleak Future?" *Cinema in India* (Mumbai, January-March 1989).

Hughes, Stephen, "The Sociology of Madras Cinema Audiences in the 1920s" (Unpublished paper, 1992).

Krishnaswamy, S, "The Major Films of My Father", Pamphlet, published on the occasion of the 80th birth anniversary of K Subrahmanyam (Madras 1984).

Murugadasa, "The Rise and Growth of Tamil Film" (Unpublished manuscript, 1976).

Shoesmith, Brian, "The Problem of Film: Reassessing the 1927/1928 Inquiry", *Continuum*, Vol.2, No.1, Asian Cinema Special (Perth, 1988-89).

Swarnavel Eswaran Pillai "*Iruvar*/The Duo" in *The Cinema of India*. Ed. Lalitha Gopalan, 2009.

Qamruddin, Mazhar, "Silent Films", *Chennai Film Society Souvenir* (Madras, 1983).

Glossary

Achkan	A longer version of the Jodhpuri coat.
Agraharam	The enclave where Brahmins live. Usually close to the temple.
Bajanai	Devotional group-singing.
Busby Berkely	Hollywood choreographer of the Thirties, known for his elaborately choreographed, geometric dance numbers.
Cinema verite	Cinema that captures life as it is. Attributed to filmmaker and theoritician Dzigo Vertov of Soviet Russia. He coined the term in 1922.
Dolly	Moving the cine camera on wooden rails while filming a scene.
Harijan	Dalits, considered to be at the bottom in the caste heirarchy.
Iris in /Iris out	A cinematic device to change shots.

Glossary

Jump cut	A cut between two shots that seems abrupt and calls attention to itself.
Kalakshepam	Musical narration of episodes from mythology.
Karagam	A folk dance in which the dancer balances a pot on his or her head.
Khadi	Handspun and handwoven cloth.
Montage	A method of editing in which a series of individual shots are connected to make a meaningful whole. This was developed by the Russian filmmaker Sergei Eisenstein.
Nagaswaram	A wind instrument on the lines of the clarinet.
Russian angle	Tilting the camera, to achieve an effect.
Thali	Symbol of marriage, a cord or gold chain worn by married women.
Themmangu	A form of folk song.
Therukoothu	Traditional street theatre of Tamil Nadu.
Villupaatu	A musical narration, sung to the accompaniment of strumming a bow.
Wipe	A transition from one scene to another in which the new scene gradually appears while "wiping" off the old.

Index

Abraham, John 153, 154
acting, stylized 19
Adults only 113
Adyar, studio in 196
Agatha Christie 185
ageing 143
Agnihothri, Rathi 159
Agnipravesam (short story) 153
Air Raid Precaution 26
alcholism 118
allegory 98
Alexander, J 193
All India Radio 49, 58, 232
Al Rm Company 98
Amala, actor 209
Amarnath, K 95
amateur actors in films 19
Ambikai, Goddess 100

Index

Ambujammal 16
Ammu Swaminadhan 239
Amusement Weekly (magazine) 236
anachronism in films 13, 132
Anandavikatan (magazine) 11, 16, 27, 60, 70, 101, 175, 176, 216
Anandhi films 164
Akkur Ananthachari 79
Ananthanarayanan K S 79
Andal, saint 151
Andaman islands 116
Angamuthu, K, actor 105
Angel Films Salem 214, 229
Anglo-Indian women in films 8
Anjali Devi, actor 112, 121
Annadurai, C N 29-32, 65, 85, 89, 106, 142, 202, 216, 230
Annamalai, E Dr 70
Annamalai University 24, 122, 208
anti-Brahmin 152
anti-capitalist 125
anti-caste appeal 15, 100
anti-child marriage 221
anti-hero 137, 178
anti-religious 33, 50, 107, 197
anti-priesthood 31, 111, 230
Anuradha Ramanan 164
Arangannal, Rama 36
Aravindaraj 165
Arutpa, devotional hymns 20
Archana, actor 169, 170
Arya Gana Sabha, 229
Asaithambi, A V P, 32, 36
Ashe, Robert William d'Escourt, District collector 135

Ashokamitran 219
Ashoka, the emperor 102
ashram, featured in films 107, 145
Associate Films 6, 202, 207, 212
As You Like It (play) 73, 175
atheistic propaganda 37, 230
audio cassettes 49, 67, 115, 130
Australian film industry 7
Avvaiyar, poetess 23, 24, 34, 218
A V M Productions 103, 160, 191, 210
Ayyamuthu, A, Kovai 23, 28, 105, 106, 176
Ayyanar, guardian deity 140

Babu Nandancode 145
Baby Saroja 99
Badami, Sarvotham 13, 27
Bagyaraj, K 159, 178-179, 186
Balachandar, K 137, 162, 180, 181, 231
Balachandar, S 119, 120, 182, 183, 196
Balaiya, T S 92, 106, 108, 116, 119, 139, 190
Balakrishnan, N, 160
Balasaraswathi, T, 79
Balasubramanian, G N 44, 125, 190, 225
Balasubramaniam, R 121
Balasundaram, Pavalar 114
Balu Mahendra 169, 170, 179, 183, 184, 193
Bannerji, Jiten 6
Bangalore, as a film production centre 6, 200
ban on films 10, 27, 28, 50, 99, 101, 172, 220
Banthulu, B R 134
Baskara Das 53, 91, 220, 221
"Battling" Mani, actor 8

Index

Batman 111
Berry, Violet, actor 8
Bhagavathi, T K, actor 127
Bhanuchandar, actor 169
Bharatanatyam 79, 139
Bharathi, *see* Subramanya Bharathi 20, 21, 103, 104, 117, 135, 136, 146, 227
Bharathiraaja 158, 159, 178, 185, 231
Bharathidasan, *see* Kanagasubbhurathinam 21, 22, 30, 53, 215, 227
Bhimsing, A 134, 135, 154, 187-188
Bhowal Sanyasi Case, 107
black market 104,105, 106, 115
Bhulabhai Desai 82
blind character in film 143, 146, 167
Bombay, Tamil films shot in 4, 6, 13, 26
bonded labour 193
Bose, Sailen 99
boycott of foreign cloth 79, 137, 200
Brahmin dialect, 66, 166
Bresson, Robert 153
British government 7, 50, 75-76, 83, 99, 221
brothel 150, 169
Buddha Pictures 134, 187
Buddhism 32
Burma 24, 25, 26, 200
bureaucracy 164
Busby Berkley, choreographer 103

cabaret 55, 165
Calcutta, Tamil films made at 13, 18, 46, 94, 98, 175, 193, 202, 205, 206, 207, 214,215
Caldwell, R 19

camera, concealed 159
camera, hand-held 168, 171
camera movement 109, 157
campus movement 11
cannabis, smoking 17
Capra, Frank 28, 30
Carnatic music, 40, 41, 79, 97, 122, 125,
Caste
    identities 150, 163
    in villages 161, 164
    see also anti-caste, low caste and Scheduled Caste
Cauvery, the delta 139, 228
censorship of films 10, 24, 101, 103
Central Board of Film Certification (*see* Film Censor Board) 25, 115, 120
Ceylon, *see* Sri Lanka 48, 107, 216
Chakrapani, M G 123
Chakravarthy, Venkatesh 61
Chalapathi Rao, T 124
Chalukyas 132
Chandamarutham (magazine) 216
Chandrababu 53
Chandragupta, the play 99
Chandrasekhar, Raja 101, 102, 206, 207
Chandrodhayam, the play 29
Chaplin, Charlie 15, 138
Chari, T V 22, 25, 64
charisma of film stars 78
charkha, as symbol of nationalism 76, 91, 101
Chatterjee, Sarat Chandra 118
Chellappa, V A 22
Chera dynasty 22

Index

Chettiar A K 177
Chettiar, P S 237
Chidambaranathan, M M 75, 87
child actors, 147, 183, 192
Chinnappa, P U 96, 97, 98, 206, 223, 227
Chipko movement 129
Chithravani (magazine) 197
Chittrarasu, C P 194
Chokkalinga Bhagavathar, M A 170, 171
Chola dynasty 21, 22, 93, 94, 113, 127, 132, 133
Cho Ramasamy 142
Christian 108, 134, 148, 149, 162, 172
Cinema Ulagam (magazine) 27, 87
Cinema
    grammar of 9, 10
    plasticity of 36
    vocabulary of 9
    specific characteristics of 57
cinema of dissent 29-30
cinema studies xiii, xiv, 10
Cinema verite 157
Cinematic
    conventions 9, 13, 171, 217
    elements 56
    experiments 67
    film 146
    kitsch 210
    language 9
Cine Technicians Associations 198, 212
circus 96, 208, 211
Civil Disobedience movement 19, 72, 79, 86, 91
civil defence 26

classical music 41, 42, 44, 45, 57, 58, 78, 226
classical music featured in films 97, 106
classical musicians 42, 44, 58
class struggle 120
Cohen 235
Coimbatore 23, 31, 68, 81, 93, 106, 108, 209, 216
coincidence in filmic narration 131
colonial rule 20
colour sequences 177, 255
colour film, first used 124, 215
commercial broadcasting 48, 49
communal harmony 134, 135
communal riots 116
Communist movement 53
Communists, using films 120
company drama 14, 18, 41, 42, 43, 44, 63, 74, 75, 86, 231
conflicts, resolution of 119
Congress party 16, 17, 24, 71, 72, 80-86, 93, 101, 224, 229, 230
Cooper, E R 98
Coppola, Francis Ford 169
Corelli, Marie, novelist 112
Count of Monte Cristo, The (novel) 31, 107
courtesan 21, 64, 112, 113, 127, 140
courtroom scenes in films 35, 172
crane shots 103, 173
Crown Theatre 4
crucifixion 144

DMK, *see* Dravida Munnetra Kazhagam
colours of DMK 143
dance drama 133, 152
Dandabani Desikar, M M, 44, 122

Index

Das, C R 80
De Sica, Vittorio 185
Delhi Ganesh 158, 159
Depression years 30
Desabakthi, the play 86
Durgabai Deshmukh 86
Devaraj -Mohan, *see* Mohan 151
Devika, actor 134
Devi Nataka Sabha 225
Devudu Aiyar 42, 79
Dey, K C, singer 222, 93, 94
Dharmalingam Mudaliar, S M, 4, 201
dialect, regional 68, 136, 164
dialogue
    delivery 68, 129
    rhetorical 32, 34, 36, 64, 65
dialogue writers 22, 30, 32, 34, 36, 37, 65, 67, 68, 114
diglossic language 65
doctors, depiction of 167
dominance of spoken words in Tamil films 31, 35, 36, 46, 63-64, 68, 69, 103, 181, 208, 217, 222
double acting 99, 177
double entendres 52
drama films 4
Draupathi, M S, 116
Dravidian movement 71, 71, 80, 84, 85, 86, 111, 198, 199, 224, 231
Dravida Munnetra Kazhagam, 29, 86, 106, 115, 127, 128, 135, 194, 210, 217, 223, 224
Dravidanadu, the magazine 231
drinking scenes in films 118, 129, 143, 156
Drum dance 104, 211
Dumas, Alexander 107

Dungan, Ellis R, 92-95, 110, 190-191
Dupont 3
Durai, filmmaker 149-151, 158, 189, 195
Durairaj, T S, 66, 108
Duraiswamy Ayyengar, Vaduvoor, novelist 15

East India Company 128, 207
Edison, 3, 235
Edwards, M 1
Eisenstein, Sergie 10
Electric Theatre 2
Elphinstone Theatre 78, 93
Empire films 7
escapist entertainment 57
eternal triangle 125, 130, 212
European Association 77
Eucharistic Congress 219
Evans, W 236
E V R, *see* Ramasamy Naicker
eye-level shots 35
Exhibitor Film Services 6, 200
"explainers" 9, 62
extraneous programmes 9

Fairbanks, Douglas 115
falling at the feet of the man 120, 131
fan clubs 210
Fatima Begum 207
feminist ideas 173
fencing 111, 124, 206, 218
fight sequences 9, 127, 137, 168
fight, stylized 168

Index

Film and Television Institute of India, Pune ix, 154, 185
Film Festival
    Cannes 196
    Tashkent 192
    Toronto 175, 193
    India, International 175, 193
Film Federation of India 218
film music 39-41, 45, 46, 48, 49, 54-58, 159, 196
Film Producers Guild 214
Films Division of the Government of Tamil Nadu, 206
Film society 11
Film songs
    as an independent product 48
    characteristics of 48
    erotic 54-55, 224
    in rural areas 55
    for propaganda 50
Film stars, involvement in politics 78-82
filmic conventions 217
filmic narration 54, 69, 186, 193, 218
First World War 10
Flaherty, Robert 200
Flynn, Errol 112, 113
folk deities 126,186
folk music 40, 42, 48, 54, 228
folk songs 26, 42, 43, 128, 227
freedom fighters 173, 194
freedom movement 16, 74
French Revolution 109

GPC – General Pictures Corporation 6, 8, 200, 204, 205
Gaiety Theatre 4

Gandhiji
    opposed by Satyamurthi 77
    Salt Satyagraha 79, 86
    77th Birthday celebrations 103
    temple entry programme 100
    tour of Tamil Nadu 91
    views on cinema 82
    visit to Palani 106
Ganga, the river 156
Gemini Ganesh 130, 132, 134, 135
Gemini Studios 24, 26, 198, 211, 217, 218
gender issues 157
George V, King 236
Gingee fort, as shooting location 99, 205
Globe Theatre 4
Gogate, G G 204
Gohar, actor 78, 96, 208
Gopalakrishnan K S (1), 177
Gopalakrishnan K S (2), 79, 88, 192
Gopalakrishnan V 108, 165, 233
Ghosh, Nemai 119, 120
gramophone 2, 3, 14, 19, 40, 44, 48, 50, 67, 74, 82
group dances 9, 125, 138, 146, 179, 210
Guhan Films 137
guillotine 127
Gujarati, language 5, 209
gymnasts in films 8

Hariharan, K, filmmaker 178, 219
Harvey, G T B 25
Havelock, Arthur, Governor of Madras 1
Hiuen Tsang 133

Index

Hindu
Hindu, The (Daily) 13, 14, 25, 63, 93
Hindustani music 41, 42, 47, 106
historical film 93, 94, 99, 102, 112, 128, 132, 133, 136
Hitchcock, Alfred 167, 184
Hollywood xii, 6, 31, 32, 92, 102, 190
housing problem 170
Huffton, T H 4, 11

Ibrahim T M 119
Ilangovan, *see* Thanikachalam T K
Ilayaraja 57, 58, 151, 152, 156, 160, 168, 170, 172, 186, 232
illiteracy 77, 80
Imperial Movietone Company 90
impotency 192
Inbasagaran, the play 106
Indian Cinematograph Act of 1918 236
India Film Company 4, 201
Indian Legislative Assembly 72
Indian Parliament, Rajya Sabha 218
Indian Peoples Theatre Association 214
indigenous productions 7
Institute of Film Technology, Madras 146, 203, 217
insurance for films 214
inter-caste marriage 85
International Year of the Handicapped 148
International Year of Shelter 170
Irani, Ardeshir 202
Irani, Bomman 96

Jainism in Tamil country 21
Jaishankar, actor 166

Jallianwala Bagh massacre 74, 221
Janaki S R, actor 142
Janakaraj, actor 168
Janaki, Sowkar 141
Janaki V N 106, 108
Javert, Seetharaman 108-110
Jayabharathi, filmmaker 173, 174, 193
Jayakanthan 141, 154, 156, 180
Jayalakshmi, T A 103
Jayalalithaa 210, 213, 142
Jeyamohan, B, 181, 196
Jeevamani (magazine) 202
joint family 92, 161, 162
Jupiter pictures 30, 33, 105, 106, 112, 211, 216
Justice Party 80, 83, 84
Jwala, group of film buffs 173

Kadarin Vetri, play 86
Kai Vilangu (novelette) 141
Kalaivanar, *see* N S Krishnan
Kalavathy, N Dr, 88, 219
Kali N Rathinam, actor 26, 96, 97
Kalki (writer) *see* Krishnamurthy R
Kalyanasundaram, Pattukottai 227-229
Kamala, Kumari (Laxman) 103, 104, 132
Kamala Kamesh 161
Kamalahasan 156, 158, 168, 170, 183
Kamaraj K, 84, 87
Kambar, poet, 22, 93
Kambadasan, 222-223
Kanagasabai Pillai V, 20
Kanagasubburathinam, *see* Bharathidasan

Index

Kannada films, 182, 185, 186, 189, 190, 195, 203, 213, 215
Kannadasan, 35, 36, 53, 127, 128, 135, 138, 211-212, 216, 223-224, 232
Kannagi, literary character, 21, 64, 152, 206
Kannan, Jalakantapuram Pa, 64, 224
Kannamba, P 64, 101, 119, 152, 206
Karachi, communal riots in 116
Karaikudi, make-shift studios in 104
Karthick, actor 186-187
Karthikeya Films 197
Karunanidhi A 110, 140
Karunanidhi M 29, 32, 35, 65, 66, 85, 111, 114, 115, 217
Kattabomman 128
kattiyakaran 122
Koundamani 160
Kesavan K P 92, 96, 97
Keskar, B V, central minister 68
Khilafat agitation 221
Kindhanar ballad 231
Ki Ra, writer 25
Kittappa, S G 42, 81
Kokko, S S 95, 96
Kothainayaki Ammal, Vai Mu, 96-97, 176
Krishnadevaraya Emperor 35
Krishnan, N S, *see* Kalaivanar 15, 25, 32, 66, 85-86, 93, 97, 101, 103, 121, 122, 124, 126, 230, 231
Krishnan-Panju, *see* Panju 34, 114, 137, 142, 187
Krishnamurthy, Ku Sa, 116
Krishnamurthy, Maharajapuram M R, 15
Krishnamurthy, R, *see* Kalki 33, 37, 38, 60, 101, 132, 133, 233
Kumaran (magazine) 202
Kumudini, T V, actor 98, 99

Kundalakesi (classic) 110
Kurosawa, Akira 184
Kutti Padmini, actor 149

Labour movement 117
Lalitha, actor 108, 111, 118
Lalitha, Tambaram, 158
Lakshmi, actor 5, 121, 141, 154, 156, 165-166, 172-173
Lakshmi, S N, actor 137
Lang, Fritz 10
Les Miserables (novel) 108, 148
Lingappa, T G 121
Loganathan, Tiruchi, singer 111
Lokanathan, B S, cinematographer 163
Loyola College, Chennai 154

Madan Company, 6
Madhavan, P, filmmaker 144, 148
Madhuri Devi 110, 111, 112
Madras Christian College 72
Madras Film Society 239
Madras Tamil dialect 158, 159
Madras United Artistes Corporation 99, 214
Mamallapuram 133, 198
Mahadevan, K J 99
Mahadevan, K V 139, 144
Mahalingam, T R 103, 227, 229
Mahendran, J, filmmaker 185, 194
Mail, The (daily) 5, 197
Mamoulin, Rouben 31
Mani Ratnam 168, 195, 196
Mani, M V 79

Index

Manikodi (magazine) 22, 197, 200
Manimekalai (epic) 21
Manoj Gyan 166
Manonmaneeyam (play) 22
Manorama, actor 139, 161, 163, 172
Maran, Murasoli 35
Marconi, T 17
Marina beach 147, 157
Marudakasi, A 225-226
Marudamuthu Moopanar 236
Marudu brothers 128, 129
Maruthi Rao, S 114, 137, 142
Masthan, M 106, 112
Meena Narayanan 219
Meenakshi Cinetone 18, 214
Melodrama 134, 151, 186, 196, 210, 212, 213, 217
Metro Studios 204
Meyyappa Chettiar, AVM 103, 202
MGR, *see* Ramachandran M G
middle class 121, 138, 162, 170, 171, 182
Modern Theatres, Salem 25, 30, 110, 123, 191, 215, 216, 223
Mohideen, S K 33
Motion Picture Combines 214, 218
Movie Mirror (magazine) 200
Mullick, Pankaj 102
Mullil Roja (play) 202
Murugadasa 197-198, 211
Murugan Talkies 90, 101, 207
music video 196
Muslim 66, 134-135
Mustafa, M K 128
Muthuraman, actor 137, 146, 149

Muthusamy Dikshithar 227
Muthusamy Kavirayar, Sarabam Udumalai, poet, 75, 118, 225, 230
Muthuswamy, T K 8, 15
mythologicals 7, 9, 12, 41, 43, 66, 92, 97, 104, 115, 192, 198, 205, 222

N S K Drama Company 104
Nadkarni, Sundararao 6
Nagaiya, V 69, 78, 101, 108, 110, 140
Nagarajan, A P 139-140, 192, 198-199
Nagarajan, S 119
nagaswaram 139, 140, 156
Nageswara Rao, A 118, 119, 130
Nagesh 137-138, 141, 154
Nambiar, M N 104, 105, 124, 139, 140
Nandanar, saint 231
Nanditha Bose 146
Narayana Kavi, Udumalai 118, 225,230-231
Narayanan, A 5, 6, 10, 18, 199, 200, 205, 206
Narayanasamy, T V 85
Narasimhabharathi, P V 11, 105
Nataraja Mudaliar 4, 5, 8, 201
Natarajan, S A 110
Nataraja Pillai, T B 11
National Movietone 96, 217
nationalist propaganda 16, 24, 76, 95, 205
nationalist songs 50, 104, 221, 230
Neelakantan, P 121, 202
Nehru, Motilal 73, 80
Netaji, 233
newsreel 116, 205
New Theatres, Calcutta 94

Index

Nizhalkal Ravi 168
Non-Brahmin movement 77
Non-cooperation movement 75

Odeon Gramophone company 230
Old men marrying young women, practice of 106
Omalev, Michael 27
opera 74, 231
Oomaithurai, Poligar 128
oriental dance 54
Orrs Gramophone and Talkies 14

Packiam, M S S 105
Padma awards 183, 196, 218, 227, 234
Padmanabhan, R xv, 6, 203-204, 208
Padmini 108, 111, 124, 125, 126, 139, 140, 144, 152
Pakshiraja Films 108
Pal, Bipin Chandra 137
Pallava dynasty 132-133
Pandari Bai 114, 149
Pandyan dynasty 21, 22, 23
Pandian, M S S 60, 89, 178
Pandithurai Thevar 136
Panju, *see* Krishnan-Panju
Parsi drama companies 41
Paari, the Tamil king 24
Parthasarathy, Y G 154
Patel Purse Fund 78
Pathe of United States 3
Pathe of France 204
patriotic cinema 98, 100
patriotic songs 81, 221

Pattammal, D K 222
Paul Muni 31, 37
period films 46, 126
period flavour 109, 169, 196,
Periyar, *see* Ramasamy Naicker, EV
Perumal, K A 33, 98
Perumal, K K 92, 98
Phalke, Dada Saheb 183
photographed drama 191
photographed variety entertainment 57
platform speech 65, 67
play, adaptation for film 13,22, 30,114, 116, 137, 138, 145, 163, 202, 211, 212
play within a film 153
playback singing 46, 53, 55,
Poddar 219
Poligars 126
Pope, G U 19
pornography 150
Prakasa, R 5-6, 200, 204
Prakasam, N 108
Prakash Rao, T 124
Premchand, Munshi 16
pre-recording 45
prohibition 77
propaganda films xiii, 16, 17, 24, 25-26, 29, 36, 49-50, 53, 65, 75-76, 78, 80, 85-86, 128, 191, 200, 205, 231
prostitute 118, 150, 159
Pudumaipithan 194
Pullaiya, C 5, 200
Pullaiya, P 186
Pune, Tamil films made in 4, 13, 201, 208

Index

Puranas 7, 63
Puttanna Kanagal 186

"quick-cutting" 186

rpm 14, 45, 48, 222
Radha, actress 186
Radha, M K 26, 92
Radha, M R 86, 215, 134, 135
Radha Bai, M M 96
Radha Ravi 163
Radio Ceylon 48
Ragini, of Travancore sisters 132
Raghunath, T R, filmmaker 206-207
Raghuvaran, actor 161
Raja, A M, singer 130
Rajaji , *see* C Rajagopalachari 23, 87, 88
Rajakumari, T R 214
Rajalakshmi,T P 90, 91
Rajam, M N 123, 128
Rajamanikkam, Nawab 106, 192, 225,
Rajambal, Thevaram 90
Rajamma M V 106
Rajan, A V M 142
Rajarathinam Pillai, musician 191
Raja Sandow 10, 14, 21, 78, 177, 204, 208-209
Rajasulochana 119
Rajender, T 209-210
Rajendran, S S 86, 114, 128
Rajesh 165
Rajnikanth 156, 158, 183

Ramachandran, M G, *see* M G R 52, 86, 101, 103, 108, 110, 111, 112, 113, 116, 117, 123, 124, 126, 127, 142, 143, 180, 182, 203, 206, 207, 212, 216, 224, 225, 228, 233
Ramaiya, B S 197
Ramaiyadas, Thanjai 229
Ramakrishna Paramahamsa 155
Ramalinga Swamigal, *see* Vallalar 20, 23, 206
Ramamurthy, *see* Viswanathan-Ramamurthy
Ramanathan, G, music director 110, 125, 126
Ramasamy, K R 85, 86, 106, 119
Ramasamy Naicker, *see* Periyar 29
Ramasamy, V, *see* Va Ra writer 108, 197, 200
Ramasamy, V K 198
Ramasamy Aiyar, C P 24
Ramayana (epic) 93, 150
Ramnoth, K, filmmaker 69, 108, 112, 197, 211-212, 223
Ranade, Ashok 47, 60
Ranga, B S 118
Ranga Rao V A K x, 59
Ranga Rao, S V 132
Randor Guy ix, 176, 177, 219, 220
Rangachari, P B 93
Rangavadivelu 4, 201
Rao, P V 119
Rao, Y V 5, 200
rape victim 117
Rathnabai, P S 15
rationalist ideas 115
Ray, Satyajit 68, 185
"record dance" 55
Reddy, B N 211
Reddy, H M 90, 98

Index

reformist ideas 16, 22, 34, 231
reservation for jobs 172, 173
retirement 144-145
Revathi, actor 186
Reynolds, G W 6
Riskin, Robert 30-31
ritualism 32
Romeo and Juliet, play 94, 191
Rudhraiya, filmmaker 156-157
Rukmani, K T, actor 96
Rukmani, actor 135
"rush directors" 191

Sattai, (magazine) 199
Sadagopan, V V 44, 197
Sahadevan, E R 141
Sahasranamam, S V 114, 140
Saigal, K L 222
saint films 14, 15, 24
Sakthi Nataka Sabha 227
Salem as a film producing centre 30, 111, 215, 223, 230
Samanna, actor 15
Sambanda Mudaliar, P 20, 47, 73, 222
Sambandam, P T 140
Sampath, E V K 37
Sangam period 20, 21, 24
Sangeet Natak Academy 227
Sankaradas Swamigal 139
Santhanalakshmi, M R 22
Saradambal, P 98
Sarangapani, K 116, 140
Saritha 163, 166

Saroja Devi 130
Saroja, M 130
Sati, practice of 129
Satyamurthi, S 71-86, 99, 200
Savithiri 153
Scheduled caste 172
Scott, Sir Walter 132
Seagull, Jonathan Livingston, 158
Second World War 23, 24, 114, 191
Self-respect movement 20, 29, 84, 231
Serukalathur Sama 8, 21, 93, 112
Sethna, Fram 96, 98, 171
Shakespeare 22, 94-95, 176, 211
Shakunthala, G 110
Shankar, K 128
Shankar-Ganesh, *see* Ganesh 158, 161
Shanmugam, T K 81, 135
Shantaram, V 19, 213
Sharada, actor 148
Sharada, Mother 155
Shekhar, A 197, 212
Shoba, actor 158-159, 190
siddhar 229
Silapathikaram (epic) 21
Simon Boycott Propaganda Committee 76
Singh, C S D 98
Sinhalese films 203, 215
Sirumalai hills 147
Sivagnanam, Ma Po 121, 122, 199
Sivaji Ganesan 35, 66, 69, 114, 121, 122, 124, 125, 134, 136, 139, 140,141, 144, 145, 148, 188, 199, 203, 234
Sivakumar 141, 151

Index

Sivan, Papanasam 44, 93, 94, 99, 101, 197, 214, 225, 226, 231
Smith, Stewart 4, 201
smoking 17, 143, 156
soap opera, 162
"socials" 14
Socrates 35
soliloquies 69, 145
Somasundara Bharathi 20
Somayajulu, A A 21
songbook 48
Sound and Shadow, magazine 197
Sound City 18
sound, in association with images 131
sound technology 45, 49
Sound track 168
Soundararajan, T M 111, 225
South Indian Artists Association 15
South Indian Film Chamber of Commerce 80, 214, 216
South India Film Corporation 14
Sridhar, C V 125, 130, 212-213
Srikanth, actor 144, 148, 151, 154, 156
Sri Lanka, *see* Ceylon also 48, 107, 216
Srinivasa Aiyar, Semmangudi 79
Srinivasa Cinetone 18, 43, 200, 205, 206, 208
Srinivasa Rao, P S 26, 95
Srinivasan, M B 146, 147, 153
Srinivasan, Stalin 33
Sri Priya, actor 156, 158
Sri Ram, P C 168
Sriranjani 114
Srividya 173
stage, influence of 14

stardom 138
star-politicians 85
Star of the East Film Company 5, 204
Stephen, George 184
studio, glass-roofed 204
stunt-comedian 96
"Stunt" Raju 8
St Joseph's College, Tiruchi 197
St Thomas 149
Subbaiya, Master 111
Subbaiya Naidu, S M, 106, 108, 112
Subbaiya, S V 105, 141, 151
Subbaraman, C R 106, 112, 118
Subramanya Aiyar, Musiri 44
Subramanya Bharathi, *see* Bharathi 20, 21, 136, 137, 147, 228
Subramania Siva 136
Subrahmayam, K 6, 26, 99, 100, 116, 204, 213
Subbulakshmi, M S 44, 191, 221, 226
Subbulakshmi, S D 26, 99
Sudarsanam, R 103, 114
Sudarsana Gana Sabha 229
Suddhanandha Bharathi 108
Suguna Vilas Sabha 4, 73, 201-202
Sujatha, actor 151, 183
Sumithra 149
Sundaram, S D 64
Sundaram Pillai 22
Sundaram, T R 25, 123, 215-216
Sundrambal, K B 46, 81, 221
Sundararajan, Major 137, 146
Sundaribai 26, 154, 156
Sushila, J 90

Index

Susheela Devi, T 90
Swadesamithran (daily) 1, 20
Swadeshi movement 136, 200
Swadeshi Steam Navigation Company 136
Swami, A S A 33, 64, 106, 107, 113, 216
Swaminatha Aiyar, U V 20
Swaminatha Sarma 86
Swaminathan, Komal 163
Swarajists 80

T K S Brothers Drama Company 116
Tamil
    classic 20, 110
    consciousness 23
    Epics 21, 63, 216
    glorification of 199
    population 24
    revivialism 20, 22, 24, 106, 113
television xi, 40, 49, 154, 226
temperance 17, 100, 222, 231
Thamizharasu Party 199
Thamizh Nadigar Sangam 279
Thamizhthai 17, 22, 50
Thangavelu, K A 123-124, 125, 130, 140, 144
Thanikachalam, T K, *see* Ilangovan 64
Thengai Srinivasan 149
Theosophical Society 8
Therukoothu 142
Thevar, O A K 126
Thirukural (classic) 21, 230
Thotta Tharani 169, 196
thriller 14-15, 167, 184, 186

title card 5, 9, 62, 113, 202
Thyagaraja Bagavathar, M K 78, 93, 94, 101, 191, 214, 227
toddy- tapper 141-142
trade union 117, 120, 167
trade union in film studios 193
Travancore sisters 108
Twelfth Night (play) 211

Uday Shankar 211
unemployment 117, 122
Universal City Studios 200
University of Madras, Senate 89
untouchability 100, 127, 198, 214

Va Ra, *see* Ramasamy, Va 108, 197, 200
Vaiyadurai, T 146-147
Vaidhyanatha Aiyar, Yanai 96
Vaidyanathan, L 173
Vairamuthu 232
Vali 233-234
Vallalar, *see* Ramalinga Swamigal
Vannanilavan 157
Varadarajan, T R 11
Varalakshmi, S 128
Vasagam, S K 236
Vasan, S S 217-218
vathiyar in company dramas 41, 198, 229
vathiyar, referring to M G R 143
vattara vazhakku 68
Vedantham Ragaviah 118
Veda, musician 132
Veerappa, P S 123, 124, 128

Index

Vel Pictures 18, 197, 211
Velan, A K 36, 182
Vendetta (novel) 112
Venkatesan, P G 90
Venkiah, R 3, 5, 204
Venus Pictures 124, 130
Victoria Public Hall, Madras 1, 2, 3
Victoria, Queen 109
Vidor, King 164
Vijaya, K R 137
Vijayakanth 116
Vijayakumari 130
Vijayan, K G 110
Vijayan, K 141
Vijayan, R 141
Vijayaraghavachariar, Salem 136
village deities 141, 142
Village life 142, 152, 164, 166, 186
Villupattu 86, 142
Vincent, A, cinematographer 124-125, 130, 213
Vincent, Swamikannu 2
violence in political life 167
violent scene 181, 196
Visu, actor 161, 162, 163
visual narration 167
Viswanatha Aiyar, Maharajapuram 78
Viswanathan-Ramamurthy, *see* Ramamurthy 128, 134, 137, 188, 213, 224
Viswanathan, M S 142, 148, 154, 163, 165, 225, 233
Viswanathan, Poornam 172
Vijayanthimala 132

Waheeda Rehman 124
war effort film 25, 216
war publicity 25-26
Warwick Major 2
Washington Post, The (daily) 167
Welsh, Col 128, 129
western music, pop 46
Western music, classical 57
widow 8, 15, 114, 117, 145, 155, 156, 165, 190
wife beating 131
Whitaker 5
Wood, Ernest 8
woman, first music director 27
woman, first sound recordist 219
woman, wronged, portrayal of 166
women, derogatory comments on 113
woman, single 155

Yama, the God of death 121, 124
Yoganand 126, 132, 189
Yogi, S D S 92

zamindar 105, 140

Index to Film Titles

Aboorva Raganga 183
Aboorva Sakodharargal (Gemini), 219
Achamillai...Achamillai 182-183
Adhiparasakthi 192
Adventures of Robinhood (English), 113
Agraharathil Oru Kazhuthai 153
Akeli (Urdu), 115
Alibabavum 40 Thirudarkalum 123
Allavudinum Arputha Vilakkum 207
Alli Arjuna 14
Amaradeepam 124, 212, 230
Ambikapathi (1937), 22, 64, 93-94, 197
Ambikapathi (1957), 203
Ammaiyappan 187, 188
Anadhaipenn (silent), 8, 10, 176
Anadhaipenn (talkie), 205
Ananthasayanam 214
Anasuya (Telugu), 127

Andal Tirukalyanam 207
Andaman Kaithi 116
Andha 7 Natkal 180
Andha Naal 120, 184
Annai 192
Annai Bhoomi 240
Annaiyin Anai 35
Annakili 57, 151, 152
Araichimani 21, 209
Arangetram 183
Arrival of the Train (silent), 1
Ashokumar 64, 101-102, 207
Athithan Kanavu 64, 216
Au Hasard Balthazar 153
Aval Appadithan 156
Avalum Penthane 149, 159
Avan 177, 181
Avana Ivan 184
Avan Amaran 119-120, 184
Avvaiyar 23, 34, 219
Ayiram Thalaivangi Aboorva Chinthamani 229
Azhagarmalai Kallan 223
Azhiyatha Kolangal 185-186

Babul (Hindi), 115
Baghdad Thirudan 216
Bagyaleela 17
Baktha Chetha 214, 227
Baktha Kabirdas 93
Baktha Kalathi 204
Baktha Kuchela 27, 214, 227
Baktha Kumanan 20

Index to Film Titles

Baktha Pothanna (Telugu), 211
Baktha Ramdas 8, 63, 198
Bakthavathsala (silent), 209
Balamani 21
Balan (Malayalam), 215
Balayogini 15, 16, 18, 19, 214-215
Battleship Potemkin (silent), 10
Bhoja 206
Bilhanan 27
Bommai 177, 184
Boolokarambai 212
Burma Rani 25, 28, 177, 215, 216,

Captain Marvel (English), 95
Catechist of Killarney, The (Silent), 205
Chakradhari 192
Chandidas (Hindi), 46
Chandrakantha 209
Chandraleka 59, 66, 104, 211, 218, 219
Chandramohan 207, 208
Chenchulakshmi (Telugu), 59
Chinnanchiru Ulagam 193
Chinthamani 229
Chithi 177
Choodamani (Telugu), 209
City Lights (English), 138
Coral Queen, The (silent), 206
Count of Monte Cristo, The (English), 31, 107

Dakshayagnam 79, 208
Danger Signal 95
Dasavatharam (1976), 193

Dasipenn 192
Deivathai 182
Deivathin Deivam 193
Desamunnetram 193
Devadas (1937), 222
Devadas (1953), 118-119
Devaki 184
Devasundari (Telugu), 205
Devil and the Damsel (silent), 209
Dhakam 146
Dharmapathini (silent), 6, 10, 200
Dharmapathini (talkie), 17
Dhuruva 98, 177
Digambara Samiyar 216
Dopatta (Urdu), 115
Draupathi Vasthiraparanam (silent), 5, 202
Draupathi Vasthiraparanam (talkie), 230
Dumbachari 15

Edhirneechal 118
Edhu Nijam 184
Elephant Boy, The (English), 200
Elephant Walk (English), 102
Ellam Inba Mayam 204
En Annan 203
Enga Veetu Pillai 233
En Kanavar 183, 184
En Magal 208
En Magan 216
En Thangai Kalyani 210
Ethiroli 183
Ethirparathathu 192, 212

Index to Film Titles

Ezhai Padum Padu 211, 212

Fire Fly, The (English), 59
Flash Gordon (English), 95

Gajendra Moksham (silent), 205
Gallatakalyanam 213
Galavarishi 13
Garuda Garva Bangam (silent), 201
Gas Light (English), 32
Geethagandhi 215
Gnanasoundari (silent), 198, 201, 208, 223
Gnanasoundari (1935), 206
Gnanavoli 148
Godfather (English), 169, 195
Gulebakavali (1935), 62, 66
Gulebakavali (1955), 53
Gunasundari 34, 176

Hamsageethe (Kannada), 189
Haridas 47, 177, 227
Harishchandra (1932), 13

Idhu Nijama? 183
Ilamai Oonjaladukiradhu 213
Indra Sabha 206
Iru Kodugal 183
Irumbu Thirai 219
Iru Sakodarargal 78, 92, 103
It Happened one Night (English), 31
Ivan the Terrible (Russian), 113
Izhandha Kathal 231

Jalaja 79, 192
Johnny 194
Jothi alladhu Srimath Ramalinga Swamigal 20
Jungle, The (English), 215

Kachadevayani 215
Kadu 190
Kaithi 183
Kalaiyarasi 228
Kalam Mari Pochu 51, 164
Kalamegam 22, 191
Kalathur Kannamma 188
Kalidas 43, 62, 63, 76, 90, 91, 221, 222
Kalinganarthanam (silent), 202
Kallukul Eeram, 187
Kalpana (Hindi), 211
Kalyana Agathikal 183
Kalyaniku Kalyanam 217
Kalyanaparisu 228, 130, 212
Kanavane Kan Kanda Deivam 206
Kanavan Manaivi 188
Kanjan 23, 105
Kankatchi 199
Kannagi 21, 64, 152, 206
Kannamma En Kathali 26
Kapal Kuntala (Hindi), 102
Kappalotiya Thamizhan 135, 136
Kathanayaki 212
Kausalya 14
Kaval Deivam 141
Kavalkaran 203
Keechakavatham (silent), 202

Index to Film Titles

Kizhake Pogum Rayil 179, 187
Kizhattu Mappillai 206
Kovalan (silent), 13
Kovalan (talkie), 205
Krishna Arjuna, 205
Krishna Leela 227, 230
Krishna Tulabaram 219
Kubera Kuchela 227
Kudisai 193, 194
Kulamagal Radhai 199
Kumari 204
Kumarikottam 203
Kurathi Magan 193, 231

Lava Kusa (silent), 202
Leaving the Factory (silent), 1
Life of Jesus Christ (silent), 3
Life of Emile Zola The, 31

Machavathar (silent), 236
Madanakamarajan 218
Madras Must Not Burn (English), 26
Madurai Veeran 35, 126, 127, 224
Mahatma Gandhi 177
Maheswari 228
Mahatma Kabirdas (silent), 205
Mahiravanan (silent), 5, 202
Maithili Ennai Kathali 210
Maitreyi Vijayam (silent), 202
Makkalai Petra Makarasi 68
Malaikallam 239
Manasamrakshanam 215

Mandhirikumari 35, 94, 110, 191, 225
Mangaiyarkarasi 223
Mangamma Sabatham 211
Manimekalai 21
Manithan 212
Manohara 35, 66, 73
Manonmani 22, 64, 215
Manvasanai 187
Mappillai Azhaippu 207
Mandhirikumari 35, 94, 110, 191, 225
Maria My Darling 190
Markandeya (silent), 5, 202
Markandeya (talkie), 198
Marmayogi 112, 212, 223
Marudanattu Ilavarasi 62, 65
Mathrubhoomi 98, 177
Maya Bazaar (1935), 204
Maya Bazaar (1957), 230
Mayajothi 204, 230
Maya Machindra 208
Mayavathi 216, 225
Meera 44, 192
Melnattu Marumagal 199
Menaka 8, 15, 208, 209
Minal Dinar (silent) 207
Minnalkodi 95, 96
Missiamma 229, 230
Miss Kamala 91
Miss Sundari 176, 222
Mohini 207, 212
Mohini Rukmangatha 207
Moonrampirai 186, 225

Index to Film Titles

Moonru Mudichu 183
Moonru Pengal 205
Mouna Geethangal 180
Mr Deeds Goes to Town (English), 30
Mullum Malarum 194, 185
Mundhanai Mudichu 52, 180
Mudhal Thedhi 121, 122, 203

Nadodoi Mannan 207, 212
Nadu Iravil 184
Nalla Idathu Sambandham 198
Nallathambi 30, 32, 231
Nallavan Vazhvan 35, 233
Nallathangal 98
Nalvar 198
Nam Iruvar 103, 202
Nanal 183
Nandanar (silent), 46, 66, 77, 78, 81, 198, 201
Nandanar (talkie 1933), 14
Nandanar (1935), 46
Nandanar(1942), 198
Nandu 195
47 Naatkal 183
Naveena Satharam 214
Nayakan 168
Neengal Kettavai 186
Neerkumizhi 182
Neethipathi 217
Nenjathai Killathe 195
Nenjil Oor Aalayam 213
Nenjil Oru Ragam 210
Netru Inru Nalai 203

Nizhalgal 232
Noolveli 182

Olivilakku 52
Oomai Janangal 193
Oomai Vizhigal 166
Oor Iravu 203
Ore Oru Gramathile 172-173
Oru Kai Osai 180
Oru Kaithiyin Diary 187
Oru Kudumbathin Kathai 190
Oru Manithan Oru Manaivi 190
Oruthalai Ragam 209
Oru Veedu Iru Vasal 183
Our Daily Bread (English), 164

Pachai Vilakku 188
Padhuka Pattabishekam 197
Padikatha Medhai 192
Paditha Penn 228
Palaivanathil Pattamboochi 190
Palum Pazhamum 224
Panam 224
Panama Pasama 192
Pandava Nirvahan (silent), 207
Pandithevan 215
Parasakthi 32, 33, 34, 35, 38, 65, 67, 114, 115
Parthiban Kanavu 132
Pasamalar 187
Paasavalai 228
Pasi 68, 158, 190
Pathala Bairavi 229

Index to Film Titles

Pathi Bakthi 18, 187
16 Vayathinile 179, 186
Pavalakodi 213
Pavamannipu 69
Pavathin Sambalam 190
Pazhani 188
Place in the Sun, A (English), 184
Policekaran Magal 213
Ponmudi 216
Poompuhar 203
Poongothai 33
Pootatha Pootukkal 194, 195
Porveeran Manaivi 206
Prahalada 222
Premsagar (Hindi), 215
Pride of Hindustan, The (silent), 204
Psycho (English), 167
Pucca Rowdy 95
Pudhaiyal 35
Punitha Malar 190
Punnagai 183
Puthiya Varpukal 160
Pudu Nellu Pudu Nathu 187

Queen Christina (English), 31

Radha Kalyanam 79
Raja Desingu 93
Rajakumari 216
Rajambal (1935), 201
Rajambal (1951), 184
Rajamohan 177

Rajarani 188
Rajarajachozhan 199
Rajarajan 50
Rajamukthi 208
Raja's Casket (silent), 3
Rajasekaran 222
Rajeswari (silent), 209
Rangoon Radha 32
Rashomon (Japanese), 184
Rasukutty 180
Rathapasam 212
Rayil Payanangal 210
Rendum Rendum Anju 193
Returning Soldier 191
Rose of Rajasthan, The (silent), 206
Rukmani Kalyanam 202

Sakata Yogam 204
Sakunthala 226
Salivahanan 177
Sampoorna Ramayanam 198
Samsaram 219
Samsaram Adhu Minsaram 161
Sandhyaragam 181, 185
Sankarabaranam (Telugu), 48
Sankaracharya 14
Sarada 146, 147, 192, 193
Santhanathevan 215
Sarvadhikari 32, 216
Sathi Akalya 215
Sathi Leelavathi 79, 191, 191, 217
Seemandhini 190

Index to Film Titles

Server Sundaram 137, 138
Sethubandhanam 204
Sevasadan 16 214, 226
Sila Nerangalil Sila Manithargal 154
Sirai 165
Siruthonda Nayanar 14
Sita Jananam 207
Sita Kalyanam 226
Sita Kalyanam (Telugu), 211
Sita Vanavasam 13
Sivagangai Seemai 128, 224
Sivakavi 22
Sollu Thambi Sollu 176
Sorgavasal 32, 231
Sri Murugan 216
Srinivasa Kalyanam 200
Sri Krishna Leela (Telugu), 227
Sri Ramanujar 22, 201
Stage Girl (silent), 205
Star of Mangrelia (silent), 6
Street Car named Desire, A (English), 125
Subadhra 30
Sugam Enge 212
Sulochana 215
Sundarakandam 180
Sundaramurthy Nayanar 197
Suneetha (Sinhalese) 203
Sunehre Din (Hindi) 115
Suvarillatha Chithirangal 179

Thabalkaran Thangai 193
Tenaliraman 35
Testament of Dr.Mabuse, The (silent), 10
Thalapathi 196

Thamizhariyum Perumal 22
Thamizhthai alladhu Mathrudharmam 17, 50
Thangapadumai 217
Thangapathakkam 194
Thangaikor Geetham 210
Thanneer...Thanneer 163, 183, 232
Tarasasankam, 206
Thavanikanavugal 180
Thai Ullam 212
Thenilavu 213
Thookuthooki (1935), 230
Thookuthooki (1954), 230
Thillana Mohanambal 139
Thirudathe 203
Thirumalai Thenkumari 199
Thirumbipaar 224
Thiruneelakantar 64, 78, 209,
Thiruvalluvar 21
Thiruvilaryadal 199
Thulivisham 217
Thyagabhoomi 16, 99, 173, 214, 227
Two Heavenly Creatures (English), 60
Thuna, 190

Uchi Veyil 173, 193, 194
Udan Khatola (Hindi), 223
Udhiripookal 194
Ulagam Sutrum Valiban 203
Unnaipol Oruvan (1965), 57, 68
Urimaikural 213
Usha Kalyanam 215
Usha Sundari 209

Index to Film Titles

Vaa Raja Vaa 198
Valaiyapathi 215
Valli 222
Valli Thirumanam (silent), 5
Valmiki 64
Vamana Avatharam 222
Vaname Ellai 183
Vaanaratham 223
Vanasundari 207
Vandematharam (Telugu), 211
Varumaiyin Niram Sivappu 183
Vasanthathin Azhaipukal 209
Vasanthasena 208
Vazhkai 88, 203
Vedala Ulagam 203
Vedham Puthithu 187
Veedu 57, 170-171, 180, 185, 186
Velaikari 30, 31, 33, 35, 65, 106, 107, 217
Venuganam 197
Vichithravanitha 215
Vidivelli 213
Vidiyumvarai Kathiru 180
Viduthalai 211 212
Vietnam Veedu 144-145
Vijayakumari 217
Vimochanam 17
Vishnu Leela (silent), 6
Vishnu Leela (talkie), 14, 208
Viswamithra 201
Vivasayi 51

Yar Paiyan 207
Yatra (Hindi) 215

www.ingramcontent.com/pod-product-compliance
Lightning Source LLC
Chambersburg PA
CBHW070528090426
42735CB00013B/2900